Real–Time and Retrospective Analyses of Cyber Security

David Anthony Bird
British Computer Society, UK

A volume in the Advances in
Information Security, Privacy, and
Ethics (AISPE) Book Series

Published in the United States of America by
   IGI Global
   Information Science Reference (an imprint of IGI Global)
   701 E. Chocolate Avenue
   Hershey PA, USA 17033
   Tel: 717-533-8845
   Fax: 717-533-8661
   E-mail: cust@igi-global.com
   Web site: http://www.igi-global.com

Library of Congress Cataloging-in-Publication Data

Names: Bird, David Anthony, 1965- author.
Title: Real-time and retrospective analyses of cyber security / by David
   Anthony Bird.
Description: Hershey, PA : Information Science Reference, an imprint of IGI
   Global, [2021] | Includes bibliographical references and index. |
   Summary: "This book explores the development of cyber security by
   drawing from events in recent history"-- Provided by publisher.
Identifiers: LCCN 2020009679 (print) | LCCN 2020009680 (ebook) | ISBN
   9781799839798 (hardcover) | ISBN 9781799856023 (paperback) | ISBN
   9781799839804 (ebook)
Subjects: LCSH: Cyberterrorism--History.
Classification: LCC HV6773.15.C97 B57 2021 (print) | LCC HV6773.15.C97
   (ebook) | DDC 363.325--dc23
LC record available at https://lccn.loc.gov/2020009679
LC ebook record available at https://lccn.loc.gov/2020009680

This book is published in the IGI Global book series Advances in Information Security and Privacy
(AISP) (ISSN: pending; eISSN: pending)

British Cataloguing in Publication Data
A Cataloguing in Publication record for this book is available from the British Library.

All work contributed to this book is new, previously-unpublished material.
The views expressed in this book are those of the authors, but not necessarily of the publisher.

For electronic access to this publication, please contact: eresources@igi-global.com.

Advances in Information Security, Privacy, and Ethics (AISPE) Book Series

ISSN:1948-9730
EISSN:1948-9749

Editor-in-Chief: Manish Gupta, State University of New York, USA

MISSION

As digital technologies become more pervasive in everyday life and the Internet is utilized in ever increasing ways by both private and public entities, concern over digital threats becomes more prevalent.

The **Advances in Information Security, Privacy, & Ethics (AISPE) Book Series** provides cutting-edge research on the protection and misuse of information and technology across various industries and settings. Comprised of scholarly research on topics such as identity management, cryptography, system security, authentication, and data protection, this book series is ideal for reference by IT professionals, academicians, and upper-level students.

COVERAGE

- Security Classifications
- Data Storage of Minors
- Computer ethics
- Technoethics
- Security Information Management
- Cyberethics
- Global Privacy Concerns
- Information Security Standards
- Cookies
- IT Risk

IGI Global is currently accepting manuscripts for publication within this series. To submit a proposal for a volume in this series, please contact our Acquisition Editors at Acquisitions@igi-global.com or visit: http://www.igi-global.com/publish/.

Titles in this Series

For a list of additional titles in this series, please visit:
http://www.igi-global.com/book-series/advances-information-security-privacy-ethics/37157

Privacy Concerns Surrounding Personal Information Sharing on Health and Fitness Mobile Apps
Devjani Sen (Algonquin College, Canada) and Rukhsana Ahmed (University at Albany, SUNY, USA)
Information Science Reference • ©2021 • 300pp • H/C (ISBN: 9781799834878) • US $215.00

Establishing Cyber Security Programs Through the Community Cyber Security Maturity Model (CCSMM)
Gregory B. White (CIAS, The University of Texas at San Antonio, USA) and Natalie Sjelin (CIAS, The University of Texas at San Antonio, USA)
Information Science Reference • ©2021 • 221pp • H/C (ISBN: 9781799844716) • US $195.00

Applied Approach to Privacy and Security for the Internet of Things
Parag Chatterjee (National Technological University, Argentina & University of the Republic, Uruguay) Emmanuel Benoist (Bern University of Applied Sciences, Switzerland) and Asoke Nath (St. Xavier's College, Kolkata, India)
Information Science Reference • ©2020 • 295pp • H/C (ISBN: 9781799824442) • US $235.00

Advanced Localization Algorithms for Wireless Sensor Networks
M. Vasim Babu (Institute of Technology and Sciences, India)
Information Science Reference • ©2020 • 300pp • H/C (ISBN: 9781799837336) • US $195.00

Social, Legal, and Ethical Implications of IoT, Cloud, and Edge Computing Technologies
Gianluca Cornetta (Universidad CEU San Pablo, Spain) Abdellah Touhafi (Vrije Universiteit Brussel, Belgium) and Gabriel-Miro Muntean (Dublin City University, Ireland)
Information Science Reference • ©2020 • 333pp • H/C (ISBN: 9781799838173) • US $215.00

Multidisciplinary Approaches to Ethics in the Digital Era
Meliha Nurdan Taskiran (Istanbul Medipol University, Turkey) and Fatih Pinarbaşi (Istanbul Medipol University, Turkey)
Information Science Reference • ©2020 • 300pp • H/C (ISBN: 9781799841173) • US $195.00

For an entire list of titles in this series, please visit:
http://www.igi-global.com/book-series/advances-information-security-privacy-ethics/37157

701 East Chocolate Avenue, Hershey, PA 17033, USA
Tel: 717-533-8845 x100 • Fax: 717-533-8661
E-Mail: cust@igi-global.com • www.igi-global.com

Table of Contents

Foreword

My job is largely playing games. This needs some unpacking. Cyber security is critical at all levels of society; from the protection of an individual's data and property, scaling up to the concerns of businesses and of nation states. Reading books and journals on cyber security, attending conferences, following key websites and twitter feeds, as well as practise-based activity, can only develop knowledge of cyber security to a certain point. Cyber wargaming can help convert that knowledge into *understanding*.

My research includes reconstruction of cyber-attacks, with the aim of attempting to get inside the mindset of the red and blue team in order to better understand the decisions made. Yesterday a firm I work with announced the outcome of a targeted phishing email used as part of a pentest. The phishing email looked plausible; of the 821 staff who opened the email, 248 clicked on the link, 149 then entered their password and their mobile phone number. I spend time considering why these figures were not higher (or lower); what could be done to change these numbers. I spent even more time gaming this situation, considering how the hackers are likely to use this information and how they *might* use it. If you can imagine scaling up this task to a whole business (including their supply chain) or a nation state, then you start to visualize how I apply games to gain potential insight. The very best outcome of this gaming effort is where unexpected insights emerge from this process.

This brings me to why I am interested in this book. For my research to have value, these games need to involve detailed, specialized, knowledge that is not readily available, even in the cyber security profession. There are a lot of people in the profession who know a great deal about the technical detail, but less about what it all means. I am referring to digital leadership in the cyber security space.

In order to understand trends, an overview that syntheses facts into knowledge is necessary and that is where this book comes in. It pulls together this detail and supported by this detail, gives an overview, which in the military is referred to as the 'helicopter view'. Essentially, this is keeping the broad thrust of developments in mind, rather than getting lost in the operational detail that is the cut and thrust of the long war between the red and the blue teams.

To me, detail needs to be summarized to inform, and that is what this book has achieved. Rather than just base this work on practise, this book pulls together published research. Each chapter is largely standalone and gives a concise summary of a topic, supported by references to research and further reading. As a whole they are an excellent survey of some of the key issues affecting cyber security today.

I hope you find the chapters as informative as I did.

John Curry
Bath Spa University, UK

Preface

The author has worked in cyber security for over a decade as his second career, and he has been an adoptee of progressive computing technology over the past 25 years. Prior to this, the author worked in what is now called Cyber and Electromagnetic Activities for the United Kingdom (U.K.) Joint Services. The author was subsequently able to bring his expertise and familiarity of this field into the dominion of Cyber Security and adapt his analytical experience from the military. Before the Cyber Security term was coined, the author worked for two of the three most highly regarded information assurance companies in the United Kingdom. These companies include the Cyber Division of a large United States (U.S.) Defense and Cyber Security corporation. Later, the author worked as researcher and cyber security architect for an acclaimed cyber and defense research group. Over the past 11 years, the author has worked within the Information and Communications Technology (ICT) engineering domain on specific tasks for U.K. Public Sector organizations. Over this protracted period of time, the author has continued to encounter similar problems in the perception and tolerance of cyber security by individuals from the wider industry. Whilst new technologies have come on stream and have been adopted by companies and government departments alike – in the author's experience – a mutual theme seems to arise. This common thread is portrayed as if it is the technology that is affecting civilization. Society therefore considers, discusses, and blames technology as if it is a living thing. Of course, this is not the case. The human desire for progress, diversity, and convenience in their interaction with cyberspace has, in the author's opinion, both positive and negative socio-technological effects. This ultimately affects users' trust in technology, their privacy, and the protection of our data.

DIVERSITY OF CHALLENGES

Now of course these facets are a topical issue in their own right with the advent of machine-learning leading civilization on a path towards an end-goal of Artificial General Intelligence (AGI) (Eslami & Shanahan, 2019). Presently, AGI is raising a number of questions, such as: (a) moral connotations and privacy; (b) affects to our democracy; (c) technical implications; and (d) ethical aspects about its use (Eslami & Shanahan, 2019). This is very important as society progresses towards true AGI; however, these aspects are already pertinent in computing today, and in the author's opinion, these aspects are not necessarily being addressed. Why does the author state this? Well, he thinks society has not quite got it right in the pre-AGI era. By this, the author means the human factor. A couple of years ago, the U.K. National Cyber Security Centre (NCSC) stated that 'users' should not be blamed where there are poor cyber security instantiations (Emma, 2017); by this, the author believes that the NCSC meant the lack of technical controls to protect an organization should not by default fall back upon the user's shoulders to make the right decision – based purely from a procedural controls perspective (Mertens, 2015). From experience, it seems there is a cyber security 'hill to climb' in the development, installation, and supporting functions of IT.

Admittedly, technology and new technological innovations hitting the mainstream take time to learn. However, users must remember that at this moment in time and until AGI has reached a satisfactory incarnation, it is people who gather requirements, develop against them, implement and test in a measurable way, and operate the technological systems. Admittedly, it is different teams who do so, but they are people, nonetheless. Security can be seen as a 'blocker,' in which to engineers it is perfectly acceptable to raise concessions rather than understand the salient security case informed by risk analysis. However, in the author's judgement, ironically, the true obstructions in the ICT project can be: (a) a lack of communication; (b) absence of reality; (c) people working in silos; and (d) abdication of responsibility. There are many variables to consider, such as cost benefit analysis, but there are many obstacles that are not necessarily constraints of technology. Security has a number of technological complexities, but one that is devalued in its importance is the human factor. For all the positive things occurring within the Information Technology (IT) industry today, human nature can be counterproductive when exhibited as: (a) lethargy to proactive cyber security thinking; (b) people playing politics to the detriment of best practice; (c) egos purely aimed at building one's self-esteem to the impairment of 'doing the right thing'; or

(d) belligerence and so many other human traits. The author has witnessed people who think that a perfectly adequate approach is to apply cyber security using 'security by obscurity' approaches. These individuals argue against perfectly implementable and proportionate security controls – all because they fear security will add expenditure to their project or, more importantly, make it harder for them to do their job.

Furthermore, the author has witnessed a mental block by software engineers who are so focused on functional aspects of design that basic security principles and simple security considerations can be missed or not even understood. Some project managers think cyber security is completely negotiable where there are gray areas or when discrete rules or regulatory requirements are not explicitly enforceable. This all adds pressure and stress to cyber security practitioners who are trying to protect an organizations' assets. All these human nuances open up deployed systems to inherent vulnerabilities, whether it be in the software, misconfigurations during implementation, inadequate hardening leading to poor cyber hygiene, or potentially inconsistent or poorly updated systems in production (Xu et al., 2013). This all adds to the fragility of cyber defenses and opens the doors to those who wish to abuse ICT systems for nefarious purposes. Evolving social norms and relentless innovation can help fuel this while regulation is catching up (Martin, 2019). All these facets can act as a catalyst for cyber harm to be undertaken by online threat actors.

Interestingly, recent research from Symantec implies that due to technological advances there is increased pressure upon the profession and a lack of the skills development to perform the job. Therefore, it is not surprising that just over two thirds of U.K. cyber security professionals find themselves struggling to respond and assess the asymmetric cyber threats (Bird, 2013b). Little wonder that almost two thirds of cyber security professionals within this shortage skillset category have become disenfranchised and are considering leaving the industry altogether (Helpnet Security, 2019a). Along similar lines, the author jointly wrote a paper that proposed a blended-learning and development approach that is underpinned by an overarching core knowledge framework. The intent here is to join up the extant silos of learning and development activities to gain an advantage from and shape a coherent core knowledgebase for the community. This should incorporate and benefit from the cacophony of skills from the wider IT industry, such as developers and solution architects along with system managers and system administrators; thus, establishing buy-in from other core skill areas in ICT upon which cyber security is dependent (Bird & Curry, 2018). Thus, barriers can be broken down to the benefit of all participants for an overarching and aligned response to what is effectively becoming a cyber security arms race. This should alleviate situations in which cyber security is not necessarily thought about through-life from the system concept phase, during the design and development phases, and into operations. By the time solution implementations are rolled out, oversights will have crept in. This makes it harder for systems to be protected during operation and leaves ICT support teams to retrofit controls in order to enhance a system's cyber security profile.

By no means is everyone negligent across the industry, but human failings cause cyber security gaps when users take shortcuts. Constraints such as time, cost, and effort are important for successful deliveries; however, these can also be used as an excuse to encourage behaviors contrary to good practice. This generates abject flaws by failing to avoid misconfigurations or undertake software updates and patches in good time whilst in service. The author conducted extensive research for a master's degree dissertation in which he found control-set weaknesses or vulnerabilities have been realized, improperly mitigated, and not adequately safeguarded through misconfiguration or implementation gaps in the public cloud. Therefore, lackadaisical implementations can result in insecure ways of working and cause real-world flaws in customer cloud deployments (Bird, 2018). The identification of misconfigurations by public cloud computing customers has also been recognized and ratified by the NCSC at the CyberUK 2019 conference (National Cyber Security Centre, 2019). For their part, cloud service providers like Amazon Web Services have resorted to automation to reliably fulfill their part of the 'shared security responsibility.' Automation removes human involvement to run their infrastructure, enhancing reliability and providing traceability. Of course, automation scripts still need to be tested; therefore, human intervention is occasionally required. However, an administrator's mistyped command allegedly caused the AWS Simple Storage Service outages of 2008 (Bramish & Brohi, 2011) and 2017 in the United States (Sverdlik, 2017). In the case of Microsoft, Azure Automation is promoted in order to automate frequent, time-consuming, and error-prone cloud management tasks (Microsoft, 2018).

THE HUMAN FACTOR

But misconfigurations are not just constrained to the Cloud, and they feature in deployments across the wider ICT and Industrial Control System (ICS) industries. This is tantamount to systems and software engineers burying their heads in the sand. Humans are purportedly the purveyors of technology, but as a species, they are locked in a cyber struggle and an undeclared war of attrition in cyberspace. Cyber security is not just a technological challenge as it is arguably portrayed, but more realistically, it is very much a socio-technical one. Before AGI starts autonomously coding our future, there are a few things that the wider IT industry needs to straighten out. From the author's experience of working across multiple disciplines - such as space and defense, transportation, and the maritime industry – he has surmised that there are misguided interpretations and repeatable mistakes that continue to beset the IT industry. Additionally, similar errors also appear to be ingrained within the ICS space. With regards to the latter, safety takes primacy, but even now within that community, studies have identified cyber security as a short-fall area. The author hopes that this this will be addressed by IEC62443 (ISA, n.d.), but standards alone like ISO/IEC27001 will not fix cyber security problems. Time and time again, cyber events reinforce what damage can be done to an organization's reputation after cyber security breaches.

All these factors discussed here contribute to a problem – a human problem. This is the inspiration behind this book to explore why this is the case and the effects of human behavior that affect the efficiency and robustness of cyber security. For all the inventions that mankind has produced in one form or another for the betterment of society, it would not be a stretch to say that people can exhibit a blasé perplexity when interacting with cyberspace (Bird, 2013a). This book will use topical subject areas to articulate the challenges in the cyber security domain, whilst drawing upon the events of recent history. The author will conduct a socio-technological analysis against a backdrop of evolutionary threats and their real-world impact – the catalysts that drive fear, uncertainty, and doubt. Ultimately, lessons need to be learned from neglectful, flawed, and/or insecure implementations in order to secure humanity's connected future. Cohesively, all elements of the wider technology industry need to be on the same page, and cyber security needs to be seen as applicable to different audiences, taking into account the differing contexts to break down barriers. Essentially, mankind needs to wake up to the fact there are always risks, but the trick is to adequately reduce them through the deployment of countermeasures. Just because they are not tangible does not diminish the threats or make them less real!

ORGANIZATION OF THE BOOK

This book provides a perspective from a front line of cyber defense perspective, and its purpose is to raise awareness to the dangers of our engagement with cyberspace. It provides coverage to enable an understanding of the pitfalls by overlooking crucial mitigation's and the enduing repercussions. Cyber security is ultimately a 'people problem,' and the book will be of interest to the layperson as well as the wider readership within the field of cyber security. The book is organized into eight chapters, generating a coherent structure on the issues affecting cyber security today. Descriptions of each chapter are as follows:

Chapter 1 scene sets a variety of human intentions from the last century into the new millennium. This is the start of the socio-technical analysis based around the Industry 4.0 hype, which highlights why cyber security is an important and relevant force for the good of our society underpinned by regulations. The author explores ethical and moral issues and how this might steer the development of AGI.

Chapter 2 investigates the risk and compliance conundrum against a public cloud use-case. Compliance-based approaches can influence or, alternatively, create a control-set vacuum when wholly relied upon to implement cyber security controls. These facets are fundamental principles that better inform governance of cyber security in organizations and safeguard users' interaction with the online realm.

Chapter 3 explores the challenges from a technical and societal viewpoint whilst contrasted against an undertow of hacker originated cyber-attacks from the past decade. This chapter provides examples of newsworthy hacks, security breaches, and sustained cyber-attacks that will provide salient contexts about the threats, vulnerabilities, and the resultant consequences.

Chapter 4 looks at the technical aspects and effects of some attributed and high-profile state-sponsored cyber-attacks that have been encountered from our interaction with the networked world. The author argues that the impact of these are directly and indirectly problematical to the advancement of the online realm as a whole.

Chapter 5 takes extant issues being encountered in the Middle East, which demonstrate a cross-over between electronic warfare and cyber-warfare. This affects ships, aircraft and unmanned aerial vehicles in real-life at the end of the second decade of the new millennium. This overview provides examples of how cyber-warfare techniques are now being used in a cross-battlespace domain against cyber-physical assets to affect geopolitical change and even escalate tensions that can have a wider reaching impact.

Chapter 6 explores the lessons that can be learned from social media, citing case-studies of incidents around the world in which the platforms have been abused and used for ulterior motives. The author justifies why a paradigm shift is required regarding users' perceptions of the risks and future engagement with the virtual worlds in cyberspace.

Chapter 7 uses a philosophical approach to discuss the frailty of the human psyche with regards to implementing systems and through our use of cyberspace. The author investigates whether society's constant exposure to the Internet desensitizes the public to inherent risks. The author discusses a number of key topical subject areas, exploring gaps, ways in which mistakes or omissions could be avoided and how education, and ways in which training can help prevent the abuse of assets interacting with cyberspace.

Chapter 8 focuses on the advantages of non-fungible blockchain technologies that can underpin and augment other existing security mechanisms to achieve validate data integrity, enhance identity, and access control mechanisms and support supply chain provenance. The author also provides a searching outlook as to whether the current cyber security approaches are contradictory and could be perceived as a negative connotation.

David Anthony Bird
British Computer Society, UK

REFERENCES

Bamish, M., & Brohi, S. (2011). Seven deadly threats and vulnerabilities in cloud computing. *International Journal of Advanced Engineering Sciences and Technologies*, *9*(1), 87–90.

Bird, D. (2013a). Open or closed? *ITNOW*, *55*(2), 32–33. doi:10.1093/itnow/bwt014

Bird, D. (2013b). Underlying dangers. *ITNOW*, *55*(4), 32–33. doi:10.1093/itnow/bwt077

Bird, D. (2018*). The creation of a conceptual framework to assist in determining the security risks associated with the use of public cloud computing environments* (Unpublished master's dissertation). Open University, Milton Keynes, UK.

Bird, D., & Curry, J. (2018). A case for using blended learning and development techniques to aid the delivery of a UK cybersecurity core body of knowledge. *International Journal of Systems and Software Security and Protection, 9*(2), 28–45. doi:10.4018/IJSSSP.2018040103

Emma, W. (2017, March 28). *People: The strongest link* [Weblog comment]. Retrieved from https://www.ncsc.gov.uk/speech/people--the-strongest-link

Eslami, A., & Shanahan, M. (2019, June 8). *What is AI anyway.* Paper presented at The Times Science Festival, Cheltenham, UK.

Helpnet Security. (2019a). *Cybersecurity professionals are outgunned and burned out.* Retrieved from https://www.helpnetsecurity.com/2019/06/28/cybersecurity-burnout/

ISA. (n.d.). *ISA99, Industrial automation and control systems security.* Retrieved from https://www.isa.org/templates/two-column.aspx?pageid=124560

Martin, C. (2019a, April). *Making the UK the safest place to live and work online.* Paper presented at CyberUK Conference, Glasgow, UK.

Mertens, X. (2015, July 14). *Don't (always) blame the user!* [Weblog comment]. Retrieved from https://blog.rootshell.be/2015/07/14/dont-always-blame-the-user/

Microsoft. (2018). *An introduction to Azure Automation.* Retrieved from https://docs.microsoft.com/en-us/azure/automation/automation-intro

National Cyber Security Centre. (2019, April). *Cloud: The latest thinking from the NCSC on Cloud.* Paper presented at CyberUK Conference, Glasgow, UK.

Sverdlik, Y. (2017). *AWS outage that broke the internet caused by mistyped command.* Retrieved from http://www.datacenterknowledge.com/archives/2017/03/02/aws-outage-that-broke-the-internet-caused-by-mistyped-command

Xu, T., Zhang, J., Huang, P., Zheng, J., Sheng, T., Yuan, D., … Pasupathy, S. (2013). Do not blame users for misconfigurations. In *Proceedings of Symposium on Operating Systems Principles (SOSP).* Association of Computing Machinery.

Acknowledgment

IGI Global would like to acknowledge the help of all the people involved in this project. More specifically, IGI Global would like to thank the author and the reviewers. Without their support and expertise, this book would not have become a reality.

The editor and author would like to acknowledge the valuable contributions of the reviewers regarding the improvement of quality, coherence, and content presentation of the chapters.

As the author, I would like to thank my partner, Jane, for her patience and contribution in proofreading the chapters. In addition, I would also like to thank my colleague and friend, Peter, for being a sounding board and who helped to develop ideas for Chapter 3.

David Anthony Bird
British Computer Society, UK

Chapter 1
An Analysis of Industry 4.0

ABSTRACT

Chapter 1 sets the scene by providing an overview of the Industry 4.0 concept that is conjoining a number of different technologies, with various levels of maturity, in order to provide an end-to-end capability. This case study is a good exemplar to tease out many pertinent socio-technical topics where the main contexts will be elaborated on throughout the remainder of the book. In short, a case is made that cyber security is first and foremost a human problem, but also highlights the importance of regulation, standards, and bodies to underpin cyber security. Examples of the opposing forces are covered here that together if unmitigated will contrive to undermine the cyber resilience of the 21st century.

INTRODUCTION

It has been more than 30 years since the public Internet was born. Society continues to transform towards an online-centric world. This utopia has been significantly tainted by the continually evolving threat landscape and the level of capability that potentially could gain unauthorized access to users' data. It is not just about the external attackers and targeted users, which in fact catch most of the press attention. It is the holistic cyber security considerations for the protection of computer-based systems that should be the preserve of many practitioners. Considerations range from software developers and programmers, system designers and solutions architects, system administrators, and system support managers (Bird & Curry, 2018). There is no better

DOI: 10.4018/978-1-7998-3979-8.ch001

protagonist to start this journey into the cyber security challenges of the 21st Century than Industry 4.0. Berting, Mills, & Wintersberger (1980) first coined the term Fourth Industrial Revolution in 1980, and it is now developing with such a technological trajectory (Swahb, 2016) that it has culminated in the coming together of various disparate technologies for a common purpose. This intersection brings an amalgamated risk from the ICT domain interfacing with Operational Technology (OT), OT interoperability with the Internet of Things (IoT), and the use of Artificial Intelligence (AI) to process big data sets. Both IoT and AI have been designated as being critical to the United Kingdom on the road to digital transformation that is engulfing the second decade of the new millennium (Violino, 2018).

BACKGROUND

Whilst it is not possible to cover every cyber security issue in one chapter, this case study will provide a compendium of general topical issues, some of which the author will explore further in this book. Many of the security principles covered here are pertinent to OT, IoT, and AI systems today because they have not only become increasingly interconnected, but most of them are also managed via ICT. This is a very large subject area that transcends private Local Area Networks (LAN), distributed wide-area networks across the Internet and Cloud Service Provider (CSP) infrastructure. Therefore, Industry 4.0 serves as a ideal paradigm to highlight the diversity of key cyber security challenges facing civilization. The remainder of the book then elaborates on many common themes and discusses how society should go about resolving them.

INDUSTRY 4.0

Information Communications Technology

Computing technology has progressed quickly from the First-Generation valve / vacuum tube-based computers to the Second Generation, which consisted of transistors, around the mid-20th century. The Third Generation consisted of integrated circuits and the Very Large-Scale Integration microprocessors of the Fourth Generation carried us forward into the 21st century (Fiegenbaum

& PMcCorduck, 1983). It is a well-known fact that the original 'open' communications protocols for Internet connectivity are based around the Internet Protocol (IP) suite. This consists of reliable and connection-orientated Transmission Control Protocol (TCP) and the connectionless User Datagram Protocol (UDP). The U.S. Defense Advanced Research Projects Agency actually designed the original concepts for a closed packetized internetworking system rather than what turned out to be a globally distributed Internet. This meant that the legacy protocol stack has been inherently insecure from the outset and more had to be done with the advent of the hypertext interlinkages that formed the World Wide Web (Bird, 2013). The online use of credentials and data exchanges across the Internet and the Web necessitated protection measures, which spawned the Secure Socket Layer (SSL) in 1994. This provided the foundations for reliable web session encryption (Bird, 2017a) and fueled what has been dubbed the first Crypto War (Soesanto, 2018). However, the execution of this technology was not necessarily completely effective, depending on how it was implemented and the cryptographic algorithm that was used. This has been heavily influenced by the Wassenaar Arrangement of 1996, which stipulated export control restrictions on both symmetric and asymmetric cryptographic products (Rbcafe, 2014).

The use of SSL also brought about the concept of Public Key Infrastructure (PKI) that was originally accredited to Whitfield Diffie and Martin Hellman in 1976 (Melone, 2012); however, the United Kingdom's Government Communications Headquarters had actually already invented it a decade earlier (Bradbury, 2001). In its simplest form, PKI can be implemented using web-served one-way or two-way mutual authentication through asymmetric cryptography using public and private key pairs. The symmetric key exchange can be conducted asymmetrically by using trusted certificates that have been signed by a Certificate Authority. Both ends then agree and initialize the symmetric key for cryptographic algorithms, such as the now favored Advanced Encryption Standard, which the United States adopted in 1999. In 2000, the participating countries under the Wassenaar Arrangement elected to remove export control criteria on mass-market 64bit symmetric key products, such as AES (Rbcafe, 2014). Subsequently, since 2006, the Electronic Frontier Foundation has been promoting secured implementations of Hypertext Transfer Protocol (HTTP) exchanges under its 'HTTPS Everywhere' campaign (Electronic Frontier Foundation, n.d.). However, it is only recently that attitudes have significantly changed toward online encryption mechanisms since the Snowden revelations of 2013, which fueled the second Crypto War (Soesanto, 2018). Transport Layer Security (TLS), a more modern derivative of SSL, has now become more prolific in protecting our interactions online. The pro-privacy stance has now rubbed off to a point at which the Padding Oracle On Downgraded Legacy Encryption and Heartbleed vulnerabilities in modern web browsers has encouraged Google to enforce TLS version 1.2 or higher in their Chrome browser. This removes the option of using earlier outmoded and arguably obsolete TLS and SSL cipher suite mechanisms (Seltzer. 2014).

Cyber Insecurities

Moreover, the Accenture and Ponemon Cost of Cybercrime Survey of 2019 stated that global cost from data losses had increased to 72% over the past five years. Additionally, the survey stated that the financial impact from cyber-crime had doubled between 2015 and 2018 ranging from 2.7 million U.S. dollars (USD) to 5.9 million USD (AccentureSecurity, 2019). The United Kingdom's existing National Cyber Strategy has stated that cyber-crime propagates malicious software (malware) for financial gain and in its pursuit of activities to steal, damage, distort, or destroy data (Her Majesty's Government, 2016). In actual fact, a prime method of infiltration by hackers is to coerce people using phishing emails to persuade them to install or download a trojan horse malware. The hackers can then use this to obtain banking details or some other information, like passwords (Bird, 2013). The level of sophistication used by cyber-crime syndicates to impersonate legitimate businesses or government organizations has become so believable that in 2013, it necessitated a warning from the U.K. Government about one campaign. This particular scam centered around a hoax tax rebate purporting to be from Her Majesty's Revenue and Customs (GOV.UK, 2013). The level of detail used to try to fool recipients, as shown in Figure 1, was quite proficient.

One of the first notable examples of malware was the Morris Worm released from the Massachusetts Institute of Technology (MIT) in 1988. Since then, hackers have continued to release viruses and worms into the 'wild,' preying upon unpatched or inadequately defended computer systems. This uncontrolled experiment that emanated from MIT became the very first cyber-attack that took down not only ten percent of the Internet, but it also ultimately became the first Distributed Denial of Service (DDOS) attack (Bird, 2013; Vaughan-Nichols, 2018). Today, Advanced and Persistent Threats (APT) use *modus operandi,* such as trojanized malware or backdoor software to gain a foothold during the first stage of a cyber-attack. This is

Figure 1. Example of a phishing email

From: "HMRC" <returns@hmr.com>
Date: 5 February 2013 08:17:48
GMT
Subject: Notice of Tax Return
Reply-To: noreply@hm1.com

 HM Revenue
& Customs

Claim Your Tax Refund Online

We identified an error in the calculation of your tax from the last payment, amounting
to £ 273.00. In order for us to return the excess payment, you need to create a Tax Gateway account after which the funds will be credited to your specified bank account.

Please click "Get Started" below to claim your refund:

Get Started

We are here to ensure the correct tax is paid at the right time, whether this relates to payment of taxes received by the department or entitlement to benefits paid.

followed by the controlled download of further weaponized malware onto the target in order to exploit vulnerabilities and escalate privileges during the second stage. Once this beachhead has been established, the malware then communicates with the Command and Control (C2) servers located elsewhere on the Internet. This enables remote attackers to manage their campaign. From this point, the attackers can maintain a persistent presence on their quarry and pivot to move laterally along the victim's network to achieve the next stage. The third stage consists of the main objective, which is generally the extrapolation of data for consolidation on a staging host, followed by data exfiltration from this subverted host; most likely, hackers use back-channel encrypted communications to avoid detection. Once the attackers have achieved their objective, they can then attempt the final stage of post-attack cleanup in an attempt to remove identifiable traces of their presence (Caban, 2019).

An example is the trojan that crept into the popular CCleaner application in 2017. Researchers have speculated that the hackers gained access to the CCleaner development environment in order to implant a backdoor into version 5.33.6162 (Yung, 2018). The objective was for the malware to communicate with C2 servers and then eventually acquire and send personal data back to the attackers. The infection potentially affected two million people before it was detected by CCleaner developers themselves (Kaspersky, n.d.a), who subsequently notified the user community and advised them to install a newer version of the application to remove the trojan.

Then of course, there is the dreaded scourge of the Internet – DDOS! Hackers have used this technique time and time again from zombie computers to bombard a target's system with a number of different messages (Somani, Sanghi, Conti, Rajarajan, & Buyya, 2017). This continues to a point at which they can no longer fulfil their primary function. The author has transposed and listed examples of DDOS type attacks in Table 1.

Table 1. Examples of DDOS techniques

Context	Message Type
Web Services attack	HTTP GET HTTP POST
Flooding attack	TCP SYN Internet Control Message Protocol ECHO
Amplification attack	Domain Name Server (DNS) Network Time Protocol (NTP) Simple Network Management Protocol (SNMP)

Source: Somani et al., 2017.

Russian Black Hat hackers allegedly used Botnets, but most likely, they were acting on behalf of the Russian State to conduct DDOS attacks against Estonia in 2007. At the time, Estonia was proudly and heavily dependent on Internet e-commerce, and such an attack significantly disrupted their economy. Similarly, in 2008, in tandem to the conflict with Russia, a coordinated DDOS attack also lambasting Georgia's infrastructure (Herzog, 2017; Plohmann, Gerhards-Padilla, & Leder, 2011). In 2015, the Chinese State subjected GitHub repository to a DDOS using the so-called Great Cannon because it hosted two projects run by anti-regime activists, known collectively as GreatFire. org (Griffiths, 2019; Jeffrey, 2018). This group developed anti-censorship applications and uses GitHub to make them available to Chinese Netizens in order to circumvent the censorship and filtering measures performed by the Golden Shield Project; this project is also known colloquially as the Great Firewall of China (Greatfire.org, 2018; Bu, n.d.). In 2018, a Chinese DDOS amplification attack running at 1.3Tbps attacked GitHub again (Griffiths, 2019). However, DDOS is not only the preserve of hackers aligned to hostile nation-states, but it is also hackers and hacking groups reacting to global issues or cyber-criminality implementing DDOS-for-hire (Cluley, 2013). The 11-hour Rackspace Domain Name Server DDOS attack of 2014 was thought to be conducted by non-state-actors, and subsequently, it encouraged the company to implement an anti-DDOS capability (Waqas, 2017; Somali et al., 2017). Such nefarious activities have resulted in cyber-criminals advertising these services on the Dark Web; it has also resulted in a range of other dubious products that are sold or exchanged, such as narcotics, stolen credentials, credit card details, and computer hacking tools or services. This has resulted in international law enforcement agencies undertaking collaborative operations to shut down these sites (Khandelwal, 2013, 2014).

There have also been cyber operations to abuse Managed Service Provider (MSP) networks and use them as a conduit to attack customers or consumers. MSPs come in various forms, but the most common model is one in which customers outsource their services to a third-party, a third-party's data center, or a third-party's environment on public cloud platforms (Gartner, n.d.). Attacking MSP's has been synonymous with nation-state cyber-attacks, such as those conducted by the Chinese group known as APT 10 in 2017 (Price Waterhouse Coopers, 2017). The methods of this APT have been to launch phishing emails in order to subvert remote hosts and then infiltrate global Managed IT Service Providers and CSP networks. During Operation Cloud Hopper, hackers deployed malware to establish a foothold, persist and propagate laterally, and identify target systems of interest. This deployment culminated in data exfiltration (Burt, 2017; Price Waterhouse Coopers, 2017). Now, it transpires that cyber-crime is following suit in their attempt to distribute ransomware. This has led to campaigns against U.S. municipalities who have been targeted with Ryuk ransomware in 2019 (Helpnet Security, 2019a; Ilascu, 2019); this is especially true since Lake City and Riviera in Florida paid hacker demands, which has encouraged cyber-criminals to continue besieging U.S. cities with ransomware campaigns (Cimpanu, 2019).

Operational Technology

Industrial networks today utilize EtherNet/IP networks to transmit standard TCP/IP as well as encapsulated legacy industrial protocols. This type of network topology is ideal to conjoin Enterprise LANs in order to manage the Supervisory Control and Data Acquisition (SCADA) LAN layer. This consists of Human Machine Interfaces (HMI), Application Servers, Database Server, Input and Output (I/O) Server, Historian, and Domain Controller. The SCADA LAN interfaces with local HMIs and Programmable Logic Controllers (PLC) and/or I/O modules that comprise the control plane of the Distributed Control Systems (DCS). In addition to commanding PLCs, messages also transit from Controller LAN to Fieldbus devices using serial communications, such as Modbus Remote Terminal Unit (RTU); within the automation industry, assets that reside on the Fieldbus Layer are the actuators or sensors. Some safety critical implementations may use a Safety Instrumented System (SIS), which connects to important actuators and performs specific actions in response to failure conditions (Obregon, 2015).

According to the MIT, recent cyber-attacks against SCADA and ICS provides proof that hackers can abuse legitimate communications to invoke an unsafe function. Cyber-attackers thereby misuse the communications exchanges that are assumed to be trusted by the processes within the system (Thomas, 2018). Therefore, data integrity should not only cover invalid or incorrect parameters but also validate or verify data exchange legitimacy. This precept delves beyond traditional techniques to check the integrity of messages through the use of checksums called 'black channel communications.' Furthermore, this precept delves into the more sophisticated area of Machine-to-Machine (M2M) authentication and authorization across the nodes of the network. Today, options include the use of PKI to perform application-level and end-point host authentication between the SCADA hosts, PLCs, and Domain Controller. However, such solutions are dependent on the maturity of technology selection and the functional context in which they are employed. Undoubtedly, this approach can be too complex for legacy industrial systems, but as systems are technically refreshed or upgraded, system architects can take advantage of approaches like PKI. The introduction of PKI mechanisms is particularly important in establishing symmetrically encrypted E2E connectivity as OT begins to interface with IoT for inter-domain communications.

Industrial Attack Landscape

IEEE 802.3 ethernet compatible networks like EtherNet/IP or ProfiNet present a richer cyber-attack landscape consisting of multiple attack surfaces. These attack surfaces range from the Enterprise LAN down to the conjoined DCS Layer. Recent history reveals that the ICS components present weaknesses in their own right. In 2014, as part of the SCADA Strangelove Project, researchers discovered flaws and zero-days that enabled remote execution opportunities across five percent of SCADA, PLC, and ICS components analyzed at the time (Pauli, 2014). This is perhaps reinforced when the Ukrainian power grid was hit by another wave of cyber-attacks that caused a significant power outage in 2016. The source of this attack was malware known as BlackEnergy 3 (New Jersey Cybersecurity and Communications Integration Cell, 2017) and was attributed to the Russian Sandworm APT. This state-sponsored group embedded email attachments with trojans as part of their objective to implant further attack packages on victim computers. The trojans that were used included Backdoor.Win32.Blakken, Backdoor.Win64.Blakken, Backdoor.Win32.Fonten, and Heur:Trojan.Win32.Generic (Kaspersky, n.d.b).

The first phase was to gain a foothold in order to subvert workstations and servers. This was followed by the second stage, which consisted of a KillDisk feature, and stage three, which comprised various plug-ins associated with data erasure and to deny legitimate use of the SCADA system (Lewis, n.d.; Zorabedian, 2016; Assante, 2016). This campaign has also been likened to other nation-state disruptive activities used against Ukraine during Russia's involvement in the conflict in Crimea (Brumfield, 2019; Ranger, 2019a). By 2019, a report by Applied Risk stated that cyber security basics are not being practiced within the CNI domain; the report implied that aspects of cyber security were still an afterthought; the most common weaknesses that were found consisted of: (a) misconfigurations; (b) vulnerabilities from lack of patches or updates; (c) identity and access management found to be wanting; (d) insecure services; and (e) architecture and network segmentations (Helpnet Security, 2019b).

Internet of Things

In 1999, the co-founder of Microsoft, Bill Gates, described the concept of a 'digital nervous system' (Gates, 1999) in which the Internet would be the bearer. Arguably, IoT is manifesting itself into his vision, but not necessarily in the form that Gates had foreseen. In the consumer space, IoT popular low-power wireless options feature short range IEEE 802.15.4 Zigbee and very short-range proprietary Z-Wave Alliance standard. 2.5G has been repurposed to carry slower data rate IoT data communications using Global System for Mobile Communications (Short, 2018). IoT is now being deployed using third Generation (3G) to fourth Generation (4G) cellular networks to carry traffic from front-end devices via Narrowband-IoT (Bird, 2018a). The radio frequency landscape extends using Narrowband-IoT Low Powered Wide Area Networks (LPWAN) followed by the 4G Long Term Evolution (LTE) for Machines (Short, 2018). In addition, there is the new medium distance 'weightless wireless communications' standard (Bird, 2015a; DesignSpark, 2016).

Industrial IoT differs from the traditional business-to-consumer telephony model used by consumer IoT, whereby industrial services form a business-to-business-to-consumer approach (GSMA, 2014). Connected and Autonomous Vehicles (CAV) are destined to use the new 802.11p Wireless Access in Vehicular Environments (WAVE) protocol. This is due to its performance over 4G and fifth Generation cellular (5G) for short range vehicle-to-vehicle communications within the 5.9GHz frequency band. Automotive long-haul communications for CAVs will also most certainly be needed for resilience in the Vehicle-to-Everything (V2X) context, so 5G cellular fits the bill in this case (Filippi et al., n.d.). In addition, 5G has been formally expressed as a transformative technology for long haul communications connecting smart factories from the manufacturing plant to back-end systems; thus, 5G enables data processing for analytics purposes (Howell, 2019) to bring greater efficiency and performance monitoring beyond the plant's physical boundary (Palmer, 2019; Ranger, 2019b).

China has been heavily represented in the 3G Partnership Project (3GPP), driving the direction of 5G standards by supplying 40% documentary input, while Huawei and ZTE have both been committed to 5G more than any other company in the world (3GPP, 2020); in fact, these Chinese firms have been readily exporting 4G and 5G to Africa, the Near East, and the Far East (Freedom House, 2018). In addition, the 5G Infrastructure Public Private Partnership (5G-PPP) is a joint initiative between the European Commission and European ICT industry. 5G-PPP also contributes toward "solutions, architectures, technologies and standards for next generation communication", highlighting the viability of 5G for goods and services (5G-PPP, 2018). 5G is set to achieve potentially greater download speeds around the 10Gbps mark with sub-1ms latency (Bird, 2015b). It is widely publicized that 5G will use Massive Multiple Input Multiple Output (MIMO) radio technologies. 5G evolves the 4G eNodeB base station concept for RAN access into the next-generation 5G-NR gNodeB (CableFree, 2019). In the United Kingdom, the frequency spectrum intended to be used for 5G includes: the 'Low Band' in the 700MHz band, 'Mid Band' between 3.4 to 3.6 GHz, and 'High Band' in the 26GHz band. The use of multiple bands will decongest the available spectrum and increase the reliability and quality of service. A heightened experience will be an enabler for mass adoption of this seamless and ubiquitous communications medium.

The 5G Core Network (5GCN) packetized approach decouples the User Plane (U-Plane) from the Control Plane (C-Plane) with 5G services abstracted in a service-based model using software defined networking (Udunuwara, 2018) for a service-orientated infrastructure. Several C-Plane Functions in the Access and Mobility Management Function (AMF) control each subscription's access to the 5G network and the User Equipment's (UE) mobile connection and mobility management tasks. User data transits via the U-Plane Function (UPF) to the external Data Network, which is effectively the Internet, and synchronizes with the AMF using C-Plane signalling (Lescuyer & Lucidarme, 2011; Giust et al., 2018; Wireless Broadband Alliance, 2018). The use of abstraction in 5G as a cloud-based radio access network technology facilitates slicing to customize available functions in order to manage commodity mobile, IoT, and commercial cellular use-cases. Within this, the following are catered for: service, usage duration, network capacity, network speed, network latency, and security configurations. The 5GCN will stretch out to include Multi-access Edge Compute (MEC) capabilities as part of the architectural design to minimize latency. This makes it proportionately scalable and capable of reducing operating costs for the Telecommunications Company (Telco) (Reznik et al., 2018).

The 5GCN has evolved from the 4G network architecture, which in turn is a progression of the 3G infrastructure. In the 4G Evolved Packet Core, services such as the Mobility Management Entity and Home Subscription Server fulfill the C-Plane requirement for UE authentication to the network and billing. A combination of the Serving Gateway and the Packet Data Network Gateway provides a number of services that enable data flows from the UEs to egress to and ingress from the public Internet or translate Voice over LTE via the Multimedia Gateway to the Public Switched Telephone Network (PSTN). Notably, in the early days of voice over 5G it will be stepped down from the 5G UPF into the 4G Multimedia Gateway and beyond. The 3G network architecture was far more node-centric rather than service orientated as a progression from the hardware focused approach used in 2G. 3G was a service orientated approach, in which voice was carried via the Mobile Services Switching Center and Gateway Mobile Services Switching Center to the PSTN. Data flows in the 3G model was distributed to and from the internet via the Serving GPRS Support Node to the Internet via the Gateway GPRS Support Node. Figure 2 shows the evolution of cellular end-to-end (E2E) connectivity.

Figure 2. Simplified architecture showing the transition from 3G to 5G

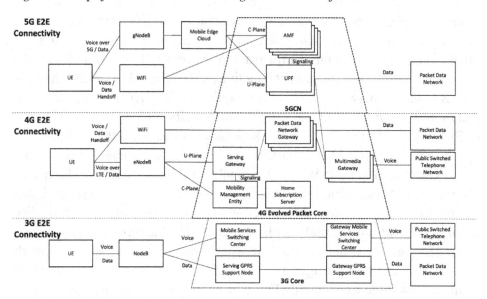

A hangover from the 3G cellular realm is the International Mobile Subscriber Identity (IMSI), in which an attacker could intercept the mobile device's handshake with the right equipment and with it attempt to access the RAN (Information Security Newspaper, 2019). This can occur even though the data passed over the air is encrypted with 128-bit block and streaming ciphers and utilize secure authentication and authenticity functions (Norrman, 2018; Information Security Newspaper, 2019). The 4G implementation tried to minimize the impact of IMSI exposure by using Globally Unique Temporary Identities (GUTI), which are correlated to the UE and protects the identity of the customer's subscription across the Telco's network (Do, 2013). In the 5G world, enhancements will include the adoption of the electronic Subscriber

Identity Module (SIM), which is already utilized by some smart watches in the 4G space. This replaces the interchangeable legacy SIMs (@Telecoms, 2018) and associates the end-user's subscription to the UE. There is also an evolution of the security measures used to identify subscribers on the RAN, called the Subscriber Permanent Identifier. 5G will use derived Authentication Key Agreement (AKA) to safeguard the subscriber's identity during a 5G smart device's handover to other nodes using a protected Subscription Concealed Identifier (SUCI) (Sauter, 2018).

Additionally, the European Space Agency is investigating the integration of satellite paths for 5G relay and therefore the dynamic use of radio spectrum to deconflict satellite and terrestrial communications in a shared spectrum environment. The intent of this investigation includes consideration of both upstream and downstream segments of satellite-borne capability. This is important for not only expanding 5G to rural expanses but also for accessibility to CAVs outside urban areas. However, 5G requires the right insertion price per bit for Telcos to adopt satellite paths and in turn augment the terrestrial base station cell coverage (Arnold & Franchi, 2019).

IoT Challenges

The concept of Industrial IoT (IIoT) by its title implies a bridge between smart automation systems and/or ethernet-based OT to enhance manufacturing and industrial processes using connectivity (DiFazio et al., 2020). In addition to the aforementioned short-haul wireless networks, IIoT will need to interoperate long-haul across networks and the Internet. An example is LPWAN network, also known as Lower Powered Radio Wide Area Network (LoRaWAN), which relies on media access control links to relay messages from end-point devices via gateways to a central server; the latter acts as a bridge between the packets carried by radio to ethernet IP networks communicating with applications. LPWAN uses a LoRaWAN protocol to communicate seamlessly and bi-directionally between manufacturers either regionally, nationally, or internationally across the Internet. This technology utilizes AES encryption for end-to-end sessions, interoperating with the server (LoRa Alliance, 2020). However, a cyber security researcher found that the implementation of the AES 128 encryption is flawed and provides non-optimal encryption that can be deciphered by an attacker with the right capability and skills (Valens, 2016).

Another protocol that is popular for this purpose is the Message Queuing Telemetry Transport (MQTT) technology developed initially for OT. MQTT is a M2M protocol transported by HTTP, and the data can be secured in transit using TLS. The lightweight stack makes it suitable for the IoT use-case to transmit data to back-end services in the public cloud (Bird, 2019). The Automotive Industry could utilize it for vehicle-to-vehicle, vehicle-to-device, and V2X communications paths in the autonomous car arena (Ryabchuk, 2018) to disseminate road congestion alerts, quality monitoring, or vehicle performance tracking data (Bird, 2015a; Speed, 2013). In addition, researchers are exploring blockchain to support the autonomous transportation industry. The Decentralized Autonomous Vehicle (DAV) Foundation has proposed that Ethereum and a transportation protocol can be utilized to manage the following: (a) autonomous transport charging network; (b) autonomous transport planning; and (c) track autonomous transportation assets. The model uses the Kademlia Decentralized Hash Table coupled with a ledger system, smart contracts, and DAV tokens for payment. The history of transactions and records are stored on a sub-chain to the Ethereum blockchain, and insurance companies would be a stakeholder of this approach. This implementation is aimed at the following categories of autonomous transportation: (a) drones; (b) CAVs; (c) autonomous boats; and (d) delivery robots (Rupp et al., 2019).

However, individuals must heed the cyber insecurity warning signs from the Jeep Cherokee hack of 2015 that was accomplished using the vehicle's over-the-air communications system. The outcome of the hack has potentially dire consequences from an attack that could be conducted through the vehicle's infotainment system (Greenberg, 2018). In addition, the following year, the same hackers also demonstrated an attack using a direct connection to the vehicle's onboard diagnostics port; in this case, they were able to disable the car's transmission and brakes by hacking the Engine Control Unit microcontroller that sat on the vehicle's Controller Area Network (Howard, 2016). Regulation would certainly be a necessity for IoT and blockchain convergence, in which smart contracts are used. In 2015, the risks associated with IoT were publicized in a U.S. Federal Trade Commission Report. The findings consisted of the following groupings: (a) unauthorized access and misuse of personal information; (b) facilitator for attacks on other systems; and (c) act as a catalyst to personal safety (FTC Report, 2015).

The rush of consumer IoT products to market in order to gain an advantage has resulted in a 'security as an afterthought' approach (Bird, 2018a). Ironically, the Zigbee Alliance and Z-Wave Alliance standards have security measures built in. Furthermore, both employ Advanced Encryption Standard 128-bit cipher suites to protect packet payload and prove authenticity (Gascón, 2009; RF Wireless World, 2012). However, these assets can by default connect to their respective hubs insecurely. Even if security options are enabled, Zigbee has a flaw that could allow devices to insecurely rejoin their network if they drop-off for some reason, like a power outage (SmartThings, n.d.). In 2012, researchers found Zigbee to be potentially susceptible to replay attacks that could force devices to perform illicit actions that will enable an attacker to gain access to the Zigbee network itself (Bowers, 2012). In 2013, researchers found Z-Wave to have a vulnerability within the device connection process dubbed Z-Shave. Even though the issuance of a new standard was an attempt to remediate a weakness through what is known as the S2 framework (Crist, 2017), devices were still susceptible to a downgrade attack that effectively resolved back to the vulnerable S0 version. This thereby allowed keys to be intercepted (Kovacs, 2018). Evidence of bugs (Boder, 2014) has led to other forms of security options being proposed, such as secure boot and securely authenticated connectivity to remote back-ends (Gamundani, 2014).

LPWAN technology is useful because it fills the gap between short range protocols and cellular network carriers using chirped spread spectrum technique below the L-band frequency range. As part of this functionality, there are two network joining mechanisms: (a) Over-the-Air Activation, which uses randomized nonce values to prevent replay attacks; and (b) Activation by Personalization, which enables devices to connect end-devices without initiating a join-request using predefined keys; unfortunately, hackers can use reverse engineering techniques or replay attacks to compromise these default keys that can enable man-in-the-middle attacks for the lifetime of the end-point device. Another risk is jamming of LPWAN communications that would deny data exchanges using this medium (Aras et al., 2017). Also, weak application session keys coupled with default device keys that should be changed through configuration could be in place, providing a vulnerability (Cimpanu, 2020).

In addition, the consumer short-range IoT hubs are connected to Wireless Fidelity (WiFi) access points and use them to communicate across the Internet. This not only makes hubs accessible for authorized remote access across the Internet, but it also puts them at risk if default passwords and default configuration are used. Existing WiFi is susceptible to the Key Re-installation Attack, which exploits a weakness in the way the WPA2 performs its four-way handshake by setting the Pre-shared Key (PSK) to zero. Vulnerable devices that have not been patched can be forced to reinitialize into this less secure state, thus enabling a man-in-the-middle attack and the interception of data over the wireless network. This is achievable without having to use previous brute force techniques that would normally be needed to crack the

PSK itself offline (Hoffman, 2017; Newman, 2017). WPA3 technology has been introduced to fix issues of the previous version. While vendors have been working hard to patch this problem on existing equipment, in mid-2019, researchers found a flaw called Dragonblood in the new WPA3 protocol stack. The WiFi Alliance hurriedly fixed this, but they did so in a manner that still presented a security flaw to other security researchers (Khandelwal, 2019).

From a 4G perspective, there is a possibility that IMSIs can be discerned from RAN handoffs to Non-3G Partnership Project (Non-3GPP) compliant nodes (O'Hanlon, Borgaonkar, & Hirschi, n.d.) such as IEEE 802.11ax IoT ready WiFi version 6 access points. Lessons have been learned in this respect, and 5G makes use of the Extensible Authentication Protocol (EAP) AKA (CableLabs, 2019) for smart-device handoff functions to non-3GPP networks and EAP-TLS for 5G enabled IoT devices. This is combined with SUCI to protect the UE identity. Researchers have proposed Internet Key Exchange protocol version 2 and Internet Protocol Security to protect traffic during hand-off operations to other networks outside the control of the 5G Telcos and rejoin the 5GCN via an Internet Gateway (Dutta, 2018; Jover & Marojevic, 2018; Zhang, 2017). Of course, security measures provided by the Telco will only be valid from the handset or device to the 5GCN; outbound traffic beyond the Telco destined for the onward Internet *per se* will require end-to-end encryption from the consumer's application(s) to the server at the other end (Wireless Broadband Alliance, 2018). However, this is particularly important, especially when experts are of the opinion that 5G Telcos will be offloading the U-Plane to the Internet WAN as soon as feasibility possible in order to achieve the best data rates and quality of service (Arnold & Franchi, 2019).

Artificial Intelligence

In the early 1980s, Fiegenbaum and McCorduck (1983) had a premonition that the new fifth generation of computing would be built on next-generation technologies centered around expert systems – now known as AI. Until recently, researchers have considered AI to be a technology of the future (Stanek, 2017). However, the dawn of cloud-based computing has helped in part to fulfil the AI prophecy. What was not so apparent is that software-based processing underlies AI's technological capability that in itself has been built using microprocessor technology. That said, beyond the hype, the real meaning of AI can be ambiguous and unintuitive to the layperson. In 2017, even though Machine-learning (ML) features were reported in the Technical Press, only nine percent of the U.K. populace had heard of it (Susskind, 2017). Landmarks in the history of AI consist of the following events: (a) Google's DeepMind that beat the world champion Fan Hui at the traditional game of AlphaGo in 2015 (Deepmind, n.d.); (b) International Business Machines (IBM) Watson that beat human contestants in the U.S. television game show Jeopardy in 2011 (Shacklett, 2017); and (c) IBM's Deep Blue that beat the champion chess player Garry Kasparov in 1997 (Levy, 2017).

Between 1997 and 2007, fabricators deployed robots into the manufacturing industry, and on average, each robot has replaced up to six workers. This is in fact the start of job redistribution through technology, revealing that the jobs of tomorrow will undoubtedly be different than the jobs of today. However, technology is the enabler but not the driver. The main culprit is the desire for efficiency and effective quality control that elaborates upon Dr W. Edward Deming's principles of Total Quality Management from the 1980s (Sherrer, 2010). To achieve this, industry implemented rule-based computing to enable automation (Hauert, Colton, & Susskind, 2017). This paradigm is called Routinization Hypothesis, in which repetitive tasks lend themselves to be codified and performed by machines operated through software (Maselli & Beblavý, 2013). Today, individuals recognize this as ML. To the layperson, computer intelligence is perceived as the speed at which mathematical calculations can be performed; but this is not true intelligence in its own right – just computation (Jamilly, 2018). AI technology today at its most complex is equivalent to the sensory cortex of the human brain, but there is more to brains than just neural networks. In an AI context, neuron networks are algorithmic modules that are needed to achieve real machine intelligence on our journey towards AGI. Embodied in this concept is our trajectory to achieve artificial abstract knowledge through hierarchical deep learning, consisting of weighted inputs and reinforcement learning through action and reward.

Experts are of the view that it takes the 'non-routine' to nurture creative empathy (Hauert et al., 2017), which is perhaps more akin to the aspirational vision by AI experts for AGI. To achieve this capability, a large range of tasks are required to learn adaptability and objective persistence. This is comparable to common sense, which in itself is hard to replicate in machines. It is a big step forward to move from reinforcement learning, gleaned from supervised learning, to learning by imitation, and this requires machines to effectively believe in their actions (Shanahan & Eslami, 2019). Taking this even further, the path to machine orientated instinct requires a replication of cognitive capabilities used by humans to assess a situation from multiple factors within an environment. To achieve this, neuroscience has found its way into the world of ML. Taking this further, algorithm-focused teaching and machine focused cognitive learning could potentially lead to the intended goal of machine consciousness and imagination. They could thereby take mankind one step further to achieving the panacea of AGI (Hassabis, 2018).

Concerns

Undoubtedly, the introduction of modern AI has generated a new philanthropic experiment based on super intelligent machines. Sceptics have expressed AI as either the worst thing for humanity or the best (Lentino, 2019). Today, cloud architectural patterns and recommended approaches for security control implementations are publicly available from CSPs, such as Amazon Web Services (AWS), Microsoft Azure, and Google Cloud Platform (GCP). All three are positioning themselves in the field of AI albeit Google has in effect been specialized in AI from the start of the GCP. AWS and Microsoft are collaborating through the growth of their Gluon open-source deep learning Application Programming Interface (API), which can be used by developers to prototype, build, train, and deploy advanced machine-learning models. AI adopters can espouse Google's TensorFlow library as a cross-platform for neural network machine-learning applications culminating in Google Cloud Vision API technology while leading companies like Deep Mind expand into deep reinforcement learning and neural reasoning. However, the security control interdependence within the cloud customer's 'shared security responsibility' generally has the potential of being interpreted incorrectly due to a reliance on compliance-based assessments. This could inadvertently enable control misconfigurations to seep into the environment and potentially expose or compromise data (Bird, 2017b; Knight, 2017; Bird, 2018b). On the other hand, CSPs themselves are not immune to failings and deficiencies. An administrator's mistyped command allegedly caused the AWS Simple Storage Service outages of 2008 (Bamish & Brohi, 2017) and 2017 in the United States (Sverdik, 2017). Additionally, Microsoft Azure has had a number of power related incidents in some of its data centers in 2018 and 2020 (Krazit, 2018; Moss, 2020). GCP faced an outage that affected several Google services that were, amongst others, in the 'U.S. West1' region (Tung, 2019). Therefore, unforeseen events need to be factored into customer utilization planning and business continuity planning, highlighting the necessity of effective governance and proper due diligence.

Since 2017, China has been stepping up its surveillance of troubled regions like Xingjang, where facial patterns are compared against a watchlist and used to thwart perceived terrorists. Other observers might call the process the victimization and oppression of the Uyghur population (Lenisa, 2018). To date, there are 200 million surveillance cameras installed across China. A number of Chinese AI and facial recognition companies, who are on a U.S. blacklist, have been involved in rolling out AI-backed surveillance in the troubled region (Yu, 2019). There have been many instances of AI implementations being used to benefit people at railway stations, in shops, and the like. However, it is also the intention of the Chinese State to conjoin video surveillance with AI for image analysis – leading towards their end goal of complete state control. This technology is already being used for pattern recognition by the Chinese police in Beijing, to enforce traffic laws in Futian, and in the trial of smart-traffic lights in Shenzhen. Police are also using smart glasses to display facial features, identity card, and vehicle identification number data from the national database; furthermore, Chinese companies are developing a real-time AI-based crowd monitoring system, which focuses on thermal mass (Chi et al., 2019a, 2019b); and technologies like those produced by Hicotech that appear to be judiciously used as part of the country's response to the Coronavirus Disease-19 pandemic (Hicotech, 2020).

In addition, 20 Chinese provincial security bureaus are using a system called Dragon Eye, which can identify a person from a 1.8-billion-person database with 95.5% accuracy. The authoritarian government in Beijing is keen to promote its approach to export its technology to help like-minded countries. Huawei has already deployed 'safe cities' technology to Kenya, which has reportedly assisted in curbing urban crime rates (Denyer, 2018). Yitu Technologies has exported the Dragon Eye facial recognition system to the Malaysian Auxiliary Force, enabling resources on the ground to match suspects faces with images held in the police database (Lentino, 2019; Chi et al., 2019a). Additionally, there have been concerns about AI and facial recognition technology being used against demonstrators in Hong Kong during the pro-democracy demonstrations of 2019. Demonstrators have been defying emergency laws by wearing face masks, destroying closed circuit television, and damaging smart-lamp posts in fear that the authorities are not adhering to Hong Kong legislation, which provides more rights than mainland China (Schmidt, 2019).

In recent years in the United States, a CAV using AI under test misidentified a cyclist as a plastic bag and therefore saw the person as posing no threat; but in reality, the risk was actually to the cyclist, and the misidentified computation actually caused a collision (Coldicutt & Harding, 2018). Hence, the vision of AI immersion is a long way off, and humans still need to be in the loop and remain accountable for control over the CAVs (Exeros, 2019). In the meantime, without some form of regulation, society could be at risk of losing control. This is especially true as Gartner estimated that 30% of Industry 4.0 projects will be conveniently sourcing algorithms from marketplaces (Gartner, 2017). Ultimately, AI algorithms must conduct computations in a reliable manner, and protective measures need to be designed from the outset to safeguard data integrity. Therefore, there is a need to protect algorithms to assure the integrity of code coupled with verifiable evidence of validity (Challen et al, 2019); and to help ensure processed outcomes are sound, reliable, and more trustworthy than spurious algorithms of lesser provenance.

SOLUTIONS AND RECOMMENDATIONS

From a security point-of-view, for many years, the confidentiality, integrity and availability of ICT systems has been in the form of the CIA triad. This has been embodied in the ISO/IEC 27000 series of information security standards and the U.S. National Institute of Standards and Technology (NIST) 800 series of standards. ISO/IEC 27002:2013 and NIST 800-171 list categories of security control types with the intention to enable organisations to comply with and adequately implement appropriate countermeasures. The OT industry provides another perspective to the importance of data integrity, which, for safety purposes, may surpass the confidentially aspect. Researchers have deemed traditional methods of quantifying hazards in OT, such as Failure Modes Effects Analysis, inefficient, and their reliability is questionable within the modern-day systems. This is driving cyber security aspects for OT through the ISA/IEC 62443:2018 standard, which supplements the IEC 61508:2010 standard of functional safety. The combination of both confidentiality and integrity has not yet fully resonated into the IoT domain, and this is particularly concerning because IoT will be the conduit to transmit OT data to backends for processing using AI techniques.

Experts have stated that IoT is already underpinning services, industries, and CNI, and there is an absolute necessity to secure IoT (Allpress & Butler, 2018) E2E. Even though there are alliances associated with front-end devices, like those for Zigbee, Z-Wave, and WiFi, experts have found flaws in technology implementations. This is because tech-businesses are possibly driven by the race for customer adoption to achieve market emersion (Minj, 2019). Researchers have argued that normalization is the key to this problem. This is coupled with IoT architectural ontologies, which drive quality and reliability from industry, and a granular model, which avoids iffy product manufacturing or provenance (Allpress & Butler, 2018). In fact, liability by default could be a consequence if cyber hygiene is compromised through the lack of preventative measures such as patching. Researchers have recognized that IT and OT teams should no longer operate in silos and should share their experience, knowledge, and lessons that can be learned for the common good of this diverse industry (Cyber-X, 2019).

In 2017, ENISA and Europol categorically argued the case for cooperation as part of an agenda to secure IoT devices (Warwick, 2017). The IoT Security Foundation took action in 2017 by releasing their IoT Security Compliance framework. Additionally, Industrial IoT Consortium released their own 'New IoT Security Maturity Model' (IIC Consortium, 2018). Some action has already been taken to remedy the cyber risks to CAVs in the form of a cyber security component of the 5StarS framework (Insurance Edge Editor, 2019) and the impending ISO/SAE 21434 Cyber Security Engineering standard that complements the Road vehicles Functional safety standard ISO 26262:2018. Both are avenues to establish a path of trust for consumers to understand the cyber security features in future vehicles.

The General Data Protection Regulation is now enshrined in the new U.K. Data Protection Act 2018. This act is applicable not only in the European Union (EU), but also globally to enforce the adequate protection of PII in non-EU countries. Where national data protection regulators find any breaches of EU PII, European organizations could end up being fined a maximum of four percent of worldwide group turnover (Schmidt, 2017). In addition, the Network and Information System Directive 2016/1148 not only delineates the requirement for cyber security incident response for each member state, but it also applies to digital service providers of essential services that includes utilities, transport, financial services, and health and digital infrastructure (Lord, 2018). However, more regulation is required. The United States has taken steps by submitting the IoT Cybersecurity Improvement Act, which is being presented for consideration to the Senate and the House in mid-2019 (Warner, 2019). In the United Kingdom, the Department of Culture, Media, and Sports has undertaken a public consultation regarding IoT (OCL, 2019) and has introduced an IoT code of practice (Manners, 2018). However, at the first PETRAS IoT conference, academics declared that greater action is required to safeguard IoT – by both Government and Industry. This would eventually lead to standardization and regulation (Zhang, Kuntz, & Schröder, 2017). Portnox, a company registered on Gartner Peerinsight's website, already concluded the importance of regulation and stated that regulatory compliance will be the biggest influencer of IoT adoption moving forward (Amitai, 2018).

On the tail of regulatory initiatives, experts in the field have made appeals for ethics, standards, and frameworks pertaining to ML and AI capabilities (Yapp, 2017). In Europe officials are considering ethical aspects for the use of technology in the form of a British Standard on Ethics in Robotics and a European Commission report that will contribute towards the ethical implementations of AI controlled robotics (Hassabis, 2018). From an algorithm perspective, AI frameworks are already being open sourced and available for use on public cloud platforms; this then raises the risk of them potentially being used for nefarious purposes by hackers once some modifications have been made. Experts using AI for space applications are categorically saying that developers or data scientists cannot simply plug in code anymore, and integrators need to make considerations on the protection of algorithms and embedding security capabilities within computing architectures used in AI. In addition to this, data scientists also need to have the right sets of skills to develop ML and AI systems (Winder, 2018) proficiently and be aware of the cyber risks in a wider socio-technical context.

FUTURE RESEARCH DIRECTION

Analysis of attack trends in this chapter has identified that various threat actors can abuse the multiple layers of differing architectures and technologies that make up today's Industry 4.0. Unfortunately, IoT presents a ferial environment that can increase the attack landscape and potentially result in unintended consequences. A concern here is the integrity of smart device applications being used in some cases to remotely access SCADA systems (Lord, 2018). For instance, in 2016, a Nokia malware report stated that out of 85% of all malicious traffic detected transiting cellular networks, Android malware comprised 74% of this traffic, while iOS only consisted of four percent (Bird, 2017c). The company F-Secure stated that cyber-attacks on IoT devices has increased three-fold in 2019 (Doffman, 2019a). Research conducted by Irdeto in 2018 identified that 80% of organizations surveyed had witnessed an IoT focused cyber-attack, and as a consequence, 90% experienced downtime, customer data compromises, or end-user safety risks (Helpnet Security, 2019c).

The dangers of cyber-attacks are prevalent, so much so that the U.S. Department of Defense is using the words 'cyber warfare' more often (Doffman, 2019b). This is because cyber-attacks are transcending attack categories not just associated with hacker groups but also associated with risks needing to consider state-sponsored attacks against commercial companies. There is also a cross-over between cyber-criminality and foreign state cyber operations that include cyber-espionage, and agendas related to the pursuit of financial, or political gain. This provides a focus of attention erring towards governance from both national and international perspectives, which sweeps up regulations, legislation, and standards often used in compliance approaches. However, researchers need to further explore the relationship between compliance and risk management. The author will cover risk versus compliance challenges in relation to the public cloud in Chapter 2. The author further explores aspects such as cyber security within the supply-chain and the rigor of control-set implementation in Chapters 3 and 4. Chapter 8 explores blockchain further in relation to a number of use-cases including IoT.

CONCLUSION

Arguably, humankind finds itself in a situation in which individuals are being blindsided by the audacity and repetition of cyber-attacks (Bird, 2013b). The rapid pace of change is outstripping existing laws and measures to apply proper legislative control that could result in serious inefficiencies in the safeguarding of our wellbeing in cyberspace. The connectivity diversity, insecurity by design and deployment, software opacity, and even security by obscurity approaches are themselves impediments to a known good state (Nurse, 2018). Therefore, insecurity is a real risk of becoming the weak underbelly of the Fourth Industrial Revolution. There are a number of cyber security issues that have been explored from not only the ICT arena but also from problems that we face today, ranging across OT, IoT, and AI. The author has used this chapter to disambiguate various levels of technological capability that together make up Industry 4.0. The diagram in Figure 3 shows the E2E connectivity from front-end clients to back-end systems.

Over the past 20 years, rapid technological development has been the main focus of ICT; in contrast, the driver for OT progression has been 'business need.' Both IT and OT have evolved towards Industry 4.0 but on parallel

Figure 3. High-level representation of atypical Industry 4.0 Architecture

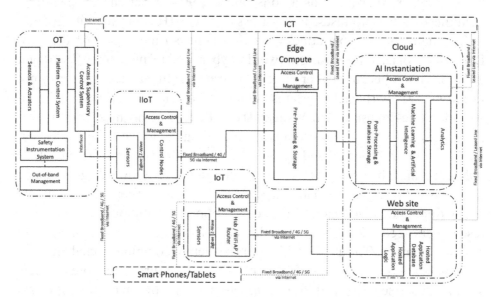

paths (Oliver, 2018). The OT standard ISA/IEC 62443:2018 will go some way to demystify cyber security in that area, but there should be a marriage of cyber understanding between IT and OT. This should be underwritten by standards to meet regulatory commitments in the both domains in order to counteract the misuse of systems and protect data. However, there is a way to go in the IoT space because the developer community is of the opinion that legislating too early in the IoT realm could hamper innovation (Green, 2018) by applying too many constraints. It will take the United Nations Economic Commission for Europe World Forum on the Harmonization of Vehicle Regulations (United Nations Economic Commission for Europe, n.d.) to at least align CAV manufacturers into one legislative framework within Europe. The enacted U.K. Autonomous and Electric Vehicle Act of 2018 will probably need to be compatible with this framework for trade purposes (Legislation.gov.uk, 2018). Independent of European-focused legislative itineraries, the U.S. House of Representatives passed the Safely Ensuring Lives Future Deployment and Research In Vehicle Evolution Act in 2017 (McCormick, 2017). Unfortunately, the bill for the American Vision for Safer Transportation through Advancement of Revolutionary Technologies Act failed to be endorsed in 2018 (Lawson, 2019), leaving a vacuum in the interim.

In addition to this, there is the subject of competing interests versus international standards alignment between the West and countries like China.

On the one hand, the Chinese have been striving towards technology leadership that contributes to their economic growth. Yet on the other hand, its national security agenda has arguably contradicted this. For example, counter-terrorism regulations have a provision for backdoors and decryption capabilities and infers that China's encryption standards may be able to be cracked by the State (Zhou, 2016) and would affect their adoption internationally. For instance, China has developed the ZUC stream cipher, and global implementations of 4G uses it. Additionally, China has integrated the SM2 PKI algorithm into OpenSSL. However, ISO and the Institute of Electrical and Electronics Engineers has rejected the Wireless Local Area Network Authentication and Privacy Infrastructure (WAPI) standard that is widely used in China (Laski & Segal, 2019; Yang, n.d.). Suspicion over Huawei and ZTE has come about since accusations over email hacking devices being placed in Zambian infrastructure and backdoors in Sri Lankan Internet Service Provider networks. This has arguably fueled the ban of Huawei and ZTE 5G equipment in Australia and heightened concerns in the United States (Freedom House, 2014, 2018). In late 2019, a new standard was proposed consisting of a new set of rules for Internet architecture, which was supported by Huawei and the Chinese government; the proposal called 'New IP' provided the pretext of more efficient space-terrestrial communications but it was rejected by the Internet technical forum Réseaux IP Européens as it favored authoritarian regimes (Kundaliya, 2020). Coupled with this is standardization and regulations (Porter 2019; Morgado, Huq, Mumtaz & Rodriguez, 2017) that will need to include new 5G standards for terrestrial and satellite use (Arnold & Franchi, 2019) and thereby influence seamless and reliable high-speed connectivity for the end-user.

Civilization needs to consider regulation for the use of AI type technology, but countries also need to combine it with an agreed set of ethics for each use-case. These will vary depending on the area of the world to which it applies. For instance, China has brought in a new law that all Chinese citizens who register a new mobile SIM card must also undergo AI-backed facial recognition scans, which usurp the previous requirement for identity cards or passports to fulfil the same purpose. Moreover, human rights activists have decreed that this is another measure that contributes towards China's dystopian agenda (Kuo, 2019). That said, the West needs to be cautious because U.S. law enforcement is implementing a facial recognition system called Clearview AI. An Australian company designed the system, which uses a database of scraped images sourced from the Internet to identify a person when compared to traditional surveillance images. Yet the system still has to be assessed for accuracy by the National Institute of Standards and Technology (Hill, 2020). Cases like this have incited U.S. lawmakers to raise concerns publicly, and the European Commission is considering a ban up to five years on the use of facial recognition in public places. This is expected to enable legislation to catch up with technology progression in this area (British Broadcasting Corporation, 2020). In contrast, in the first quarter of 2020, Washington state has endorsed the first law in the United States that regulates facial recognition. This is at a time when the Department of Homeland Security is considering deploying more of this intrusive technology into airports and along the border (Staff, 2020). The use of face recognition has been muted in the United States during the Coronavirus Disease-19 pandemic, but House Oversight Committee hearings on the subject have been delayed, causing any federal legislation to be delayed (SecurityMagazine, 2020).

With the veritable regulatory vacuum in the West, designing software-defined architectures to fulfil regulatory requirements must reach beyond cyber security mapping against standards to avoid purely compliance orientated approaches. This is because glossing over the details obscures the identification of necessary countermeasures for secure-by-design. Understanding data and code or technology provenance must be considered to address the risk of authoritarian influences seeping into our integrated AI systems as it allegedly has already for network infrastructure. It will also help mitigate cyber-criminals or nation-states abusing AI through adversarial techniques to poison data or manipulate algorithms – cyber security can no longer be an afterthought in the AI context (Europol, 2019). To this end, the European Commission has published their guidelines on ethical and trustworthy AI (Bergmann et al., 2018). Without ethics and regulation, Industry 4.0 could become one big experiment in its own right (Xu, David, & Kim, 2018).

REFERENCES

AccentureSecurity. (2019). *The cost of cybercrime* [PDF document]. Retrieve from https://www.accenture.com/_acnmedia/PDF-96/Accenture-2019-Cost-of-Cybercrime-Study-Final.pdf#zoom=50

Allpress, S., & Butler, J. (2018). *IoT discussion panel*. PETRAS Internet of Things Conference, IET, London, UK.

Amitai, O. (2018). *Is IoT security being regulated?* Retrieved from https://www.itproportal.com/features/is-iot-security-being-regulated/

Aras, E., Ramachandran, G., Lawrence, P., & Hughes, D. (2017). Exploring the security vulnerabilities of LoRa. *Proceedings of the 3rd IEEE International Conference on Cybernetics.* doi: 10.1109/CYBConf.2017.7985777

Arnold, K., & Franchi, A. (2019). 5G parallel stream. UK Space Conference, Newport, UK.

Assante, M. (2016). *Confirmation of a coordinated attack on the Ukrainian power grid* [Weblog comment]. Retrieved from https://ics.sans.org/blog/2016/01/09/confirmation-of-a-coordinated-attack-on-the-ukrainian-power-grid

Bamish, M., & Brohi, S. (2011). Seven deadly threats and vulnerabilities in cloud computing. *International Journal of Advanced Engineering Sciences and Technologies, 9*(1), 87–90.

Bergmann, U., Bonefeld-Dahl, C., Dignum, V., Gagné, J., Metzinger, T., Petit, N., Steinacker, S., ... Yeung, K. (2018). Ethics guidelines for trustworthy AI-independent high-level expert group on artificial intelligence. Brussels: European Commission.

Berting, J., Mills, S., & Wintersberger, H. (1980). *The socio-economic impact of microelectronics.* Pergamon Press.

Bird, D. (2013). Underlying dangers. *ITNOW, 55*(4), 32–33. doi:10.1093/itnow/bwt077

Bird, D. (2015a). Buckle up. *ITNOW, 57*(2), 24–25. doi:10.1093/itnow/bwv038

Bird, D. (2015b). The need for 5G speed. *ITNOW, 57*(3), 34–35. doi:10.1093/itnow/bwv071

Bird, D. (2017a). Collaborative effects of cyberspace. In S. Crabb (Ed.), Current practices and trends in technical and professional communication (pp. 252-274). ISTC Books.

Bird, D. (2017b). *A shared responsibility.* Retrieved from: https://www.bcs.org/content/conWebDoc/58147

Bird, D. (2017c). Mobile threat. *ITNOW, 59*(4), 46–47. doi:10.1093/itnow/bwx132

Bird, D. (2018a). Industry 4.0 – The accumulative risks. *CyberTalk, 20,* 58–60.

Bird, D. (2018b). AI in the Cloud. *ITNOW, 60*(2), 38–39. doi:10.1093/itnow/bwy048

Bird, D. (2019). Cybersecurity considerations for Internet of things small satellite systems. *Current Analysis on Communications Engineering Journal, 2,* 69–79.

Bird, D., & Curry, J. (2018). A case for using blended learning and development techniques to aid the delivery of a UK cybersecurity core body of knowledge. *International Journal of Systems and Software Security and Protection, 9*(2), 28–45. doi:10.4018/IJSSSP.2018040103

Boder, R. (2014). *Can hackers unlock my z-wave door lock.* Retrieved from https://suretyhome.com/can-hackers-unlock-my-z-wave-door-lock/

Bowers, B. (2012). *ZigBee wireless security: A new age penetration tester's toolkit* [Weblog comment]. Rtrieved from https://www.ciscopress.com/articles/article.asp?p=1823368&seqNum=4

Bradbury, D. (2001). *Why public key infrastructure is a good idea.* Retrieved from https://www.computerweekly.com/feature/Why-public-key-infrastructure-is-a-good-idea

British Broadcasting Corporation. (2020). *Facial recognition: EU considers ban of up to five years.* Retrieved from https://www-bbc-com.cdn.ampproject.org/c/s/www.bbc.com/news/amp/technology-51148501

Brumfield, C. (2019). *Russia's Sandworm hacking group heralds new era of cyber warfare.* Retrieved from https://www.csoonline.com/article/3455172/a-new-era-of-cyber-warfare-russias-sandworm-shows-we-are-all-ukraine-on-the-internet.html

Bu, R. (n.d.). *The great firewall of China.* Murray State University.

Burt, C. (2017). *Report: China-based attacked targeting MSPs, cloud hosts.* Retrieved from http://m.talkincloud.com/cloud-computing-security/report-china-based-attacks-targeting-msps-cloud-hosts

Caban, D. (2019). *Triton malware case study: FireEye, Schneider Electric & NCSC.* Paper presented at CyberUK Conference, Glasgow, UK.

CableFree. (2019). *5G terminology: The gNB.* Retrieved from https://www.5g-networks.net/uncategorized/5g-terminology-the-gnb/

CableLabs. (2019). *A comparative introduction to 4G and 5G authentication.* Retrieved from https://www.cablelabs.com/insights/a-comparative-introduction-to-4g-and-5g-authentication

Challen, R., Denny, J., Pitt, M., Gompels, L., Edwards, T., & Tsaneva-Atanasova, K. (2019). Artificial intelligence, bias and clinical safety. *BMJ Quality & Safety Journal, 28*(3), 231–237. doi:10.1136/bmjqs-2018-008370 PMID:30636200

Chi, C., Yu, G., Yeh, J., Li, X., Pen, J., … Kai-Fu, L. (2019a). *China internet report 2019.* Hong Kong: South China Morning Post.

Chi, C., Yu, G., Yeh, J., Li, X., Pen, J., … Kai-Fu, L. (2019b). *China internet report 2019.* Retrieved from https://www.scmp.com/china-internet-report#secondSubscriptionForm

Cimpanu, C. (2019). *Second Florida city pays giant ransom to ransomware gang in a week.* Retrieved from https://www.zdnet.com/article/second-florida-city-pays-giant-ransom-to-ransomware-gang-in-a-week/

Cimpanu, C. (2020). *LoRaWAN networks are spreading but security researchers say beware.* Retrieved from https://www.zdnet.com/article/lorawan-networks-are-spreading-but-security-researchers-say-beware/

Cluley, G. (2013). *Second Dutch teenager arrested for WikiLeaks-related DDoS attacks.* Retrieved from https://nakedsecurity.sophos.com/2010/12/12/second-dutch-arrest-wikileaks-ddos-attacks/

Coldicutt, R., & Harding, V. (2018). *The ethics of artificial intelligence.* Paper presented at The Times Science Festival, Cheltenham, UK.

Crist, R. (2017). *Your Z-Wave smart home gadgets just got more secure.* Retrieved from https://www.cnet.com/news/your-z-wave-smart-home-gadgets-just-got-more-secure/

Cyber-X. (2019). *Global ICS & HoT risk report* [PDF document]. Retrieved from www.cyberx-labs.com

Denyer, S. (2018). *Beijing bets on facial recognition in a big drive for total surveillance.* Retrieved from https://www.washingtonpost.com/news/world/wp/2018/01/07/fature/in-china-facial-recognition-is-sharp-end-of-a-drive-for-total-surveillance

DesignSpark. (2016). *11 Internet of Things (IoT) protocols you need to know about*. Retrieved from https://www.rs-online.com/designspark/eleven-internet-of-things-iot-protocols-you-need-to-know-about

DiFazio, G., Poulos, K., Authier, G., & Biodorn, K. (2020). *Navigating industrial cyber security* [PDF document]. Retrieved from https://www.tripwire.com/-/media/tripwiredotcom/files/book/tripwire_navigating_industrial_cybersecurity_a_field_guide.pdf

Do, M. (2013). *LTE: User identifiers - IMSI and GUTI* [Weblog comment]. Retrieved from https://www.netmanias.com/en/post/blog/5929/lte/lte-user-identifiers-imsi-and-guti

Doffman, Z. (2019a). *Cyberattacks on IOT devices surge 300% in 2019, 'measured in billions', report claims*. Retrieved from https://www.forbes.com/sites/zakdoffman/2019/09/14/dangerous-cyberattacks-on-iot-devices-up-300-in-2019-now-rampant-report-claims/

Doffman, Z. (2019b). *Cyber warfare: U.S. military admits immediate danger is 'keeping us up at night'*. Retrieved from https://www-forbes-com.cdn.ampproject.org/c/s/www.forbes.com/sites/zakdoffman/2019/07/21/cyber-warfare-u-s-military-admits-immediate-danger-is-keeping-us-up-at-night/amp/

Dutta, A. (2018). *Mobility protocols and handover optimization* [PDF document]. Retrieved from Lecture Notes Online Website: http://sites.ieee.org/denver-com/files/2018/05/Boulder-DL-Talk.pdf

Electronic Frontier Foundation. (n.d.). *HTTPS everywhere*. Retrieved from https://www.eff.org/https-everywhere

Europol. (2019). *Trustworthy AI requires solid cybersecurity*. Retrieved from https://www.europol.europa.eu/newsroom/news/trustworthy-ai-requires-solid-cybersecurity

Exeros. (2019). *Advanced driver assistance system explained*. Retrieved from https://www.exeros-technologies.com/advanced-driver-assistance-system-explained/

Fiegenbaum, E., & McCorduck, P. (1983). *The fifth generation: Artificial intelligence & Japan's computer challenge to the world*. Reading, MA: Addison Wesley Publishing Co.

Filippi, L., Moerman, K., Daalderop, G., Alexander, P., Schober, F., & Pfliegl, W. (n.d.). *Ready to roll: Why 802.11p beats LTE and 5G for V2x* [PDF document]. Retrieved from https://assets.new.siemens.com/siemens/assets/public.1510309207.ab5935c545ee430a94910921b8ec75f3c17bab6c.its-g5-ready-to-roll-en.pdf

Freedom House. (2014). *Freedom on the net: Tightening the net: Governments expand online controls* [PDF document]. Retrieved from https://freedomhouse.org/sites/default/files/FOTN_2014_Full_Report_compressedv2_0.pdf

Freedom House. (2018). *Freedom on the net: The rise of digital authoritarianism* [PDF document]. Retrieved from https://freedomhouse.org/sites/default/files/FOTN_2018_Final%20Booklet_11_1_2018.pdf

Gamundani, A. (2014). An algorithmic framework security model for Internet of things. *International Journal of Computer Trends and Technology, 12*(1), 16–20. doi:10.14445/22312803/IJCTT-V12P105

Gartner. (2017). *Gartner says by 2020, at least 30 percent of industrie 4.0 projects will source their algorithms from leading algorithm marketplaces.* Retrieved from https://www.gartner.com/en/newsroom/press-releases/2017-03-21-gartner-says-by-2020-at-least-30-percent-of-industrie-4-projects-will-source-their-algorithms-from-leading-algorithm-marketplaces

Gartner. (n.d.). *Managed service provider.* Retrieved from https://www.gartner.com/it-glossary/msp-management-service-provider

Gascón, D. (2009). *Security in 802.15.4 and ZigBee networks* [Weblog comment]. Retrieved from http://www.libelium.com/security-802-15-4-zigbee/

Gates, B. (1999). *Business @ the speed of thought.* Grand Central Publishing. doi:10.1111/1467-8616.00097

Giust, F., Verin, G., Antevski, K., Chou, J., Fang, Y., Featherstone, W., … Zhou, Z. (2018). *MEC deployments in 4G and evolution towards 5G* [PDF document]. Retrieved from https://www.etsi.org/images/files/ETSIWhitePapers/etsi_wp24_MEC_deployment_in_4G_5G_FINAL.pdf

GOV.UK. (2013). *Don't get caught on the net by tax rebate phishing scam.* Retrieved from https://www.gov.uk/government/news/don-t-get-caught-on-the-net-by-tax-rebate-phishing-scam

3.   GPP. (2020). *3rd generation partnership project: The mobile broadband standard*. Retrieved from https://www.3gpp.org/

Greatfire.org. (2018). *We monitor and challenge internet censorship in China*. Retrieved from https://en.greatfire.org

Green, E. (2018). *Commodity IoT review*. Paper presented at CyberUK, Manchester, UK.

Greenberg, A. (2018). *Hackers remotely kill a jeep on the highway—With me in it*. Retrieved from https://www.wired.com/2015/07/hackers-remotely-kill-jeep-highway/

Griffiths, J. (2019). *When Chinese hackers declared war on the rest of us*. Retrieved from https://www.technologyreview.com/s/612638/when-chinese-hackers-declared-war-on-the-rest-of-us/

GSMA. (2014). *Understanding the Internet of Things* [PDF document]. Retrieved from https://www.gsma.com/iot/wp-content/uploads/2014/08/cl_iot_wp_07_14.pdf

Hassabis, D. (2018). *AI deep mind*. Paper presented at The Times Science Festival, Cheltenham, UK.

Hauert, S., Colton, S., & Susskind, D. (2017). *Living in a machine world*. Paper presented at The Times Science Festival, Cheltenham, UK.

Helpnet Security. (2019a). *Cyberthreats targeting municipalities are on the rise*. Retrieved from https://www.helpnetsecurity.com/2019/07/23/cyberthreats-targeting-municipalities/

Helpnet Security. (2019b). *Cybersecurity should not be an afterthought within industrial environments*. Retrieved from https://www.helpnetsecurity.com/2019/07/09/cybersecurity-industrial-environments/

Helpnet Security. (2019c). *IoT cyberattacks are the new normal, the security mindset isn't*. Retrieved from https://www.helpnetsecurity.com/2019/05/29/iot-cyberattacks/

Her Majesty's Government. (2016). *National cyber security strategy 2016-2021*. HM Government.

Herzog, S. (2017). Ten years after the Estonian cyberattacks: Defense and adaptation in the age of digital insecurity. *Georgetown Journal of International Affairs*, *18*(3), 67–78. doi:10.1353/gia.2017.0038

Hicotech. (2020). *Facial Recognition Temperature Instrument Thermal Infrared Imaging CCTV Digital IP Monitoring PC Controller Web WDR Camera with 8" Display Screen*. Retrieved from https://hicotek.en.made-in-china.com/product/kZfQCHyjrnVM/China-Facial-Recognition-Temperature-Instrument-Thermal-Infrared-Imaging-CCTV-Digital-IP-Monitoring-PC-Controller-Web-WDR-Camera-with-8-Display-Screen.html

Hill, K. (2020). *The secretive company that might end privacy as we know it*. Retrieved from https://www.nytimes.com/2020/01/18/technology/clearview-privacy-facial-recognition.html?smid=nytcore-ios-share

Hoffman, C. (2017). *Your Wi-Fi's WPA2 encryption can be cracked offline: Here's how*. Retrieved from https://www.howtogeek.com/202441/your-wi-fi%E2%80%99s-wpa2-encryption-can-be-cracked-offline-here%E2%80%99s-how/

Howard, B. (2016). *The Jeep Cherokee hack gets worse — at least if hackers can get physical access to the car first*. Retrieved from https://www.extremetech.com/extreme/232947-jeep-cherokee-hack-gets-worse-at-least-if-hackers-can-get-physical-access-to-the-car-first

Howell, D. (2019). *Future factory: How 5G will transform industry, networking and communications*. Retrieved from https://www.silicon.co.uk/cloud/5g-will-transform-industry-networking-communications-262419/amp

IIC Consortium. (2018). *IoT security maturity model: Description and intended use* [PDF document]. Retrieved from https://www.iiconsortium.org/pdf/SMM_Description_and_Intended_Use_2018-04-09.pdf

Ilascu, I. (2019). *Hackers ask for $5.3 million ransom, turn down $400k, get nothing*. Retrieved from https://www.bleepingcomputer.com/news/security/hackers-ask-for-53-million-ransom-turn-down-400k-get-nothing/

Information Security Newspaper. (2019). *New attack variant against 4G and 5G networks*. Retrieved from https://www.securitynewspaper.com/2019/02/25/%EF%BB%BFnew-attack-variant-against-4g-and-5g-networks/

Insurance Edge Editor. (2019). *Autonomous tech: 5StarS consortium on driverless cars welcomed by Thatcham*. Retrieved from https://insurance-edge.net/2019/06/27/autonomous-tech-5stars-consortium-on-driverless-cars-welcomed-by-thatcham/

Jamilly, M. (2018). *Limitations of AI.* Retrieved from https://www.bcs.org/content-hub/limitations-of-ai/

Jeffrey, C. (2018). *GitHub falls victim to largest DDoS attack ever recorded.* Retrieved from https://www.techspot.com/news/73522-github-hit-massive-ddos-attack.html

Jover, R., & Marojevic, V. (2018). *Security and protocol exploit analysis of the 5G specifications* [PDF document]. Retrieved from https://arxiv.org/pdf/1809.06925.pdf

Kasperksy. (n.d.b). *BlackEnergy APT attacks in Ukraine.* Retrieved from https://www.kaspersky.com/resource-center/threats/blackenergy

Kaspersky. (n.d.a). *CCleaner malware* [Web log comment]. Retrieved from https://www.kaspersky.com/resource-center/threats/ccleaner-malware

Khandelwal, S. (2014). *Silk road dealer plead guilty for selling illegal drugs for Bitcoins* [Web log comment]. Retrieved from https://thehackernews.com/2014/04/silk-road-dealer-plead-guilty-for_25.html

Khandelwal, S. (2017). *Feds seize AlphaBay and Hansa markets in major dark-web bust* [Web log comment]. Retrieved from https://thehackernews.com/2017/07/alphabay-hansa-darkweb-markets-seized.html

Khandelwal, S. (2019). *Researchers discover new ways to hack WPA3 protected WiFi passwords.* Retrieved from https://thehackernews.com/2019/08/hack-wpa3-wifi-password.html?m=1

Knight, W. (2017). *AI is taking over the Cloud.* Retrieved from https://www.technologyreview.com/s/608678/ai-is-taking-over-the-cloud/

Kovacs, E. (2018). *100 million IoT devices possibly exposed to Z-Wave attack.* Retrieved from https://www.securityweek.com/100-million-iot-devices-possibly-exposed-z-wave-attack

Krazit, T. (2018). *Microsoft releases details on last week's big Azure outage, during which servers were damaged but no data was lost.* Retrieved from https://www.geekwire.com/2018/microsoft-releases-details-last-weeks-big-azure-outage-servers-damaged-no-data-lost/

Kundaliya, D. (2020). *Internet governance body RIPE opposes Chinese proposal to change core internet protocols*. Retrieved from https://www.computing.co.uk/news/4014383/internet-governance-body-ripe-opposes-chinese-proposal-change-core-internet-protocols

Kuo, L. (2019). *China brings in mandatory facial recognition for mobile phone users*. Retrieved from https://www.theguardian.com/world/2019/dec/02/china-brings-in-mandatory-facial-recognition-for-mobile-phone-users

Laski, L., & Segal, A. (2019). *The Encryption debate in China*. Retrieved from https://carnegieendowment.org/2019/05/30/encryption-debate-in-china-pub-79216

Lawson, S. (2019). *AV START is dead, but feds have given an inch on regulation*. Retrieved from https://www.tu-auto.com/av-start-is-dead-but-feds-have-given-an-inch-on-regulation/

Legislation.gov.uk. (2018). *Automated and electric vehicles act 2018*. Retrieved from http://www.legislation.gov.uk/ukpga/2018/18/contents/enacted

Lenisa, Y. (2018). *Facial recognition – The future of mobile payments in China* [Weblog comment]. Retrieved from https://www.it-consultis.com/blog/facila-recongition-future-mobile-payments-china

Lentino, A. (2019). *This Chinese facial recognition start-up can identify a person in seconds*. Retrieved from https://www.cnbc.com/2019/05/16/this-chinese-facial-recognition-start-up-can-id-a-person-in-seconds.html

Lescuyer, P., & Lucidarme, T. (2008). *Evolved Packet System (EPS): The LTE and the SAE evolution of 3G UMTS*. John Wiley & Sons Ltd. doi:10.1002/9780470723678

Levy, S. (2017). *What deep blue tells us about AI in 2017*. Retrieved from https://www.wired.com/2017/05/what-deep-blue-tells-us-about-ai-in-2017/

Lewis, N. (n.d.). *Is BlackEnergy malware a threat to U.S. utility companies?* Retrieved from https://searchsecurity.techtarget.com/answer/Is-BlackEnergy-malware-a-threat-to-US-utility-companies

LoRa Alliance. (2020). *What is the LoRaWAN® specification?* Retrieved from https://lora-alliance.org/about-lorawan

Lord, N. (2018). *What is the NIS Directive? Definition, requirements, penalties, best practices for compliance, and more.* Retrieved from https://digitalguardian.com/blog/what-nis-directive-definition-requirements-penalties-best-practices-compliance-and-more

Manners, D. (2018). *DCMS launches code of practice for IoT security.* Retrieved from https://www.electronicsweekly.com/news/business/dcms-launches-code-practice-iot-security-2018-10/

Maselli, I., & Beblavý, M. (2013). *Should there be rage against the machine?* [PDF document]. Retrieved from http://www.neujobs.eu/sites/default/files/D4.4.3%20Routinisation%20Hypothesis.pdf

McCormick, C. (2017). *What's in the SELF DRIVE Act?* Retrieved from https://medium.com/@cfmccormick/whats-in-the-self-drive-act-6c090e8a2e9a

Melone, M. (2012). *Basics and history of PKI* [Weblog comment]. Retrieved from https://blogs.technet.microsoft.com/option_explicit/2012/03/10/basics-and-history-of-pki/

Minj, V. (2019). *Perils of trivialising IoT security.* Retrieved from https://iot.electronicsforu.com/content/tech-trends/perils-of-trivialising-iot-security/

Morgado, A., Huq, K., Mumtaz, S., & Rodriguez, J. (2017). A survey of 5G technologies: Regulatory, standardization and industrial perspectives. *Digital Communications and Networks, 4*(2), 87–97. doi:10.1016/j.dcan.2017.09.010

Moss, S. (2020). *"Isolated power event" causes small Azure outage in West Central US cloud region.* Retrieved from https://www.datacenterdynamics.com/en/news/isolated-power-event-causes-small-azure-outage-west-central-us-cloud-region/

New Jersey Cybersecurity and Communications Integration Cell. (2017). *BlackEnergy.* Retrieved from https://www.cyber.nj.gov/threat-profiles/ics-malware-variants/blackenergy

Newman, L. (2017). *The 'secure' Wi-Fi standard has a huge, dangerous flaw.* Retrieved from https://www.wired.com/story/krack-wi-fi-wpa2-vulnerability/

Norrman, K., Nakarmi, P., & Fogelström, E. (2018). *5G security - enabling a trustworthy 5G system.* Retrieved from https://www.ericsson.com/en/white-papers/5g-security---enabling-a-trustworthy-5g-system

Nurse, J. (2018). *The reality of assessing security risks in IoT systems*. Paper presented at PETRAS Internet of Things Conference, IET, London, UK.

O'Hanlon, P., Borgaonkar, R., & Hirschi, L. (n.d.). *Mobile subscriber WiFi privacy* [PDF document]. Retrieved from https://www.ieee-security.org/TC/SPW2017/MoST/proceedings/OHanlon_MoST17.pdf

Obregon, L. (2015). *Secure architecture for industrial control systems*. The SANS Institute.

OCL. (2019). *DCMS consultation on regulatory proposals for consumer IoT security*. Retrieved from https://isoc-e.org/dcms-consultation-iot-security/

Oliver, A. (2018). *Improving cyber security for industrial control: Rebuilding the OT/IT relationship* [PDF document]. Retrieved from https://www.defenceiq.com/events-icscybersecurity/downloads/improving-cyber-security-for-industrial-control-systems-rebuilding-the-otit-relationship

Palmer, D. (2018a). *SCADA security: Bad app design could give hackers access to industrial control systems*. Retrieved from https://www.zdnet.com/article/scada-security-bad-app-design-could-give-hackers-access-to-industrial-control-systems/

Palmer, D. (2018b). *SCADA security: Bad app design could give hackers access to industrial control systems*. Retrieved from https://www.zdnet.com/article/scada-security-bad-app-design-could-give-hackers-access-to-industrial-control-systems/

Palmer, D. (2019). *5G use cases for the enterprise: Better productivity and new business models*. Retrieved from https://www.zdnet.com/article/5g-use-cases-for-the-enterprise-better-productivity-and-new-business-models/?ftag=TRE3e6936e&bhid=25938706913849853718443426927355

Pauli, D. (2014). *Hackers gain 'full control' of critical SCADA systems*. Retrieved from https://www.itnews.com.au/news/hackers-gain-full-control-of-critical-scada-systems-369200

Plohmann, D., Gerhards-Padilla, E., & Leder, F. (2011). *Botnets: Detection, measurement, disinfection and defence*. Retrieved from http://www.enisa.europa.eu/activities/Resilience-and-CIIP/critical-applications/botnets/botnets-measurement-detection-disinfection-and-defence

Porter, J. (2019). *Huawei's 5G equipment is a manageable risk, British intelligence claims*. Retrieved from https://www.theverge.com/2019/2/18/18229111/uk-huawei-5g-security-risk-concerns-ncsc-gchq

5G.PPP. (2018). *About the 5G PPP*. Retrieved from https://5g-ppp.eu

Price Waterhouse Coopers. (2017). *Operation cloud hopper* [PDF document]. Retrieved from https://www.pwc.co.uk/cyber-security/pdf/cloud-hopper-report-final-v4.pdf

Ranger, S. (2019a). *This 'most dangerous' hacking group is now probing power grids*. Retrieved from https://www.zdnet.com/article/this-most-dangerous-hacking-group-is-now-probing-power-grids/?ftag=TRE3e6936e&bhid=2593870691384985371844342692735

Ranger, S. (2019b). *5G and the IoT: The UK's first smart factory just switched on*. Retrieved from https://www.zdnet.com/article/5g-and-the-iot-the-uks-first-smart-factory-just-switched-on/?ftag=TRE620e144&bhid=24734138609373909185025257836691

Rbcafe. (2014). *Wassenaar arrangement / COCOM*. Retrieved from https://www.rbcafe.com/wassenaar/

Report, F. T. C. (2015). *Internet of things privacy & security in a connected world* [PDF document]. Retrieved from https://www.ftc.gov/system/files/documents/reports/federal-trade-commission-staff-report-november-2013-workshop-entitled-internet-things-privacy/150127iotrpt.pdf

Reznik, A., Miguel, L., Murillo, C., Fang, Y., Featherstone, W., & Filippou, M. ... Zheng, Z. (2018). *Cloud RAN and MEC: A perfect pairing. White Paper 23*. Sophia Antipolis, France: European Telecommunications Standards Institute.

Rupp, M., Kumar, P., Scholten, U., & Turner, D. (2019). *Autonomous vehicles and a Blockchain-based transportation protocol* [Weblog comment]. Retrieved from https://content-hsm-utimaco-com.cdn.ampproject.org/c/s/content.hsm.utimaco.com/blog/autonomous-vehicles-and-a-blockchain-based-transportation-protocol?hs_amp=true

Ryabchuk, P. (2018). *How can the automotive industry use Internet of Things (IoT) technology?* [Weblog comment]. Retrieved from https://www.intellias.com/how-can-the-automotive-industry-use-internet-of-things-iot-technology/

Sauter, M. (2018). *The 5G core network (5GC) – Part 2 – Identifiers.* Retrieved from https://blog.wirelessmoves.com/2018/04/the-5g-core-network-5gc-part-2-identifiers.html

Schmidt, B. (2019). *Hong Kong police already have AI tech that can recognize faces.* Retrieved from https://www.bloomberg.com/news/articles/2019-10-22/hong-kong-police-already-have-ai-tech-that-can-recognize-faces

Schmidt, S. (2017). *AWS and the general data protection regulation.* Retrieved from https://aws.amazon.com/blogs/security/aws-and-the-general-data-protection-regulation/

SecurityMagazine. (2020). *Should facial recognition be used to identify individuals with coronavirus?* Retrieved from https://www.securitymagazine.com/articles/91953-can-facial-recognition-identify-individuals-with-coronavirus

Seltzer, L. (2014). *Google advances SSL with new Chrome versions.* Retrieved from https://www.zdnet.com/article/google-advances-ssl-with-new-chrome-versions/

Shanahan, M., & Eslami, A. (2019). *What is AI Anyway.* Presented at The Times Science Festival, Cheltenham, UK.

Sherrer, A. (2010). *Deming's 14 points and quality project.* Retrieved from https://www.projectsmart.co.uk/demings-14-points-and-quality-project-leadership.php

Short, M. (2018). *Plenary panel session: International IoT – Worldwide initiatives.* PETRAS IoT Conference, London, UK.

SmartThings. (n.d.). *ZigBee "insecure rejoin" FAQ.* Retrieved from https://support.smartthings.com/hc/en-us/articles/208201243-ZigBee-Insecure-Rejoin-FAQ

Soesanto, S. (2018). *No middle ground: Moving on from the crypto wars.* European Council on Foreign Relations. https://www.ecfr.eu/page/-/no_middle_ground_moving_on_from_the_crypto_wars.pdf

Somani, G., Sanghi, D., Conti, M., Rajarajan, M., & Buyya, R. (2017). Combating DDOS attacks in the Cloud: Requirements, trends, and future directions. IEEE Computer Society.

Speed, J. (2013). *M2M MQTT for connected car*. Retrieved from https://www.automotiveworld.com/articles/m2m-mqtt-for-connected-car/

Staff, D. (2020). *COVID-19 opens door to facial recognition skills surge*. Retrieved from https://insights-dice-com.cdn.ampproject.org/c/s/insights.dice.com/2020/04/09/covid-19-opens-door-facial-recognition-skills-surge/?amp

Stanek, R. (2017). *Getting real business value from artificial intelligence*. *Retrieved* from http://www.dbta.com/BigDataQuarterly/Articles/Getting-Real-Business-Value--From-Artificial-Intelligence-118226.aspx

Susskind, D. (2017). *The future of work*. Paper presented at The Times Science Festival, Cheltenham, UK.

Sverdlik, Y. (2017). *AWS outage that broke the Internet caused by mistyped command*. Retrieved from http://www.datacenterknowledge.com/archives/2017/03/02/aws-outage-that-broke-the-internet-caused-by-mistyped-command

Swahb, K. (2016). *The fourth industrial revolution: What it means, how to respond*. Retrieved from https://www.weforum.org/agenda/2016/01/the-fourth-industrial-revolution-what-it-means-and-how-to-respond/

@Telecoms. (2018). *IoT and eSIM: Connecting the future* [Weblog comment]. Retrieved from https://telecoms.com/opinion/iot-and-esim-connecting-the-future/

Thomas, J. (2018). *Lessons from safety engineering – Applying systems thinking to cyber security*. Paper presented at CyberUK Conference, Glasgow, UK.

Tung, L. (2019). *Google details 'catastrophic' Cloud outage events: Promises to do better next time*. Retrieved from https://www.zdnet.com/article/google-details-catastrophic-cloud-outage-events-promises-to-do-better-next-time/

Udunuwara, A. (2018). *SDN and NFV: Are they the same?* Retrieved from https://www.bcs.org/content-hub/sdn-and-nfv-are-they-the-same/

United Nations Economic Commission for Europe. (n.d.). *WP.29 – Introduction*. Retrieved from https://www.unece.org/trans/main/wp29/introduction.html

Valens, C. (2016). *LoRaWAN security vulnerabilities exposed*. Retrieved from https://www.elektormagazine.com/news/lorawan

Vaughan-Nichols, S. (2018). *The day computer security turned real: The Morris Worm turns 30*. Retrieved from https://www.zdnet.com/google-amp/article/the-day-computer-security-turned-real-the-morris-worm-turns-30/

Waqas (2017). *Cyberhitmen hired for sustained DDoS attacks against mans ex-employer* [Weblog comment]. Retrieved from https://www.hackread.com/cyberhitmen-hired-for-ddos-attacks-against-ex-employer/

Warner, M. (2019). *A bill to leverage federal government procurement power to encourage increased cybersecurity for Internet of Things devices, and for other purpose*. Retrieved from https://www.govtrack.us/congress/bills/116/s734

Warwick, A. (2017). *Cooperation vital to securing internet of things, says Europol*. Retrieved from https://www.computerweekly.com/news/450428597/Cooperation-vital-to-securing-internet-of-things-says-Europol

Winder, D. (2018). *Can AI smarts replace humans in the Security Operations Centre?* Retrieved from https://www.scmagazineuk.com/ai-smarts-replace-humans-security-operations-centre/article/1472608

Wireless Broadband Alliance. (2018). *Unlicensed integration with 5G Networks WBA 5G workgroup*. Retrieved from https://wballiance.com/unlicensed-integration-with-5g-networks/

Wireless World, R. F. (2012). *Basics of z-wave security in zwave networks*. Retrieved from https://www.rfwireless-world.com/Tutorials/z-wave-security.html

Xu, M., David, J., & Kim, S. (2018). The Fourth Industrial Revolution: Opportunities and Challenges. *International Journal of Financial Research, 9*(2), 90–95. doi:10.5430/ijfr.v9n2p90

Yang, P. (n.d.). *International adoption of Chinese cryptography algorithms* [PDF document]. Retrieved from Lecture Notes Online Web site https://cabforum.org/wp-content/uploads/CABTalks.pdf

Yapp, C. (2017). *The road ahead: Navigating AI's pitfalls*. Retrieved from https://www.bcs.org/content-hub/the-road-ahead-navigating-ais-pitfalls/

Yu, Y. (2019). *Why China's AI players are struggling to evolve beyond surveillance*. Retrieved from https://asia.nikkei.com/Spotlight/Cover-Story/Why-China-s-AI-players-are-struggling-to-evolve-beyond-surveillance

Yung, P. (2017). *Security notification for CCleaner v5.33.6162 and CCleaner Cloud v1.07.3191 for 32-bit Windows users* [Weblog comment]. Retrieved from https://www.ccleaner.com/news/blog/2017/9/18/security-notification-for-ccleaner-v5336162-and-ccleaner-cloud-v1073191-for-32-bit-windows-users

Zhang, X., Kuntz, A., & Schröder, S. (2017). *Overview of 5G security in 3GPP.* Paper presented at IEEE Conference on Standards for Communications and Networking, Helsinki, Finland. doi 10.1109/CSCN.2017.8088619

Zhou, Z. (2016). *China's comprehensive counter-terrorism law.* Retrieved from https://thediplomat.com/2016/01/chinas-comprehensive-counter-terrorism-law/

Zorabedian, J. (2016). *Ukrainian power grid was hit by "co-ordinated cyberattack".* Retrieved from https://nakedsecurity.sophos.com/2016/01/14/ukrainian-power-grid-was-hit-by-coordinated-cyberattack/

ADDITIONAL READING

Burns, L. (2018). *Autonomy: The quest to build the driverless car – And how it will reshape our world.* Harper Collins Publishers.

Fry, H. (2018). *Hello world: How to be human in the age of the machine.* Transworld Pubishers.

Kaplan, J. (2015). Humans need not apply. Yale University.

Kobes, P. (2017). *Guideline industrial security: IEC 62443 is easy.* VDE Verlag GMBH.

McCullough, M. (2004). *Digital ground: Architecture, pervasive computing, and environmental knowing.* Massachusetts Institute of Technology.

McEwen, A., & Cassimally, H. (2014). *Designing the Internet of Things.* John Wiley & Sons.

Norden, J., O'Kelly, M., & Sinha, A. (2019). *Efficient black-box assessment of autonomous vehicle safety.* arXiv preprint arXiv:1912.03618.

Sautoy, M. (2019). *The creativity code.* London: 4th Estate.

Susskind, D., & Susskind, R. (2017). *The future of the professions.* Oxford University Press.

Yaqoob, I., Khan, L. U., Kazmi, S. A., Imran, M., Guizani, N., & Hong, C. S. (2019). Autonomous driving cars in smart cities: Recent advances, requirements, and challenges. *IEEE Network.*

KEY TERMS AND DEFINITIONS

AGI: Mature AI capabilities in which the machine thinking ability is more comparable to human intelligence.

APT: Proficient hackers working for cyber-criminality or foreign state threat actors working towards various goals in order to achieve nefarious outcomes such as data exfiltration or extortion.

CIA: The triad of confidentiality, integrity, and availability are the underpinning factors in considering mitigating control-sets to treat cyber security problem areas.

Coronavirus Disease-19: Known as COVID-19. This is a viral and novel coronavirus that was detected in 2019 and that spreads to the lungs once the Severe Acute Respiratory Syndrome Coronavirus 2 pathogen has been incubated by an infected human host.

Dark Web: An underground marketplace consisting of a series of obscured websites that are accessed using anonymization techniques such as The Onion Router network.

DDOS: A means of overloading servers using a range of protocols in order to successfully starve the victim of computational resources and the ability to operate effectively.

IoT: A scale of technologies that span a variety of front-end sensors/ devices using lightweight protocols to remotely distribute data through fog computing edge devices to back-end processing systems in the Cloud.

Malware: Specially crafted code/software used to subvert or compromise a computerized asset, which may include viruses, worms, or trojan horses.

Man-in-the-Middle Attack: An attacker who has gained unauthorized access to a network can intercept dataflows across that network fabric, whether ethernet-based or wireless.

Phishing: Use of emails to entice users to either open an attachment containing embedded malicious code or 'click on a link' representing a URL of a server under an attacker's control that can land malware onto the victim's client. Spear phishing is the targeted distribution of spoof emails to a target audience.

Signaling: Is part of the C-Plane used in modern architectures to synchronize and track utilization of U-Plane for billing and subscription purposes.

Chapter 2
The Challenge of Adequately Defining Technical Risk

ABSTRACT

Chapter 2 investigates the risk and compliance conundrum as fundamental principles that better inform the governance of cyber security in organizations. Public cloud computing examples are used to highlight the deficiencies of legacy risk assessment methods but also to provide a stark warning about using compliance mapping approaches instead of considered security control implementations. Ultimately using blanket compliance frameworks does not necessarily influence, but rather conversely, creates a vacuum that does not drill deep enough into the controls needed to safeguard cloud environments; this is particularly relevant since public cloud systems are connected to and accessed via the internet and therefore exposed to external threats. This chapter explores the use of threat modelling to contextualize risks more accurately in order to mitigate them more effectively.

INTRODUCTION

Public cloud platforms provide a number of different deployment formations comprising a range of service models (Smith, 2012). Customers are then able to lease or purchase processing, storage, and services from different global regions. Today, researchers use several methods of virtualization in cloud formations (Symons, 2016), and they host them on Cloud Service Provider (CSP) third-party infrastructure. Following sets of defined and publicized CSP

DOI: 10.4018/978-1-7998-3979-8.ch002

service criteria, the customers are ultimately accountable for the protection of their data under their own control. This is called the 'shared security responsibility' (Alert Logic, 2016; Trend Micro, 2016; Provos, 2016). The importance of cloud computing has now reached a turning point with end-user organizations deploying systems and applications into the Cloud more readily and using Software-as-a-Service (SaaS) in some cases to replace customer on-premises productivity applications. Additionally, the innovation of cloud-based database management systems is drawing wider end-user adoption (Ronthal, 2019). Inherently, the datacenter and configuration of the underlying hardware or software infrastructure for cloud computing are under the control of third-party CSPs. This is a step change compared to normal enterprise solutions, in which the responsibility lies either with customer IT support teams or a contracted outsourced service provider utilizing dedicated infrastructure; in such cases, customers usually articulate, as part of their contract with the supplier, specific requirements criteria that can be auditable by the customer.

The top three CSPs are Amazon Web Services (AWS), Microsoft Azure, and Google Cloud Platform (GCP). AWS is renowned for its breadth of services, Azure for its enterprise feel, and Google for its Big Data offerings (Harvey & Patrizio, 2020). As discussed in Chapter 1, cloud platforms have come to the fore in recent years with regard to AI led by Google and Amazon in particular (Stanek, 2017) with Microsoft Azure also breaking into this market (InsideBIGDATA, 2020). CSPs provide supporting documentation and evidence of their conformity to global certifying standards. Tables 1 and 2 illustrate this. Trusted Third Parties (TTP), such as Ernest and Young, audit the CSPs (Ernest & Young, 2014) rather than the customers themselves. Therefore, it is up to the customer to check TTP certifications prior to contracting with the CSP. The Internet has global reach, so it is feasible for customers to access regional CSP datacenters within or outside their own country in which services can differ from region-to-region. In addition, the configuration, context of implementation, continued support, management, and policy of controls required from the customer perspective can be obscured. The CSPs provide recommended configuration and guidance on how to use their platform, yet data stored in cloud-hosted databases and storage were inadvertently exposed in 2017 (Bird, 2017).

SkyHigh Networks (Abel, 2017) found that seven percent of AWS Simple Storage Service (S3) buckets have been exposed, which may explain a surge of newsworthy data leaks throughout 2017. One of the most infamous episodes was the exposure of secure remote login credentials and 60,000 files by

Table 1. Compliance to United Kingdom and international standards

CSP	Compliance to U.K. and International Standards							
	CSA Security Trust	ISO27001	ISO27017	ISO27018	Payment Card Industry Data Security standard (PCI-DSS)	System Organizational Controls 1, 2, 3	Cyber Essentials Plus	Government Cloud
AWS	X	X	X	X	X	X	X	X
Azure	X	X	X	X	X	X	X	X
GCP	X	X	X	X	X	X		

Sources: Amazon Web Services, 2020; Google, 2020; Microsoft, 2020.

Table 2. Compliance to U.S. standards and regulations

CSP	Compliance to US Standards and Regulations							
	Criminal Justice Information Services	Defense Information Systems Agency	Federal Risk & Authorization Management Program	Health Insurance Portability & Accountability Act (HIPAA)	International Traffic in Arms Regulations	NIST 800-53	Securities Act Rule 17a-4(f)	Motion Picture Association of America
AWS	X	X	X	X	X	X	X	X
Azure	X	X	X	X	X	X	X	X
GCP	X	X	X	X		X	X	

Sources: Amazon Web Services, 2020; Google, 2020; Microsoft, 2020.

Booz-Allen. This deficiency was not evident during internal and external audits (Daniels, 2017), and therefore it could be concluded that Booz-Allen was undertaking compliance mapping rather than risk assessments. Deep Root Analytics also inadvertently made between 150 and 198 million records containing PII of potential U.S. Republican voters available to the public Internet. Verizon exposed client PII data due to a cloud storage configuration error (Mascarenhas, 2017; Ragan, 2017). Accenture left private keys, certificates, authentication credentials, secret API data, and customer data unprotected in an unsecured S3 bucket (Paganini, 2017).

Furthermore, Deloitte's email servers were compromised on Microsoft Azure Cloud through the company's email server administrator account (Hopkins, 2017). In 2017, a cyber researcher discovered 93.4 million Mexican voter records due to an inappropriately configured MongoDB database

(Paganini, 2016). Additionally, in 2018, McAfee identified that one in 20 S3 buckets had been accessible to the Internet (Nichols, 2018). By 2020, cyber security researchers found another S3 bucket that stored thousands of scanned U.K. passports, tax documents, job applications, proof of address, background checks, expense forms, scans of signed contracts, salary information, emails, and more to be accessible from the Internet. AWS has subsequently taken it offline and is actively notifying customers when they detect unprotected S3 buckets (Kobie, 2020). In late 2019, a cyber security researcher discovered 1.2 billion records of PII on an unsecured Google Cloud server using web-scanning techniques, and the researcher assumed the records originated from a data broker. The data contained landline and cellular numbers, social media profiles, and email addresses, which could be used to assume somebody's identity (Newman, 2019). By early 2020, a database holding 800 gigabytes of data was found to be publicly accessible by researchers on a Google Cloud server. Thus, enabling researchers to gain access to emails, credit ratings, mortgage and tax details, and investments; at the time of discovery the owner was not known, but it could have been a marketeer or census organization (Doffman, 2020).

Then, researchers found that AWS customers exposed snapshots of Elastic Block Store volumes related to virtual machines in AWS's Elastic Cloud Compute known as EC2. These snapshots are a form of point-in-time backups that can contain access keys, certificates, and sensitive files (Pham, 2018). Such eventualities demand that customer organizations specify backup and business continuity policies through a customer Authoritative Governance regime. All this occurred even though AWS provides tomes of information advising how to adequately use their services. Consequently, they have added S3 bucket file encryption by default (Amazon Web Services, 2020a) and 'public access settings' in order to avoid further inadvertent public exposures (Barr, 2018). Admittedly, cloud users can intentionally leave some S3 buckets open for public consumption, but there are ways and means of doing this safely.

In 2019, the Magnecart hacking group known, for credit card skimming attacks (Whitaker, 2018), were modifying Javascript files hosted in public S3 buckets. This is achievable because they have been configured in a way that the hackers can not only access them but also edit the contents as well. This is proving fruitful for them, and more than 17,000 static websites hosted in S3 have been compromised in 2019, enabling credit card details to be extrapolated (Zorz, 2019). Hence, for accessible websites in S3 buckets, protective controls should include access control lists and rules to control 'read' and 'write' capabilities as a means to avoid unfettered access and modification (Amazon Web Services, 2020b). Similarly, in 2019, hackers also subverted a provider of cloud-hosted online stores with 20,000 customers by using the same hallmark modified Javascript file. This provider is the first one traced to GCP hosted storage (Cimpanu, 2019). But the misconfiguration of cloud storage is not the only trend. A worrisome prediction by Gartner in the recent past is that 95% of cloud security failures will be the fault of the customers by 2020 (Pettey, 2016). This is proving true at the moment, and change is required to represent cloud security risk adequately and avoid customer control-set selection ambiguities.

BACKGROUND

Over recent years, the European Union Agency for Network and Information Security (ENISA) undertook research of risks to the Cloud (Haeberlen & Dupré, 2012) using multi-source analysis. ENISA formulated their findings in their *Threat Landscape Report* (Marionos & Sfakianakis, 2012; Marionos, 2013; Marionos, 2014; Marionos, Belmonte, & Rekletis, 2016; Paganini et al., 2017, 2018). Year-on-year similar issues re-occur in their report: (a) threats such as DDOS except in this case of using cloud to conduct DDOS; (b) web application injection attacks against assets in the Cloud; (c) data leakage has been a particular problem as a consequence of using cloud computing. The Cloud Security Alliance (CSA) provided a list of threats associated with cloud computing based on a survey in 2018:

- Abuse and nefarious usage of cloud services;
- Insecure graphical user interface and APIs;
- Shared technology vulnerabilities;
- Sudden information leakage;
- Insufficient due diligence;
- Cloud account hijacking;
- System vulnerabilities.

In tandem with threat actors such as APTs and DDOS attacks, a number of potentially serious issues are being shortfalls by customers such as software misconfigurations or other implementation weaknesses that cause vulnerabilities (Reynolds, 2016; Admin, 2018). For example, in 2014, hackers attacked the online search service One More Cloud, and experts blamed the attack on an out-of-date key associated with an Application

Programming Interface (API) dating back to 2006; in this case, researchers think that a collaborative partner who used One More Cloud's private GitHub environment (Blevins, 2016) compromised the key. In the event, One More Cloud had a recovery strategy, so they were able to resume a full service due to their business continuity decisions (Rossi, 2014). The Redlock study of 2017 goes further with their analysis of the root-causes of security breaches in the Cloud, and these can be summarized by the following: (a) inadvertent data and access key/credential exposures; (b) user account compromises; (c) ability of suspicious Internet Protocol addresses to probe hosted databases; (d) unpatched host vulnerabilities; and (e) lack of database encryption (Bird, 2018a). The public exposure of object storage that is not wide-open by default is the equivalent to scoring an own goal in the cyber security realm.

Figure 1. Formal systems model of cloud environment

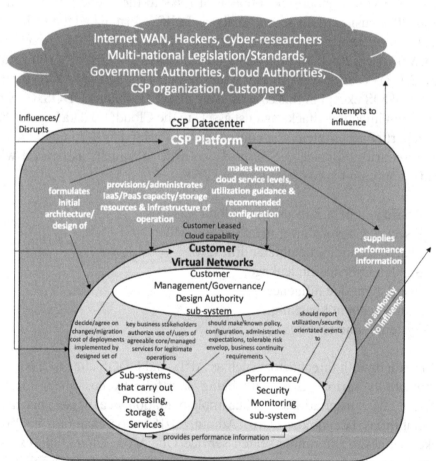

A major root-cause could be that users are naïve or do not understand the consequences of their setup. To better understand the problem, the author used a Formal System Model (FSM) in Figure 1 to provide a cloud system view and comparative analysis of the AWS, Google, and Microsoft Azure Cloud Platforms. Table 3 details the areas of responsibility for a cloud environment within the CSPs' platform and the salient control-set perspectives associated with each. The analysis focuses mainly on configurable Infrastructure-as-a-Service (IaaS) and Platform-as-a-Service (PaaS) models while retaining acknowledgement that bolt-on services can be selected as SaaS offerings.

Table 3. Analysis of cloud environment formal system model

FSM aspect	Analysis
Environment	The environment comprises the CSPs themselves, their compliance to certificating bodies, standards organizations and legislation influenced by Government bodies. CSPs make guidance available to encourage understanding of the 'shared security responsibility' using various means, such as documentation and web pages. CSP customers implement Virtual Machine (VM) instances or utilize services for business or private use. Customers and CSPs themselves are potential targets of hackers or cybersecurity researchers. CSPs simplify the complexity of the public cloud is simplified into guidance – for ease of customer use, CSPs publish CSP declarations of conformity/ compliance to certifying bodies, standards organizations, and legislation. Third-party organizations promote frameworks from which customers can seek to achieve compliance on their implementation of relevant controls for cloud utilization online.
Formulates initial design/ decides upon transformations	In line with their 'shared security responsibility,' CSPs are responsible for the platform architectural design. CSPs advertise their commitment through compliance and certifications coupled with TTP audits within their area of responsibility. Customer management and governance functions are responsible for deciding on the design for their deployments, use of instances, and services. Controls to protect virtual instances or data in storage, access control to their data, employing adequate authentication/authorization measures, accounting, and audits of their environments. Customer administrators need to ensure adequate controls are applied as part of their 'shared security responsibility' depending on the cloud model utilized.
Provides resources and legitimates area of operation	CSPs are responsible for the implementation of platform systems hardware and baseline soft-infrastructure, including hypervisor for IaaS host and middleware. Middleware includes provisioning of application capability for PaaS, the full software stack for SaaS, and all physical aspects of the datacenter. The customer governance function is responsible for communicating with their own stakeholders and authorizing their own staff to use the cloud depending on use-cases across IaaS, PaaS, and SaaS service models. Customers deploy VMs in IaaS and/or introduce applications to PaaS and PaaS-like services, such as microservices to conduct legitimate operations within the Cloud. The customer management and governance function should make their policy for the following known: the use of cloud services; their access management; configuration control and administrative expectations to support the processing; storage and use of cloud services; and undertakings of performance and security monitoring.

continues on following page

Table 3. Continued

FSM aspect	Analysis
Makes known expectations	CSPs are responsible for the following: providing the Cloud platform; defining service level agreements and staff resourcing to administrate the service; providing guidance on the use of their Cloud platform based on their core services and managed services; and providing recommendations on necessary configuration needed to utilize their service offerings. The customer management and governance function should make their policy for the following known: the use of cloud services, their access management, configuration control and administrative expectations to support the processing, storage and use of cloud services, and provisions for performance and security monitoring.
Supplies performance information	CSPs undertake security operations center and threat intelligence analysis on connections and data-flow throughput across their Cloud platforms; additionally, they undertake service performance monitoring with regards to data-rate and throughput purposes. CSPs can make available some performance data on dataflows across their infrastructure to customers for assessment purposes. Customer administrators can perform log analysis to analyze ingress and egress data flows across the cloud environment into their virtual instances. VM administrators can also deploy their own internal monitoring tools/logging servers to conduct both performance and security monitoring of their IaaS.
Decision-making subsystem	Customer key stakeholders, such as Chief Information Officer (CIO), Chief Information Security Officer (CISO), project/program managers, commercial managers, and information security managers should take a business view and understand the risks associated with using the public cloud. Customers should translate a risk appetite into policy and procedures for cloud use and make it available to projects teams within their business. Customer management should define following: (a) authorization to use cloud or a particular purpose; (b) commercial authority to purchase capacity/capability in the cloud; (c) expectations for operations in the cloud; and (d) a disaster recovery regime. In addition, an organizational account and associated structure should be explored with the CSP so that least privilege can be applied at the project level rather than default to the overarching business account level.
Subsystems that carry out transformations	Administrators and users need to adhere to the expected security risk envelope for their respective project and follow organization policy and procedures. In addition to CSP guidance and configuration recommendations, customer organizations should architect the design of infrastructure/services including: (a) access control based on role; (b) configuration of security groups; (c) network access control lists; (d) Key Management System; (d) specific measures such as boundary controls and protective monitoring; and (e) definitions for encryption to protect data-in-transit and at-rest. Customers can set up their own domain controllers in their IaaS or utilize the options provided by the Cloud platform.
Boundaries	CSPs provide boundary controls, including anti-DDOS and Cloud platform firewalls and bastion host templates, consoles, isolation measures through hypervisor/security groups, and sandboxing technologies. CSPs are responsible for their respective regional datacenter access management, maintenance and support, security, and governance. Customers need to implement their own boundary protections, network access controls, and subnet segmentation (isolation) within their boundary, including network access control lists and fine-grained security groups in IaaS and PaaS components.
Others	CSPs can apply some influence in publishing their controls and through their certification by external TTP audits. This aspect should be a part of any due diligence check by customers. Customers do not have any direct influence upon the environment.

RISK VERSUS COMPLIANCE APPROACHES

Risk Assessment

A pretext to this chapter is the author's argument that there has been: (a) an over-reliance upon or expectation on the CSP TTP certifications by customers; (b) compliance-orientated framework attributes that can hide technical complexities (National Cyber Security Centre, 2016a); and (c) risk assessment models that pre-date the Cloud and obscure the associated technical risks. Traditional methods used for risk assessments and compliance adherence include:

- **Operationally Critical Threat, Asset, and Vulnerability Evaluation (OCTAVE):** OCTAVE concentrates on the anticipated threat profiles, threat actor motivations, and system vulnerabilities against critical assets in order to represent the risk in an outcome-based manner established from threat actors, motives, and vulnerabilities. (Caralli, Stevens, Young, & Wilson, 2007). This method satisfies National Institute of Standards and Technology (NIST) 800-30 Guide to Risk Assessments (Woody, 2016). Control-set implementations can then be justified against a Statement of Applicability considering the CIA triad centered around a standard such as ISO/IEC 27001 Information Security Management as part of an information security management system. This method is in-depth and flexible but laborious.
- **Information Assurance Standard Number 1 (IAS No. 1):** IAS No. 1 is a risk assessment method that uses defined assets to model the system. It also considers threat source types, threat actor motivations, and impacts based on asset valuations against the CIA triad (CESG, 2012). The resulting output is generic and arbitrary risks drawn from a catalog of different attack vectors that an attacker could use to subvert or undermine the system. The analyst performs risk mitigation by considering control-sets from a standard like ISO/IEC 27002:2013 Security Techniques from the code of practice for the application of information security controls. This method requires a control mapping matrix against ISO/IEC 27002:2013 to reveal gaps by applying categories of technical controls, policy, and governance. It is time-consuming to complete all stages of analysis, and although technical, it is not granular.

- **Annualized Loss Expectancy (ALE):** ALE is a quantitative risk model that assigns monetary values to assets and calculates the risk based on exposure factors. By working out the Single Loss Expectancy (SLE), which is a monetary value of the total cost of the risk, the ALE can be quantified by multiplying the SLE with the Annualized Rate of Occurrence (ALO). The ALO is the likelihood of the risk occurring within a year. These variables constitute a formula that can be used to establish the ALE risk using values (Czagen, n.d.). This method does not provide a technique of meaningful technical mitigation.

- **Factor Analysis of Information Risk (FAIR):** FAIR is a high-level quantitative method that works out the risks to assets based on threat event frequency, threat capability, and strength of controls based on a matrix of predefined frequencies, percentages, and granular risk categories, respectively. Researchers use it to work out the loss magnitude that can be represented in monetary terms (Dixon, n.d.). Again, this method does not provide a technique orientated toward technical mitigation.

- **Damage, Reproducibility, Exploitability, Affected users, Discoverability (DREAD) Method:** DREAD is a risk assessment method that can be used to assign a numerical scale to work out a risk rating posed by a threat using a scale of low, medium, or high. This is performed by asking questions about the meaning of each separate category represented by each letter of the DREAD mnemonic. The sum of the risk ratings provides the overall figure that correlates with a risk scale. DREAD requires a context of potential threat vectors that threat actors may be able to exploit. Researchers can perform this using data flow diagrams to work out the threats against identified weaknesses for each major asset within a system. The author considers the following aspects during this analysis: CIA triad, authorization, authenticity, and non-repudiation. This method requires another approach in order to mitigate the risks such as Spoofing, Tampering, Repudiation, Information Disclosure, Denial of Service, and Elevation of Privilege (STRIDE) (Mahood, 2017). This method provides a way of representing risk on a qualitative scale but requires a preliminary analysis using STRIDE to provide context.

- **Guide to the Assessment of IT risk:** This is a business focused risk assessment method that treats technical risks as another business risk. It applies a number of principles using a top-down approach and breaks down IT to a component level, such as applications, databases, operating systems, and network infrastructure. Researchers use a number of questions to understand the risk from the likelihood and impacts, but at such a high-level of technology focus, it is deemed to be quite subjective. This method requires supplementary products, such as the Control Objectives for Information and Related Technologies (COBIT) to be effective (Institute of Internal Auditors, 2008).

- **COBIT 2019:** This is not a risk assessment methodology in its own right but rather an IT governance framework that is useful for defining a business governance system and governance framework. It covers a number of areas including processes, organizational structure, policies, culture, and behaviors. It has been better aligned to many different standards, frameworks, and best practices rather than place dependency on them as COBIT 5 did (Business Beam, n.d.; Koparkar & McKrell, 2015). This is still an organizational maturity and management model that is used to address organizational gaps and is aimed at people and processes.

- **NIST cyber security framework:** This provides a means for organizations to align to a profile of categorized control functions defined in the framework core to ensure controls are in place. The functions comprise the following: identify, protect, detect, respond, and recover. Each has a number of categories and sub-categories of controls. A risk assessment approach is specified to discern likelihood and impact of potential cyber security event(s) that in turn enable(s) modifications to function control implementations to be identified, thereby determining and prioritizing gaps. These are then articulated in a remedial action plan (National Institute for Standards and Technology, 2018). This approach caters for the organizational risk level and supply chain management in a similar fashion to the U.K. approach for defense contracts found in the Defence Cyber Security Partnership Programme (DCPP). This is centered around the cyber risk levels for contracts to provide adequate protection statement for an assessed threat profile and highlight any organizational gaps that need to be remedied. In contrast, the DCPP is underpinned by Cyber Essentials Plus certification that involves a penetration test requirement (GOV. UK, 2020). Both approaches, however, are aimed at the organizational level rather than orientated towards technical solution level.

- **Open governance, risk and compliance maturity management methodology:** This is a method that is aimed at asset protection and management by measuring the compliance of implemented controls against regulations, standards, guidelines, and best practices. Researchers establish compliance by measuring the compliance level. This approach refers to itself as a risk assessment, but it does not truly delve into the technical controls required to protect assets and how they are implemented; rather, it is limited to gauging an organization's compliance implementation measures (Security Officers Management & Analysis Project, 2020).

Causal Capital recently criticized a reliance on risk matrices to assess enterprise or operational risk as a failed construct of business, and they stipulated the use of alternatives (Davies, 2019). Risk methodologies, such as the ones explored here, are quite high-level. Risk matrices can veil technical complexities in cloud computing environments, and therefore, they may conceal the true associated risks. Islam (2017) argues that legacy approaches to security are becoming obsolete in the Cloud. He states that traditional on-premise controls have been complex and cumbersome, and they leave a gap in control coverage that had to be filled with layers of complexity.

Compliance Confusion

The use of matrix mapping approaches can veil technical complexities in cloud computing environments, and therefore, its use can conceal the true associated risks (National Cyber Security Centre, 2016a). Information security standards originally designed for enterprise perspectives can be difficult and confusing to cross-reference. This is particularly true of NIST 800-53 Security and Privacy Controls for Federal Information Systems and Organizations applied as a mitigating controls matrix and the ISO/IEC 27000 series of standards. Progressively, standards bodies have devised the need for standards to adjust to an online, cloud-focused paradigm by bolstering the original control-sets from the founding standards such as:

- ISO/IEC 27017:2015 Security Techniques code of practice for ISO/IEC 27002 information security controls for cloud services;
- ISO/IEC 27018:2019 Security Techniques for the protection of PII in public clouds processors, and;
- NIST 800-171 Protecting Controlled Unclassified Information in Nonfederal Systems and Organizations (Ross et al., 2015), respectively.

ENISA provided 'Technical Guidelines for the implementation of minimum-security measures for Digital Service Providers (DSP),' which maps across a number of schemes, standards, matrices, and frameworks. This then provides guidelines for CSPs to establish mitigating controls compliance (ENISA, 2016). Consequently, CSPs have been reinforcing the 'shared security responsibility' message (Lynch, 2017) and reiterating customer responsibilities for accountability (Schmidt, 2017) to protect EU PII hosted both nationally and internationally. The Cloud Control Model (CCM) (CSA, 2016) is a framework that provides several security domains, requisite controls, policy and governance and their relevance to the cloud service models, and comparisons to global standards. However, it is dependent upon compliance to other frameworks and standards for mitigating controls.

The U.S. Healthcare Information and Management Systems Society (HiMSS) produced a risk matrix for the processing/storing of PII/medical data in compliance with the HIPAA 1996 (Greene, 2013). HiMSS uses predefined vulnerabilities and threat sources diminished by a speculative/ subjective risk, likelihood, and impact scoring system. This method also relies on compliance to standards for mitigating controls. Her Majesty's Government (HMG) 14 Cloud Security Principles (National Cyber Security Centre, 2016b) is a framework that focuses on key areas such as: (a) identity and access control; (b) customer separation; (c) data-in-transit protection; (d) secure external interfaces; (e) customer secure use of service; (f) CSP governance and management; and (g) CSP service operation. Enabling the recognition of more specific technical controls, policy, and some governance aspects to aide CSP selection.

Standards like the new ISO/IEC 27005:2018 provide an update to ISO/IEC 27001:2013 and provide a structured process to establish the risk management context and to utilize quantitative or qualitative assessments to establish a level of risk in order to treat them appropriately (ISO27001Security, n.d.). CSA provides a structure to apply security and business controls to mitigate risk. However, they do not facilitate the characterization of the security mitigation interdependence through shared security responsibilities. Inevitably, there are various technical complexities associated with public cloud computing that can introduce cybersecurity risk; as a result, new or existing customers may not fully understand the associated risks and consequences of using cloud service models may not necessarily be fully understood. In addition, the information security risk context may be confused by the cascading mire of security controls from standards-based, monetary, or regulatory compliancy mapping approaches (TechTarget, 2017). Cloud customers can overlook gaps due to the onerous number of controls that are presented and the use of a checklist mentality (Ashford, 2017; standards should be thought of as a measure of information assurance maturity.

SOLUTIONS AND RECOMMENDATIONS

Revoredo de Silva et al. (2013) explored the threats to cloud computing, established mitigating control groups, and then used CSA, ISO/IEC 27002:2013, and NIST standards to propose risk treatments. The authors conducted a compliance mapping exercise to mitigate the threat on a case-by-case basis. By doing so, they revealed through their analysis that customers can typically apply mapping of system-agnostic controls with some cloud-focused control-measures without focusing on the details of control implementation rigor. For example, Rama (2017) argued that not locking down assets properly in the Cloud may mean that organizations can risk falling out of compliance with key regulations and consequently break legislative criterion.

Nurse (2018) highlighted that existing risk assessment methods are ineffective for risk establishment in the IoT domain, which also utilizes cloud technologies to process data collected and disseminated from edge nodes. The layers of abstraction employed by CSPs in their implementation can blur the cybersecurity focus using traditional risk assessment and compliance mapping approaches. This thereby obscures the associated security risks to the uninitiated and makes it difficult to understand the implications of using the public cloud and consequently, the customers' requisite security responsibilities. Consequently, White (2014) implied that the risks to the CSP reside with the customers that it hosts.

Without contextualizing the risks, the required controls from the customer perspective could be obscured. Bodungen et al. (2017) stated that in the OT domain, there is a relationship between threat event, likelihood, consequence, or impact to establish a risk rating. Leveson (2019) stated that severity or impact can be hard to credibly define, and the likelihood of cyber-attacks occurring may vary depending on the varying threats and context of system operations in the environment. She also suggested that effective impact and likelihood due to their linkage can be changed through the rigor of control-set implementation, and past security incidents are not necessarily a measure for future security events. Djemame et al. (2016) identified that atypical derivations of risk using likelihood and consequence or impact can be problematical because events need to be analyzed properly rather than using statistical analysis or subjective reasoning.

Therefore, these views are slightly different from traditional risk assessment methods because generally, these approaches amount to second guessing the impact and any arbitrary likelihood or probability estimates are based on conjecture; certainly, with vulnerability search engines like Shodan the risks will soon become evident when researchers find weakened systems to be accessible from the Internet. Therefore, threat modelling is perhaps a more effective approach to assess the potential risks in order to truly understand the context in which risk(s) may lurk in cloud environments. Changing the stereotypical risk perspective and considering the outcomes from a Shodan use-case, threat modelling can: (a) identify threats and/or relevant threat vectors; (b) identify potential vulnerabilities; (c) establish the sophistication of cyber-attacks; and (d) identify potential mitigations. The author lists examples of threat models and their application below:

- **System-Theoretic Accident Model and Processes (STAMP):** MIT devised STAMP to replace methods such as Failure Mode and Effects Analysis (FMEA) and Failure Modes, Effects and Criticality Analysis (FMECA), which were deemed time consumingly tabular in nature; in these examples analysts apply formulae to calculate the risk and criticality using their arguably arbitrary likelihood and probability assessments respectively (American Society for Quality, 2020; ReliaSoft, 2020). Researchers are now proposing STAMP as a system modelling approach that can be adopted for wider use by the cyber security profession (Bird, 2018b). The method provides a process-based approach adopted from the safety domain as a means of identifying hazards or threats primarily in cyber-physical system domains. STAMP relies on model diagrams and supporting tables of analytical data rather than the traditional reams of documentation normally used to build a safety case for industrial systems bound by regulation. The focus of this method is around the controllers and control algorithms, the control-system processes, the control actions performed by actuators, and the feedback from sensors (Thomas, 2018). While STAMP naturally lends itself well to the OT cyber-physical space, it has been adapted to conduct privacy risk analysis for an IoT use-case (Riedel, 2017) and could be adopted for end-to-end connectivity between IoT sensors frontend components and the cloud backend. MIT researchers use the following analytical processes as part of STAMP, and they have proposed that they can be as applicable for a cyber security use-case:

- **Causal Analysis-based on STAMP (CAST):** Researchers have used CAST to retrospectively work through security incidents or breach events that have occurred to identify failings. CAST is based on the following criteria: (a) assessment of system and hazard threat definition; (b) identification contributory physical system level security requirements; (c) drawing of control structure using the STAMP approach; (d) identification of the proximate events that contributed to the event/breach using dataflows and/or cause-and-effect diagramming; (e) work up the levels of control structure to identify any failings that include technical constraints, system dependencies, influencing factors, and external influences related to the operational system; (f) analysis of coordination and communications related to organizational policy, oversight, external influencing factors, such as compliance to regulatory requirements; (g) establishing the dynamics and mitigations that could have caused security incident/breach, (h) generate recommendations (Madnick, 2015).

- **System-Theoretic Process Analysis for Security (STPA-Sec):** Researchers can use this as a forward-looking process in order to proactively seek out potential system control risks and use the STAMP systems approach to identify causal factors that could contribute to the system control risks. Researchers have successfully used STPA to identify risks that had previously been considered improbable using traditional risk assessment methodologies in the cyber-physical world (Leveson, 2019). STPA-Sec is conducted over three phases: (a) concept analysis to define the security problem, hazards, potential losses and constraints; (b) architectural analysis where the functional control structure and relationships are modelled to identify controls and control actions; and (c) design analysis to derive indicators that can trigger a control action, sensors that provide feedback to the controller, collaborative brainstorming to identify compromise scenarios and critical sensors, and wargame scenarios to select control requirements and identify constraints in order to eliminate or mitigate unsafe/unsecure conditions (Young, 2019). Therefore, researchers can use STPA-Sec to mitigate technical threats, identify systematic organizational flaws in management, inform decision making, influence culture and policy, and identify applicable regulation.

- **Attack tree analysis:** The Attack Tree Analysis methodical technique pictorially articulates credible threat vectors caused by a number of vulnerabilities. Analysts can use attack tree analysis to identify proposed mitigating controls (Schneier, 1999) and explore attack profiles based on fault tree analysis (Wang, Lin, Wang, Lin, & Kuo, 2012). Attack trees are composed of root nodes, which represent the main objective of a cyber-attack, and leaf nodes that represent core constituents of the attack itself (Beccaro, n.d.). Therefore, threat profiles can be broken down into their constituent parts using 'and' and 'or' decision points throughout the hierarchical structure spanning out from the root node (Ingoldsby, 2013). This method is again effective in cyber-physical systems but is also suitable for most cybernetic systems contexts. Researchers could use it to pre-emptively establish attack profiles against cloud environments based on correlated evidence. Either retrospectively or pre-emptively, the following cyber-attack components can be discerned from this technique: (a) threat actor source; (b) one or more attack vectors used to pursue an attack objective; (c) methods of attack execution used to gain a foothold and/or prosecute a cyber-attack; and (d) any identified mitigations. A similar approach is the Cause-Consequence Analysis used in the safety domain to recognize consequence chains from failures or unwanted events (Faye, n.d.). CCA has been transposed into Deductive Cause-Consequence Analysis, which is a generalization of FMEA and FMECA outcomes (Ortmeier, and Schellhorn, 2006).

- **Data flow diagrams:** The author has already mentioned Data Flow Diagrams (DFD) in this chapter. Researchers can use this technique to delve into the E2E connectivity between nodes of the system; therefore, the data flows between entities can be identified in the model as well as the protocols used to transport/exchange data between defined boundaries of trusted and less trusted zones (McGrath, 2013). This approach provides a diagrammatic representation of inter-node or entity communications whilst highlighting exploitable vulnerabilities in communications that can be used as attack vectors. This thereby provides a context to the threats and an idea of system weak points and compromise scenarios that will assist the application of mitigating measures for most networked systems.

FUTURE RESEARCH DIRECTION

This research illustrates that reliance upon compliance for cybersecurity is a lazy, ineffective way of trying but not necessarily succeeding in risk reduction. Researchers have seen in the case of cloud computing that user misconfigurations have gone undetected. This is more than likely caused by the unreliability or false sense of security from compliancy assessments. Therefore, researchers need to further explore the consequences of inadvertently introducing weaknesses ranging from the software supply chain to standing up systems with inbuilt vulnerabilities and inefficiencies in supporting systems during operation. Chapter 3 delves into this area using case-studies covering successive years of hacker attacks to highlight the magnitude of getting it wrong against a number of differing systems.

CONCLUSION

Seven years ago, Westervelt (2013) identified the phenomenon of customer data exposures and security breaches. Westervelt highlighted customer misconfigurations that risked exposing data to the wider Internet. Hospitals in the United States have a tendency to concentrate on the technical security control-sets at the expense of security management processes in order to comply with HIPAA regulatory compliance (Plato, 2019); however, the level of control-set granularity within standards and frameworks alone has become less specific over time in an attempt to turn technical language into business speak – so the true essence of what they represent has been devalued as a risk mitigation measure. Although practitioners have developed cloud-centric compliance frameworks, Dedeke (2017) recognizes that cybersecurity threats and challenges are too diverse to be remedied by a single list of controls measured in a compliancy manner. Compliance mapping against standards is not security but rather a measure on the application of security. If solely relied upon, this can provide false assurance (Kwon & Johnson, 2017). When there is a temptation to use compliance mapping approaches against standards, the relevance of the risk context can be missed in the deployment of subsequent cyber security strategy. Thus, this means effective cyber security will not necessarily be effectually deployed due to a dependency on the fixed categories contained in standards rather than their adequate implementation in the real-world.

The U.K. National Cyber Security Centre argued that more is needed than just a compliance tick-box culture (Susan, 2017). An analysis of concerns about compliance raised the point that security breaches are still occurring even though enterprises invest time and resources into being compliant. It would appear that blindly adopting a strategy to perform governance, risk management, and compliance can more often than not be used at the expense of adequate security provision, (Fredsall, 2015) which gives a false sense of security. In reality, compliance should be an audit function to check that security components have been adequately defined and implemented in line with standards rather than being the definition of salient controls needed to be used out of context to the system implementation. Therefore, the author asserts that traditional risk assessment and compliance approaches can obfuscate the finer detail needed to adequately implement and configure control-measures in the public cloud – whether they are directly security orientated or security dependent. While cyber security, data privacy, and regulatory compliance are interdependent (Abadir, 2016), Samani (2018) stated that compliance should not drive security, but rather security should drive compliance. In effect, not focusing on the technical details in light of the past ENISA threat reporting amounts to the IT equivalent of gross negligence. This is particularly important because the 2020 Trustwave Global Security Report indicates that cyber-attacks against public cloud environments have increased from seven percent in 2018 to 20% in 2019; a Trustwave expert has said, "more organizations across all industries are adopting cloud services so it is becoming a bigger target for criminals." (Waldman, 2020).

It all comes down to the level of detail in the processes and data exchange mechanisms in system designs, and researchers can identify these aspects using threat modelling. Certainly, practitioners can use DFDs and attack trees together to contextualize the various threats that can be imposed upon customer environments in the public cloud. The author argues that this approach can influence defense-in-depth approaches through the analysis of data flows that articulate the protocols in use and attack trees that can contextualize the threat vectors and assist in highlighting potential mitigations. Cloud customers can thereby avoid negligent misconfigurations, which is one of the main causes of online data exposures (National Cyber Security Centre, 2019) and drives the deployment of appropriate and adequate controls. Hence, researchers see threat modelling as an alternative method to gauge potential risks customers face in public cloud-based systems. Threat modelling is more technical in nature, concentrates on specific interactions and dependencies, and can be used to discern adequate countermeasures to curtail the perceived threats and facilitate cyber resilience. A consequential application of this approach is the use of automated workflows in the public cloud that can ensure that resources are deployed in accordance with defined security policies and thereby help reduce the risk of misconfiguration (Kelly, 2019). This is why AWS automates a majority of processes within their own area of responsibility.

REFERENCES

Abadir, S. (2016). *Consequences of non-compliance.* Retrieved from https://www.lawtechnologytoday.org/2016/06/consequences-non-compliance-finding-security-grc/

Abel, R. (2017). *Researchers find 7 percent of all Amazon S3 servers exposed.* Retrieved from https://www.scmagazine.com/study-found-7-percent-of-amazon-s3-servers-are-exposed/article/696199/

Admin. (2018). *Biggest cloud security breaches in 2018.* Retrieved from https://www.cloudcodes.com/blog/biggest-cloud-security-breaches-in-2018.html

Alert Logic. (2016). It's not you, it's me: Understanding the shared responsibility of Cloud security. Houston, TX: Alert, 2.

Amazon Web Services. (2020). *AWS compliance programs.* Retrieved from https://aws.amazon.com/compliance/programs/

Amazon Web Services. (2020a). *Amazon S3 default encryption for S3 buckets.* Retrieved from https://docs.aws.amazon.com/AmazonS3/latest/dev/bucket-encryption.html

Amazon Web Services. (2020b). *How can I secure the files in my Amazon S3 bucket?* Retrieved from https://aws.amazon.com/premiumsupport/knowledge-center/secure-s3-resources/

American Society for Quality. (2020). *Failure mode and effects analysis.* Retrieved from https://asq.org/quality-resources/fmea

Ashford, W. (2017). *End complacency and help address cyber crime threat, NCA tells business.* Retrieved from http://www.computerweekly.com/news/450412817/End-complacency-and-help-address-cyber-crime-threat-NCA-tells-business

Barr, J. (2018). *Amazon S3 block public access – Another layer of protection for your accounts and buckets.* Retrieved from https://aws.amazon.com/blogs/aws/amazon-s3-block-public-access-another-layer-of-protection-for-your-accounts-and-buckets/

Big Data Inside. (2020). *Microsoft announcements on Azure artificial intelligence.* Retrieved from https://insidebigdata.com/2020/02/29/microsoft-announcements-on-azure-artificial-intelligence/

Bird, D. (2017). A shared responsibility. BCS, United Kingdom: Digital Leaders Magazine – Securing the Cloud edition.

Bird, D. (2018a). A conceptual framework to identify cyber risks associated with the use of public cloud computing. In *Proceedings of 11th International Conference on Security of Information and Networks* (pp. 14). New York, NY: ACM International. 10.1145/3264437.3264466

Bird, D. (2018b). Information Security risk considerations for the processing of IoT sourced data in the Public cloud. In *Proceedings of PETRAS Living in the Internet of Things Conference* (vol. 2018, pp. 1-7). IEEE Xplore. 10.1049/cp.2018.0040

Blevins, B. (2014). *Old AWS API key led to search provider's cloud security breach.* Retrieved from http://searchcloudsecurity.techtarget.com/news/2240224543/Old-AWS-API-key-led-to-search-providers-cloud-security-breach

Bodungen, C., Singer, B., Shbeeb, A., Hilt, S., & Wilhoit, K. (2017). *Hacking exposed industrial control systems: ICS and SCADA security secrets & solutions.* New York, NY: McGraw Hill Education .

BusinessBeam. (n.d.). *Cobit 5 VS. Cobit 2019.* Retrieved from https://www.businessbeam.com/blog/cobit-5-vs-cobit-2019/

Caralli, R., Stevens, J., Young, L., & Wilson, W. (2007). *Introducing OCTAVE allegro: Improving the information security risk assessment process. Carnegie Mellon University.* Software Engineering Institute. doi:10.21236/ADA470450

Cimpanu, C. (2019). *Hackers breach Volusion and start collecting card details from thousands of sites.* Retrieved from https://www.zdnet.com/article/hackers-breach-volusion-and-start-collecting-card-details-from-thousands-of-sites/

Cloud Security Alliance. (2019). *Cloud Control Matrix version 3.0.1.* Retrieved from https://cloudsecurityalliance.org/download/cloud-controls-matrix-v3-0-1/

Communications & Electronic Support Group. (2012). *HMG IA standard numbers 1 & 2: information risk management.* Crown Copyright, Issue 4.0.

Czagan, D. (2014). *Qualitative risk analysis with the DREAD model.* Retrieved from https://resources.infosecinstitute.com/qualitative-risk-analysis-dread-model/

Daniels, J. (2017). *Booz Allen stock plummets on word of federal government probe.* Retrieved from https://www.cnbc.com/amp/2017/06/15/booz-allen-stock-plummets-on-word-of-federal-government-probe.html

Davies, M. (2019). *Risk matrices failures* [Weblog comment]. Retrieved from https://www.causalcapital.club/single-post/2019/01/09/Risk-Matrices-Failures

Dedeke, A. (2017). Cybersecurity framework adoption: Using capability levels for implementation tiers and profiles. *IEE Privacy & Security, 15*(1), 48.

Dixon, B. (n.d.). *Understanding the FAIR risk assessment* [PDF document]. Retrieved from https://www.certconf.org/presentations/2009/files/TA-2.pdf

Djemame, K., Armstrong, D., Guitart, J., & Macias, M. (2016). A risk assessment framework for Cloud computing. *IEEE Transactions on Cloud Computing, 4*(3), 265–278. doi:10.1109/TCC.2014.2344653

Doffman, Z. (2020). *Beware—This open database on Google Cloud 'exposes 200 million Americans': Are you At risk?* Retrieved from https://www.forbes.com/sites/zakdoffman/2020/03/20/stunning-new-google-cloud-breach-hits-200-million-us-citizens-check-here-if-youre-now-at-risk/#c36137a85879

Ernest, A., & Young, A. (2014). *Building trust in the Cloud: Creating confidence in your cloud ecosystem, insights on governance, risk and compliance* [PDF document]. Retrieved from https://www.ey.com/Publication/vwLUAssets/EY_-_Building_trust_in_the_cloud/$FILE/EY-grc-building-trust-in-the-cloud.pdf

European Union Agency for Cybersecurity Cloud Security and Resilience expert group. (2016). *Technical guidelines for the implementation of minimum security measures for digital service providers.* Heraklion, Greece: ENISA.

Faye, C. (n.d.). *Cause consequence*. Retrieved from https://www.scribd.com/document/264506115/Cause-Consequence

Fredsall, A. (2015). *Go beyond compliance checklists to avoid information security breaches*. Retrieved from https://searchcompliance.techtarget.com/news/4500246275/Go-beyond-compliance-checkboxes-to-avoid-information-security-breaches

Google. (2020). *Compliance resource center*. Retrieved from https://cloud.google.com/security/compliance

GOV.UK. (2020). *Defence cyber protection partnership*. Retrieved from https://www.gov.uk/government/collections/defence-cyber-protection-partnership

Greene, A. (2013). *HiMSS Cloud security toolkit*. Retrieved from www.himss.org/file/1305316/download?token=jauR3zAT

Haeberlen, T., & Dupré, L. (2012). *Cloud computing: Benefits, risks and recommendations for information security*. ENISA.

Harvey, C., & Patrizio, A. (2020). *AWS vs. Azure vs. Google: Cloud comparison*. Retrieved from https://www.datamation.com/cloud-computing/aws-vs-azure-vs-google-cloud-comparison.html

Hopkins, N. (2017). *Deloitte hit by cyber-attack revealing clients' secret emails*. Retrieved from https://www.theguardian.com/business/2017/sep/25/deloitte-hit-by-cyber-attack-revealing-clients-secret-emails

Ingoldsby. (2013). *Attack tree-based threat risk analysis*. Calgary, Canada: Amenaza Technologies Ltd.

Institute of Internal Auditors. (2008). *GAIT for business and IT risk* [PDF document]. Retrieved from https://www.interniaudit.cz/download/ippf/GAIT/GAIT_for_Business_and_IT_Risk.pdf

Islam, J. (2017). *Cloud solutions can transform network security*. Retrieved from https://gcn.com/articles/2017/06/09/trusted-access-control.aspx

ISO 27001Security. (n.d.). *ISO/IEC 27005*. Retrieved from https://www.iso27001security.com/html/27005.html

Kelly, B. (2019). *PayThink operational holes cause breaches more than security glitches* [Weblog comment]. Retrieved from https://www.paymentssource.com/opinion/operational-holes-cause-breaches-more-than-security-glitches

Kobie, N. (2020). *An unsecured database exposed thousands of British passports.* Retrieved from https://www.wired.co.uk/article/uk-passports-exposed-data-breach

Koparkar, P., & McKrell, D. (2015). How fluffy is the Cloud?: Cloud intelligence for a not-for-profit organisation. In *Proceedings of Australasian Conference on Information Systems.* Adelaide, Australia: Faculty of Business Government & Law.

Kwon, J., & Johnson, A. (2013). Security practices and regulatory compliance in the healthcare industry. *Journal of the American Medical Informatics Society, 20*(1), 44–51. doi:10.1136/amiajnl-2012-000906 PMID:22955497

Leverson, N. (2019). *Improving the risk matrix.* Paper presented at Partnership for Systems Approaches to Safety and Security (PSASS), Massachusetts Institute of Technology, Boston, MA.

Lynch, B. (2017). *Get GDPR compliant with the Microsoft Cloud.* Retrieved from https://blogs.microsoft.com/on-the-issues/2017/02/15/get-gdpr-compliant-with-the-microsoft-cloud/

Madnick, S. (2015). *Cyber safety: A systems thinking and systems theory approach to managing cyber security risks.* Paper presented at International Conference on Computer Security in a Nuclear World, Vienna, Austria.

Mahood, H. (2017). *Application threat modeling using DREAD and STRIDE.* Retrieved from https://haiderm.com/application-threat-modeling-using-dread-and-stride/

Marionos, L. (2013). *ENISA Threat Landscape, 2013*, 45–51. Heraklion, Greece: ENISA.

Marionos, L. (2014). *ENISA Threat Landscape, 2014*, 65–67. Heraklion, Greece: ENISA.

Marionos, L., Belmonte, A., & Rekletis, E. (2016). *ENISA threat landscape 2015.* ENISA.

Marionos, L., & Sfakianakis, A. (2012). *ENISA threat landscape 2012.* ENISA.

Mascarenhas, H. (2017). *Dow Jones data leak: Over 2 million customers' personal details exposed in Cloud storage error.* Retrieved from http://www.ibtimes.co.uk/dow-jones-data-leak-over-2-million-customers-personal-details-exposed-cloud-storage-error-1630733

McGrath, M. (2013). *Threat modelling for legacy enterprise applications* (Unpublished master's thesis). Letterkenny Institute of Technology, Donegal, Ireland.

Microsoft. (2020). *Microsoft compliance offerings*. Retrieved from https://docs. microsoft.com/en-us/microsoft-365/compliance/offering-home?view=o365-worldwide

National Cyber Security Centre. (2016a). *A critical appraisal of risk methods and frameworks*. Retrieved from https://www.ncsc.gov.uk/guidance/critical-appraisal-risk-methods-and-framework

National Cyber Security Centre. (2016b). *Implementing Cloud security principles*. Retrieved from https://www.ncsc.gov.uk/guidance/implementing-cloud-security-principles

National Cyber Security Centre. (2019). *Cloud: The latest thinking from the NCSC on Cloud*. Paper presented at CyberUK Conference, Glasgow, UK.

National Institute of Standards and Technology. (2018). *Framework for improving critical infrastructure cybersecurity* [PDF document]. Retrieved from https://nvlpubs.nist.gov/nistpubs/CSWP/NIST.CSWP.04162018.pdf

Newman, L. (2019). *1.2 billion records found exposed online in a single server*. Retrieved from https://www.wired.com/story/billion-records-exposed-online/

Nichols, S. (2018). *McAfee says cloud security not as bad as we feared... it's much worse*. Retrieved from https://www.theregister.co.uk/2018/10/30/mcafee_cloud_security_terrible/

Nurse, J. (2018). *The reality of assessing security risks in IoT systems*. Paper presented at PETRAS Internet of Things Conference, IET, London, UK.

Ortmeier, F., Reif, W., & Schellhorn, G. (2006). *Deductive consequence analysis* [PDF document]. Retrieved from https://www.researchgate.net/publication/200505982_Deductive_Cause-Consequence_Analysis_DCCA

Paganini, P. (2016). *MongoDB DB containing 93.4 million Mexican voter records open online*. Retrieved from https://securityaffairs.co/wordpress/46588/data-breach/mexican-voter-records.html

Paganini, P. (2017). *Accenture – Embarrassing data leak business data in a public Amazon S3 bucket*. Retrieved from www.securityaffairs.co/wordpress/64150/data-breach/accenture-data-leak.html

Paganini, P., Samwel, P., Finlayson, J., Armin, J., Häberlen, T., Thacker, N., … Sfakianakis, A. (2017). ENISA threat landscape 2017. Heraklion, Greece: ENISA.

Paganini, P., Samwel, P., Finlayson, J., Armin, J., Häberlen, T., Thacker, N., … Hemker, T. (2018). ENISA Threat Landscape 2018. Heraklion, Greece: ENISA.

Pham, T. (2018). *Exposed AWS resources leaked sensitive data.* Retrieved from https://duo.com/decipher/exposed-aws-resources-leaked-sensitive-data

Plato, A. (2019). *The problem with compliance.* Retrieved from https://www.msspalert.com/cybersecurity-breaches-and-attacks/compliance/the-problem-with-compliance/

Provos, N. (2016). *Google security model.* Retrieved from https://cloud.google.com/security/

Ragan, S. (2017). *Republican data analytics firm exposes voting records on 198 million Americans.* Retrieved from https://www.csoonline.com/article/3201201/rnc-data-analytics-firm-exposes-voting-records-on-198-million-americans.html

Rama, G. (2017). *Study: Lax security enforcement behind rise in Amazon S3 exposures.* Retrieved from https://awsinsider.net/articles/2017/10/11/redlock-lax-cloud-security.aspx

ReliaSoft. (2020). *Failure modes, effects and criticality analysis.* Retrieved from https://www.reliasoft.com/resources/resource-center/failure-modes-effects-and-criticality-analysis

Revoredo de Silva, C., Cost da Silva, J., Rodrigues, R., Marques do Nascimento, L., & Garcia, V. (2013). Systematic mapping study in security threats in Cloud computing. *International Journal of Computer Science and Information Security, 11*(3).

Reynolds, M. (2016). *Keeping Britain safe: how GCHQ's new cyber security agency will protect us from hackers.* Retrieved from http://www.wired.co.uk/article/national-centre-cyber-security-ian-levy

Riedel, F. (2017). *Applicability analysis: Elicitation of privacy risks through STPA (-Priv) in a selected IoT scenario* (Unpublished bachelor's thesis). Institute of Software Engineering, University of Stuttgart, Stuttgart, Germany.

Ronthal, A. (2019). *The future of database management systems is Cloud!* [Weblog comment]. Retrieved from https://blogs.gartner.com/adam-ronthal/2019/06/23/future-database-management-systems-cloud/

Ross, R., Viscuso, P., Guissanie, G., Dempsey, K., & Riddle, M. (2020). Protecting controlled unclassified information in non-federal information systems and organizations. Gaithersburg, MD: NIST Computer Security Division (Information Technology Laboratory).

Rossi, B. (2014). *Catastrophe in the Cloud: What the AWS hacks mean for Cloud providers.* Retrieved from http://www.information-age.com/catastrophe-cloud-what-aws-hacks-mean-cloud-providers-123458406/

Samani, R. (2018). *Q&A with Raj Samani, IET.* Retrieved from https://events.theiet.org/cyber-ics/raj-samani.cfm

Schmidt, S. (2017). *AWS and the general data protection regulation (GDPR).* Retrieved from https://aws.amazon.com/blogs/security/aws-and-the-general-data-protection-regulation/

Schneier, B. (1999). *Attack trees* [Weblog comment]. Retrieved from https://www.schneier.com/academic/archives/1999/12/attack_trees.html

Security Officers Management & Analysis Project. (2020). *OGRCM3 - Open governance, risk and compliance maturity management methodology.* Retrieved from https://somap.org/methodology/default.html

Smith, S. (2012). Cloud computing: Moving IT out of the office, Section 1: What is the cloud? Swindon, UK: British Computer Society.

Stanek, R. (2017). *Getting real business value from artificial intelligence.* Big Data Quarterly.

Susan, A. (2017). *Delivering the strongest link.* Paper presented at CyberUK Conference, Liverpool, UK.

Symons, P. (2016). *A wonderful relationship? Part 3: Cloud and data management.* British Computer Society.

TechTarget. (2017). *Navigating cloud computing regulations and compliance requirements.* Retrieved from http://searchcloudprovider.techtarget.com/essentialguide/Navigating-cloud-computing-regulations-and-compliance-requirements

Thomas, J. (2018). *Lessons from safety engineering – Applying systems thinking to cyber security*. Paper presented at CyberUK Conference, Manchester, UK.

Trend Micro. (2016). *The 10 step action plan: Meeting your shared security responsibility with Microsoft Azure*. Trend Micro.

Waldman, A. (2020). *Ransomware, cloud attacks more than doubled in 2019*. Retrieved from https://searchsecurity.techtarget.com/news/252482012/Ransomware-cloud-attacks-more-than-doubled-in-2019

Wang, P., Lin, H., Wang, T., Lin, W., & Kuo, P. (2012). Threat risk analysis for cloud security based on attack-defence trees. *International Journal of Advancements in Computing Technology, 4*(17), 607–617. doi:10.4156/ijact.vol4.issue17.70

Westervelt, R. (2013). *Amazon S3 users exposing sensitive data, study finds*. Retrieved from http://m.crn.com/news/security/240151857/amazon-s3-users-exposing-sensitive-data-study-finds.htm?itc=xbodyrobwes

Whitaker, Z. (2018). *Meet the Magecart hackers, a persistent credit card skimmer group of groups you've never heard of*. Retrieved from https://techcrunch.com/2018/11/13/magecart-hackers-persistent-credit-card-skimmer-groups/?guccounter=1&guce_referrer_us=aHR0cHM6Ly9kdWNNrZHVja2dvLmNvbS8&guce_referrer_cs=hiKL3rvpZvJoSYUdrizPxQ

Woody, C. (2006). *Applying OCTAVE: Practitioners report. Technical Note CMU/SEI-2006-TN 010*. Carnegie Mellon University.

Young, B. (2019). *System-theoretic process analysis for security (STPA-SEC): Cyber security and STPA*. Paper presented at STAMP Conference, Massachusetts Institute of Technology, Boston, MA.

Zorz, Z. (2019). *Magecart compromised 17,000+ sites through unsecured Amazon S3 buckets*. Retrieved from https://www.helpnetsecurity.com/2019/07/11/magecart-unsecured-s3-buckets/

ADDITIONAL READING

Aljawarneh, S., & Yassein, M. (2016). A conceptual security framework for cloud computing issues. *International Journal of Intelligent Information Technologies, 12*(2), 12–24. doi:10.4018/IJIIT.2016040102

Balmakhtar, M., Persson, C. J., & Ragagopal, A. (2019). *Secure cloud computing framework*. U.S. Patent No. 10,243,959B1. Washington, DC: U.S. Patent and Trademark Office.

Bird, D. (2020). Derivation of a conceptual framework to assess and mitigate identified customer cybersecurity risks by utilizing the public Cloud. *In Proceedings of 4th International Congress on Information and Communications Technology* (pp. 249-265), Singapore: Springer. 10.1007/978-981-32-9343-4_20

Chertoff, M. (2018). *Exploding data: Reclaiming our cyber security in the digital age*. Grove Press UK.

Tariq, M. (2019). Agent based information security framework for hybrid cloud computing. *Transactions on Internet and Information Systems (Seoul)*, *3*(1), 406–434. doi:10.3837/tiis.2019.01.023

KEY TERMS AND DEFINITIONS

Asset: A standalone computer or a component of a larger system that can process, transmit, or store data that has some intrinsic value to a person or organization.

Cloud Computing: A fundamental principle of public cloud computing is the division of security responsibility between the CSP infrastructure-led perspectives and that of the customers depending on the model used. Cloud computing models comprise Infrastructure-as-a-Service, Platform-as-a-Service and Software-as-a-Service in which the customer has more responsibility for the former than for the latter.

Compliance Mapping: Is a technique using a table or spreadsheet to correlate an organization's implementation of control-set types against defined control-set categories through a standard or some other kind of framework.

Impact: The potential consequence if an attacker can persecute an identified and exploitable vulnerability.

Infrastructure-as-a-Service: This Cloud model enables customers to deploy VM instances comprising operating systems and applications to interoperate with hosted servers, storage, and networking infrastructure.

Platform-as-a-Service: Is a cloud model that provides the hardware and software computing capability for customers to deploy their applications and process their data.

Risk: Traditionally is considered to be the likelihood and impact of one or more vulnerabilities being realized.

Shodan: An online security search tool that fingerprints open ports and misconfigurations of computerized systems revealing vulnerable devices exposed to the Internet.

Simple Storage Service: Is an object-based storage service in AWS that can be used to store files or host simple websites.

Software-as-a-Service: A cloud model that provides the entirety of the hardware and software stack including applications from which customers can process their data.

Threat Actor: An attacker who undertakes a cyber-attack based on their skillset to achieve their aims.

Threat Source: A category of threat actor based on allegiances or political or financial motivations, such as nation-state or cyber-crime hacker.

Threat Vector: Is the approach a threat actor may take to exploit a vulnerability.

Vulnerability: A weakness to an asset or system that can be exploited by a threat actor.

Chapter 3
Hacker and Non-Attributed State Actors

ABSTRACT

Chapter 3 sets the scene by exploring some challenges from both a technical and societal viewpoint and contrasts situations against an undertow of cyber-attacks. This chapter investigates various cases of how vulnerabilities originating from the software supply chain can have catastrophic outcomes when weaknesses slip through the net such as unpatched software or software misconfigurations during an organization's software maintenance regime. Examples are provided of high-profile hacks, security breaches, and cyber-attacks undertaken by hackers suspected of being affiliated to foreign states. These case studies provide various salient contexts as well as examples of threats, vulnerabilities, and their resultant impacts; ultimately, the consequence of flaws that create vulnerabilities occur through misconfigurations or from unpatched software weaknesses.

INTRODUCTION

This chapter explores high-profile and newsworthy security breaches that have not been directly attributed to nation-state entities. The author discusses these events over successive years. Additionally, the author identifies and discusses each root cause. This approach will build a picture of key catalytic circumstances behind these security breaches.

DOI: 10.4018/978-1-7998-3979-8.ch003

BACKGROUND

A colleague, who has worked in the cyber security profession for a considerable number of years, provided a view regarding the existing *status quo* and the ongoing defensive battle to protect oneself against ensuing cyber-attacks. He called this 'peak cyber.' 'Peak cyber' refers to the legacy vulnerabilities found in code that could top-out in the near future and potentially regress; this is because past weaknesses in code could be phased out due to rigor instilled by agile practices and regimes used as part of Development Operations (DevOps). This view has some credence on the basis that in 2015, 70% of vulnerabilities could be predated to at least 2013, and 44% of security breaches caused by vulnerabilities were at least two to four years old (Dignan, 2015). This was true of the infamous Heartbleed vulnerability (Synopsys Inc, 2019) that had been introduced as far back as 2011. It had the effect of discrediting Open SSL version 3 to the point that bodies such as the Payment Card Industry dropped legacy SSL as an adequate means of encrypting E2E communications in favor of TLS (Man, 2015).

Another offender was the Shellshock bug that, at the time that FireEye identified it in 2014, had been around for two decades. Shellshock was related to the Bourne Again Shell that is used extensively in a multitude of Linux servers connected to the Internet. The wider online adoption of such operating systems made this remotely exploitable vulnerability a serious problem (Lin & Seltzer, 2014). A more recent vulnerability reinforced the point that there are still problems. Dubbed the Mutagen Astronomy Integer Overflow Vulnerability, it resided within the Linux kernel and could enable an unprivileged user to gain superuser privileges. This weakness affected kernels 2.6.x, 3.10.x, and 4.14.x released between 2007 and 2017 and affected Red Hat Enterprise Linux, CentOS, and Debian distributions (Mitre, 2015; Kumar, 2018).

In addition, researchers have found that VxWorks, which is a Unix-like closed Real-Time Operating System (RTOS), has at least eleven vulnerabilities reaching back thirteen years. Industry deploys this RTOS across a variety of equipment ranging from commodity devices to aerospace assets (Khandelwal, 2019a). This has been surmounted by the panic caused by the Bluekeep vulnerability in May 2019. This flaw is associated with the Remote Desktop Services of legacy Microsoft Windows systems going back to Windows XP. Within two months, a weaponized exploit was available to attack unpatched systems (Cimpanu, 2019a). Subsequently, Microsoft found two Bluekeep-like bugs that affected older systems from the Windows 7 generation upwards (Cimpanu, 2019b). Microsoft feared that if this was exploited, it could provide a wormable vulnerability on a par with WannaCry, and with the correct hard-coded credentials exploit Samba, which was also ripe for a ransomware attack using methods dubbed SambaCry. In 2017, both vulnerabilities were over five years old, but unlike, WannaCry, which was a Windows vulnerability, the Samba 3.5 vulnerability was linked to Linux. Thus, this potentially enabled remote attackers write access that could be used to execute Samba permissions (Goldberg & Greitser, 2017).

From a 2016 survey, Veracode found that 52.5% of web developers were worried about sensitive data exposure. Yet by 2018, researchers found 67% of applications to be prone to data leakage. The 2016, survey also identified that 39% of software had cryptographic issues in their implementation, and by 2018, this had increased to 64% (Veracode, 2016a; Veracode, 2016b; Veracode, 2018). These statistics occurred even though there is best practice to assist in the reduction of weaknesses, such as the Software Assurance Maturity Model (Open Web Application Security Project, 2016), and various tools to assist developers in the generation of acceptable code, like Sonotype (Lemos, n.d.).

HACKER CYBER-ATTACKS

Yahoo Hacks

Yahoo encountered the largest and inherently infamous series of security breaches of all time between 2012, 2013, 2014, and 2017. The 2012 attack was based on a server site Cross-Site Script (XSS) vulnerability on the Yahoo Mail services combined with the susceptibility of some modern client-side browsers to be redirected during the login process. This resulted in end-user accounts being hijacked. Initially, Yahoo attributed this to a single hacker, but in reality, a hacker group used it to compromise up to 400 million accounts (Protalinski, 2013; Wheatley, 2013). In 2014, hackers used a combination of attack vectors. The first was related to the details of usernames and passwords known to have been exfiltrated from a third-party into the hands of a coordinated hacker group. Secondly, hackers were also able to access consumer accounts by using 'forged cookies' implanted into the cache of web browsers replicating legitimate users' single sign-on credentials. Yahoo used legitimate cookies so that every time end-users visited their web site, they did not have to enter a password. Researchers speculated that the attackers could have acquired proprietary code from Yahoo, which provided an understanding of how this mechanism worked (Thielman, 2016). Researchers also thought that this was the attack profile used in the 2013 attacks.

The security researcher Brian Krebs previously criticized Yahoo for inadequate spam blocking and ineffective safeguards against email-based attacks such as phishing (Krebs, 2016). Interestingly, this occurred even though Yahoo had provided a Two-Factor Authentication (2FA) mechanism since 2012. Yet in 2013, it seems that a considerable number of users had not registered to use 2FA. Consequently, they were almost certainly susceptible once their standard credentials had been obtained. However, in 2017, once Yahoo had encouraged users to utilize 2FA after the 2013/2014 hack-fest, researchers also reported that hackers were still able to fool users using phishing attacks; that is, legitimate users were directed to a phishing server that was used to capture user login details. They achieved this by conducting an automated man-in-the-middle attack where the server automatically replayed captured user credentials to the legitimate Yahoo login page. This triggered a legitimate Short Message Service (SMS) 2FA code to be sent to the user out-of-band. The user then entered this into the spoof Yahoo login page, which again was replayed, allowing the attackers to gain full access to the user's legitimate Yahoo Mail account. This technique was used to undermine the security mechanism of not only Yahoo but also other reputable companies, like Google (Amnesty International, 2018; Cox, 2018). This is why in 2018, Yahoo changed their primary authentication method to an 'in-app 2FA' mechanism, thereby relegating the SMS method as a secondary option (Danchev, 2011).

On top of the 400 million hacked accounts in 2012, one billion user accounts were thought to be compromised in the summer of 2013, followed by 500 million by the late summer of 2014. Yet on reflection and after experts have trawled through the data, by 2017, this figure had grown to three billion – the entire Yahoo Mail user-base. This caused serious reputational damage and significant consternation by consumers, resulting in lawsuits, resignations, a considerable amount of spam and phishing emails targeting the Yahoo's customers. This in turn resulted in a devaluation of the company as it was being bought by Verizon. Senior members of the board lost earnings or resigned over the debacle. That said, it is only fair to say that Yahoo took action to inform customers quite quickly using 'Sign-in Alert' emails during May and August of 2013. This was followed by email requests for customers to change account passwords (Rushe, 2017). In 2016, researchers revealed that the cyber-attack had been undertaken by a Russian hacker group suspected of orchestrating activities aligned somewhat to a state-sponsored agenda. In the United Kingdom, the Information Commissioner's Office conducted an investigation and found inadequacies, as well as security lapses, in the processing of PII by Yahoo in the United States. The ensuing investigation culminated in a nominal £250,000 fine on the basis that names, dates of birth, email addresses, telephone numbers, hashed passwords, and encrypted/unencrypted security questions/answers had been compromised. However, investigators thought that payment card data had not been affected. (Hern, 2016; Thielman, 2016; Gibbs, 2018). All this occurred during the same time period, when Twitter and Linkedin accounts were also hacked (Pagliery, 2016; Shu & Conger, 2016). Therefore, this case reveals the lengths to which hackers will go to exfiltrate PII online.

Code Spaces

In 2014, hackers attacked an online developer repository hosted on AWS after a DDOS; this preceded the real attack that was used to hijack the main account. For a period of time, Code Spaces staff and the hackers played a game of cat and mouse; each attempted to change passwords linked to the Elastic Compute Cloud (EC2) Control Panel in their attempt to regain control. Meanwhile, the attackers also tried to simultaneously extort money from the company. Unfortunately for Code Spaces, the attackers had created backup logins that gave them the advantage, and when Code Spaces would not make payment, the hackers proceeded to cause unrecoverable damage (Lucian, 2014). The hackers deleted all the Elastic Block Storage (EBS) snapshots and some EBS instances. The hackers also deleted all AWS Machine Images used by Code Spaces to build their EC2 Virtual Machines (VM) as well as several VM instances and the Simple Storage Service (S3) buckets too (Lucian, 2014).

Code Spaces had poorly architected their cloud environment, which resulted in severe data losses exasperated by a lowly back-up regime. The crisis was catastrophic and ultimately resulted in the company being dissolved (Prince, 2014). Experts have formulated an assertion that a password may have been phished during the DDOS attack or alternatively recovered from a brute force dictionary attack (Williams, 2014). This security breach was ultimately successful because a robust technical authentication and authorization mechanism had not been applied to Code Space's AWS account (Mimoso,

2014). The implementation of 2FA would have significantly stifled or more than likely halted attempts to gain control of the account.

XCodeGhost

During 2015, a hacker group released a subverted version of a genuine Software Development Kit (SDK) on to the popular hosting platform Baidu in China. Baidu is one of the top three most popular brands in the Chinese mobile application space. Other top companies are Tencent and Alibaba. The purpose of the Xcode SDK is to assist developers in creating applications for Apple's iOS devices. The attackers knew that downloads from Apple took a long time in China, so they were savvy to the fact that developers would be all too willing to download the SDK from a speedier third-party site (Reed, 2015). It worked, and what the unsuspecting developers were not aware of was that once the application development had finished, the malicious code XcodeGhost was incorporated into each application at compile time. This effectively created embedded software that was able to seep through Apple's robust inspection regimes – first in China and then internationally, fooling Apple into allowing them to be hosted as legitimate applications in their application stores.

The most prominent iOS applications to succumb to this rouse was Winzip and Weixin (known as WeChat in the West). Winzip has a large global presence with WeChat's footprint consisting of at least 500 million users across China and Asia (Rossignol, 2015). Apple end-users were then able to download these compromised applications onto their devices. Hackers used this malware campaign to capture sensitive user information and send it to the hackers' C2 servers. Not only that, but the attackers also could use the C2 servers to: (a) initiate a fake alert dialog in order to phish user credentials; (b) hijack the exchange of data when applications link out to Uniform Resource Locators (URL) on the World Wide Web, potentially leading to URL redirection attack opportunities; and (c) read the clipboard which may contain a user's password after it had been copied from a password management tool.

At the time, there was a huge furor in the Tech Press, and the MacRumors magazine advised end-users to either update their applications in order to remove the malicious code or uninstall the affected applications (Rossignol, 2015). FireEye found that XcodeGhost was initially targeting older versions of iOS, in which end-users had not updated their devices or were running equipment that was unable to be updated to the latest version of the operating system. Even with remedial action that was taken quite quickly by Apple, hackers developed a new strain called XcodeGhost S that targeted iOS version 9, which was the latest operating system at the time. Therefore, XcodeGhost was able to persist to the point at which Apple had to take down thousands of infected applications. XcodeGhost targeted multiple application consumers ranging from e-commerce at the lower end of the scale to education at the higher end (Kang, Chen, & Wei, 2015).

Linux Mint

In 2016, Linux Mint was a popular Linux distribution and was most certainly targeted because of this popularity. A hacker using the handle Peace subverted the Linux Mint forum by using a flaw in a WordPress Theme to acquire the details of users and passwords. This then enabled them to compromise the Linux Mint website, affording them the opportunity to deploy a Hypertext Preprocessor (PHP) file onto the website for the specific purpose of redirecting users from the legitimate site URL to a web server under the control of the hacker (Leyden, 2016). The server was based at Sofia, Bulgaria and contained a subverted build of Linux Mint 17.3 in the form of a counterfeit ISO image (Kerner, 2016). The embedded malware comprised the Tsunami trojan, also known as Kaiten backdoor, and Backdoor.linux.Tsunami.bh, which contained a hidden Internet Relay Chat (IRC) capability.

Once the distribution had been downloaded and installed by the user, the IRC would have been used to communicate with the hacker's C2 IRC servers (Anderson, 2016). The intention of the hacker was to use these malicious builds for TCP and UDP based DDOS attacks (Dey, 2016). The attackers utilized a MD5 hash of the ISO to fool the users into believing that the download was authentic and genuine. By February 20, hackers had duped over 200 users into downloading the malicious version of the Linux build before Linux Mint realized something was wrong (Anderson, 2016). The following day, Linux Mint warned users to change their passwords because hackers were selling their credentials, which had been seized from the Linux Mint User Forum database, on the Dark Web (Dey, 2016).

Researchers have argued that a pseudo-hobbyist approach had been taken by the Linux Mint Project, which certainly lacked security rigor (Hoffman, 2016; Sanders, 2016). The community came together to help Linux Mint with its incident response. This is actually a worthy example of successful collaboration between multiple like-minded people and organizations in the face of adversity (Linux Mint, 2016). Linux Mint is based on Ubuntu and was popular due to its elegance. However, it is a downstream variant of the Ubuntu distribution (Kumar, 2020); therefore, this scenario highlights the pitfalls, and calls into question the provenance of downstream distributions. Like the XSS issues encountered by Yahoo, users should remain vigilant against site redirection attacks and generally follow the resulting rule of thumb: if it does not feel right or looks suspicious, it probably is (Rashid, 2016; Watson, 2016)! Unfortunately, this kind of attack profile is not uncommon. In 2011, the Kernel.org Linux repository was hacked. It became infected with malware that enabled the hackers to gain root access to host system files and modify passwords (Goodin, 2011).

Arch Linux User Repository

By 2018, Arch Linux User Repository (AUR) team found an open source community repository for Arch Linux to be hosting malware in an 'acroread package'; acroread is used by developers to view pdf files. The concept of the AUR is to share packages and allow other developers to modify code and then use AUR to disseminate it to other users. However, a particular issue with AUR is that orphaned packages are permitted to be updated by anyone with an account. According to a Github commit, a trojan downloader was incorporated into the 'acroread package.' The intention was to use a 'dropper' to conduct data exfiltration and forward it to a remote Pastebin website only accessible using the hacker's private Pastebin API key.

- **Exfiltrated Data:** Consisted of at least the following data and time stamped artefacts:
  - Machine identity;
  - Package management utility information;
  - The output of the "uname-a" command;
  - CPU information;
  - The output of "systemctl list-units" command.

The main objective of the attacker was to collate data about subverted hosts as part of a Stage 1 attack to learn the specifics of each system in order to progress onto Stage 2 (Cimpanu, 2018). At least two other packages were affected but were reversed back to their original state by the AUR team. However, the damage had already been done. Because AUR is not the official Arch Linux repository, the support team made it clear that users need to verify packages for malware and advised the developer community as part of best practice that this should happen on a more regular basis (Khandelwal, 2018). Basically, hackers tried to covertly slip malware laden software into the AUR in order to conduct further hacking operations at a later date. Open source repositories provide an attractive opportunity for hackers to undertake malware propagation (Bird, 2017), and the use of untrusted sources in open source development can therefore have unsavory consequences.

Capital One Breach

During the first quarter of 2019, banking giant Capital One suffered a security breach consisting of 70 PII folders dating back to 2005; this included 140,000 U.S. social security numbers, 80,000 bank account numbers and one million social insurance numbers of Canadian customers. Capital One hosted their online application process for its financial services on an AWS hosted web server. A hacker using the handle Erratic appeared to have worked for Capital One as a contractor and more latterly, AWS as a S3 software engineer between 2015 and 2016. With inside information from both organizations, the hacker, assisted by a misconfigured web application firewall, used a single command to acquire delegated access to the web server hosted in an S3 bucket. After an anonymous tip-off to Capital One an investigation was conducted before contacting the U.S. Federal Bureau of Investigation (FBI). The FBI was subsequently able to establish the identity of Erratic from a GitLab account associated with the extrapolated data and her intent from comments made on the Slack messaging service and Twitter social media. Together, this ultimately led to her demise, revealed her identity as Paige Thompson. Additionally, this brought about other misdemeanors, such as blockchain crypto jacking (Khandelwal, 2019b).

The resulting legal case brought against Thompson resulted in a five-year prison term and a 250,000 USD fine. It transpired that the stolen PII contained: (a) names; (b) addresses; (c) dates of birth; (d) phone numbers; (e) email addresses; (f) credit scores; (g) credit limits; (h) balances; and (i) payment history. The hack affected up to 106 million customers. Capital One stated that full credit card numbers, log-in credentials, and 99% of U.S. social security numbers held by the company had not been exposed during the security breach. The company estimated that the PII had not yet been disseminated to the criminal underworld or the Dark Web (Khandelwal, 2019b; Wright, 2019; Wei, 2019). AWS decreed that their infrastructure was not compromised during the hack (Flitter & Weise, 2019; McLean, 2019). The reputational damage incurred by Capital One also included 150 million USD in costs and resulted in a class-action lawsuit against them (Dellanger, 2019). This scenario highlights the importance of configuration governance across the enterprise (Kelly, 2019).

Global Medical Infrastructures Targeted

The fear instilled by the press that the recent global COVID-19 pandemic will be exploited by hacking groups has been realized. The National Cyber Security Centre of the United Kingdom has provided evidence of multiple actors abusing human traits to force erroneous decisions by using influencing factors such as: implying authority, instilling urgency, drawing upon emotion, and scarcity as part of their manipulation. Techniques in the hacker toolset include social engineering in which hackers use phishing emails, SMS phishing, and spoofed or imposter websites to fool people into revealing their personal and banking details. In addition, flaws in virtual private networks are also ripe for exploitation as the world's population seeks to use online communications during national lockdowns (National Cyber Security Centre, 2020). Such campaigns have been reiterated by the Cybersecurity and Infrastructure Security Agency (CISA) in the United States (Palmer, 2020a) and substantiated by examples of phishing attacks that have been detected in the wild, including SMS phishing attacks (Gatlan, 2020; Griffin, 2020; Stransky, 2020).

In February, hackers were spreading malware in China through phishing emails using a malicious attachment. When these emails are opened on a Windows machine, a remote access trojan dropper is landed that set up a TLS connection. The dropper then download a Visual Basic Script and executable. The script calls the executable, enabling the virus to persist by modifying the Windows registry and start collating data into a log file for exfiltration later (Paganini, 2020a). Additionally, a suspected Chinese group called PANDA, which was identified by the technology firm Crowdstrike, is trying to spread malware through attachments on the back of Coronavirus scaremongering (Herridge, 2020). The target may be Japan based on the Japanese language being used in the emails and a reference to the Kyoto Prefectural Yamashiro Minami Public Health Center (CybersecAsias Editors, 2020). This is a similar tactic being used by a suspected Chinese APT, which was detected by the cyber security firm Checkpoint. The technique used to target the

Mongolian government is to distribute Rich Text Format files weaponized by the RoyalRoad dropper that downloads a Dynamic Link Library file. This abuses a flaw in Microsoft Word to set up a C2 connection as part of the first Stage. Once persistence is attained, hackers can conduct further activities on the compromised host (Checkpoint Security, 2020).

In addition, shadow IT is likely to introduce risks to many organizations through lack of cyber security hygiene (Palmer, 2020b), including unpatched vulnerabilities in Virtual Private Networks (VPN) (Palmer, 2020c). Furthermore, Microsoft Threat Intelligence has reported that hackers associated with the REvil ransomware are scanning the Internet for vulnerable endpoints, including VPN clients of health workers who are now working from home during the pandemic (Zorz, 2020). This situation has caused Microsoft's Threat Intelligence team to instigate its first-ever targeted ransomware warning to hospitals using vulnerable VPNs (Tung, 2020). Not only that, Sonicwall's security researchers have detected a new strain of Master Boot Record (MBR) erasing malware that targets Windows systems. The destructive malware disables Windows Task Manager and User Access Control and persists by altering Windows registry settings. It is activated once the system is rebooted and then performs an overwriting of the MBR.

In March, within a single week, cyber-attacks had despicably targeted health care institutions across the globe in many sovereign nations. First, the Brno University Hospital in the Czech Republic was hit by a cyber-attack (Lyngaas, 2020) that forced a shutdown of the entire network. This halted urgent surgical interventions and laboratory testing, and acute patients had to be transferred to nearby St. Anne's University Hospital (Paganini, 2020b). At the time of writing this book, the technical details of the attack have been withheld, but it has the hallmarks of a ransomware attack. Next, the Maze hacker group targeted the United Kingdom's Hammersmith Medicines Research organization, which was previously involved in developing vaccines for Ebola and Alzheimer's. Even though the hackers landed the ransomware, the IT staff were able to recover and restore the computer systems without having to pay any ransom whatsoever. Unfortunately, in just one day, the attackers were able to exfiltrate PII of 2,300 patients including copies of passports, driving licenses, medical questionnaires, and national insurance numbers. This cyber-attack follows the Tū Ora Compass Health hack in October 2019, in which the group exfiltrated PII of nearly one million people in New Zealand (Eddy, 2020; Jay, 2020; Winder, 2020a). Another group called DarkHotel set up a website mimicking the United Nations' World Health Organization (WHO) email system in an attempt to acquire account details from its employees. The number of impersonation attempts against WHO had doubled by that moment in time during the international COVID-19 crisis (Davis, 2020; Reuters, 2020). While state-sponsored actors such as China and Russia might be suspected by the United States, there is either a hesitance or lack of convincing evidence to support any suspicions. However, FireEye has provided evidence that APT 41, attributed to China, has been quite active, and this might be indicative of nation-state campaigns using COVID-19 as a smoke screen (Cohen & Marquardt, 2020).

Furthermore, the Health and Human Services Department in the United States was hit by a DDOS attack that used a botnet to flood servers with millions of requests over several hours (Santucci et al., 2020). The sustained cyber-attack was not successful in slowing down the department's response to COVID-19. The culprits could have been a number of suspects, and an unknown state-actor has not been ruled out as being the perpetrator (Clarke, 2020; Sanger, Perlroth, & Rosenberg, 2020). Following this, the United States was hit with Netwalker ransomware that took down the website of the Champaign-Urbana Public Health District in Illinois. The U.S. company NRC Medical and the Maroof International Hospital in Islamabad, Pakistan were also hit by ransomware (Gyles, 2020). Another strain being used to target U.S. health care providers is the Ryuk ransomware. In response to the global situation Interpol issued an alert and provided advice on measures needed to help mitigate cyber-attacks. Notably, the situation has encouraged volunteers in Canada and the United Kingdom to offer their services to a bid to protect their respective nation's healthcare systems (Brewster, 2020; Paganini, 2020c; Winder, 2020b).

SOLUTIONS AND RECOMMENDATIONS

France, Germany, and the Netherlands hold a view that such cyber operations violate international law that specifies a prohibition of interference in other states' affairs. The United Kingdom considers attacks against 'essential' medical services as breaking international law. Furthermore, the United States might consider an attack against critical national infrastructure during a national crisis as an aggressive act warranting retaliation if a state-actor is involved (Mačák, Gisel, & Rodenhäuser, 2020; Williams, 2020). Generally, cyber-criminals are using multi-stage methods to conduct cyber-attacks from a range of techniques covering exploits that target vulnerabilities from one end of the spectrum through to the supply chain at the other (Helpnet Security,

2019). Carbon Black's Quarterly Incident Threat Report has espoused that 50% of cyber-attacks from criminal elements occur from techniques such as Island Hopping (National Cyber Security Centre, 2017; Thorpe, 2019). Skillful cyber-crime groups can also be attributed to the APT category, as indicated by Crowdstrike (Meyers, 2019), which is not necessarily the preserve of state-sponsored groups. Commonly used techniques (Shekhar, 2020), many of which the author has covered in this and the previous chapters, are as follows:

- Cookie theft;
- Redirection attacks;
- Malware;
- Phishing;
- Keylogger;
- Rogue Access Points;
- Watering Hole attacks; and
- DDOS.

Techniques used by hackers are not limited to those listed in the case studies from this book. The software lifecycle is particularly complex (Bird, 2017) and necessitates the timely deployment of security patches and software updates as part of an effective preventative maintenance regime. Since at least 2012, a mantra used by the U.K. government has highlighted the importance of patching as a critical aspect of preventing common cyber-attacks (Cyber Emergency Response Team UK, n.d.). In 2017, an independent survey supported this approach (Smith, 2017). This survey identified that over 80% of breaches were caused by poor patch management, and up-to-date patching can minimize the resultant effects of deploying trojans to subvert systems. The importance of patch management reaches back further to 2008, when NIST promoted the patching of ICS (US Department of Homeland Security, 2008). From personal experience penetration testing, specialists have been known to say, "Defenders must counter multiple threat vectors, but it only takes one vulnerability of the right kind to facilitate a cyber-attack." Table 1 summarizes a number of methods drawn from the examples that feature prominently in this Chapter – as well as the lessons that can be learned.

Table 1. Methods and lessons learned

Cyber Security Risk	Compromise Method	Lesson Learned
Phishing and redirection attacks	• URLs included in emails can have malicious intentions to deploy a trojan as part of an initial compromise of a host. • Subverted websites can redirect users to malicious sites and thereby entice the downloading of malware-laden software/code.	• One should not click on any email URLs unless expecting a password reset or something similar from an individual or a known organization. • One should always check the URLs and consider manually typing web links into web browsers when visiting sites of important institutions like online banks; or use a dedicated smart device app. • End-users should be provided with up-to-date web browsers to help prevent XSS attacks. Update them regularly, and users should be on their guard against redirection attacks. • Users should report suspicious emails to their computer incident response team.
Malware	• Like trojans, hackers can deploy malware through redirection attacks, and they can use them to strengthen the hacker's position to persecute the victim further using additional downloaded tools.	• One should not open unknown email attachments. • Downloads and removable media should always be antivirus swept when imported to a system and this should become a habit for end-users in order to mitigate the risks. • Any modern anti-malware product should be able to scan into ISOs and detect known malware like Tsunami, which was not new at the time of the Linux Mint hack.
Unauthorized access	• The adequate selection and configuration of access controls must not be overlooked – especially in the Cloud.	• The lack of 2FA has enabled cyber-criminals to take control of cloud environments. • The Capital One hack demonstrates the risks posed by former employees if access mechanisms are not changed/refreshed.
Malicious code infiltration	• Free and open source software, just like proprietary software, are not immune to flaws; it is a myth that open source development projects are more secure because of the larger community of people scrutinizing the code. • Hackers can alter codes unintentionally, inadvertently, or maliciously without proper authorisation or review. • Software must be updated; otherwise, vulnerabilities will eke into the supply chain or operational software deployments.	• Code reviews (manual / automated) syntax checking. • Experienced developers should undertake staged secure code reviews. • Programmers should use checksums wherever possible. • One should not open email attachments from unknown or suspicious originators. One should antivirus sweep email attachments even from a trusted source, removable media, downloaded executables, and archive file formats containing code and libraries. • One should use integrity verification methods for downloading, importing, and exporting of software libraries. • One should apply digital digests to exported code. • One should always patch operating systems and applications. • One should source code from trusted sources of known provenance and vendors should use reliable digital digests, such as SHA-256 upwards. Where possible, one should verify Source Code and check hashes / check certificate details. • The downloading of developer tools from untrusted sources poses a risk of malicious code being incorporated into baseline and being built as part of the software supply chain.
DDOS	• Hackers can use this as a distraction to precede the real cyber-attack. In the case of Code Spaces, hackers could have also used this to acquire credentials in order to hijack the cloud environment.	• One should seek to employ DDOS protection from a third-party, like Cloud Flare. • Where a CSP hosting environment is used, one should consider anti-DDOS controls provided by their cloud platform.

FUTURE RESEARCH DIRECTION

Ransomware has been prominent since mid-2000 (De Groot, 2019), and the distribution of ransomware has become *en vogue* as a tool of choice for cyber-criminals; consequently, there was a significant increase in file-encrypting attacks in the first quarter of 2019 (Palmer, 2018; Ranger, 2019). In fact, the ShadowBrokers leak of weaponized tooling, like ExternalBlue distributed by WikiLeaks, has certainly made it easier. This has not only given cyber-criminals an advantage (Milmo, 2017), but it also naturally provides a means of conducting higher level exploits and potentially, a means to obfuscate nation-state cyber-attacks. Suffice to say, the WannaCry incident of 2017 used the EternalBlue exploit to propagate through Microsoft Windows file sharing mechanism provided by the Server Message Block protocol (Islam, Oppenheim, & Thomas, 2017). The United States Cyber Emergency Response Team actually attributed this action to the North Korean state (Bird, 2018) rather than cybercriminals, and the author discusses it further in Chapter 4. Yet this is not an isolated incident.

In 2017, Kaspersky Lab reported that trojan initiated ransomware attacks were a particular problem. They identified that end-users' failure to receive or install smart device operating system updates caused Android smart devices to become infected (Rayome, 2017). Recently Google's Project Zero team declared that iPhones have been suspectable to Watering Hole attacks since iOS 10 (Shukla, 2019), and the cyber security firm Malwarebytes suspects that state-sponsored attackers are behind the exploitation of at least 14 vulnerabilities (Greenberg, 2019). Therefore, although these incidents at face value appear to be cyber-crime, they provide examples of a cross-over of tactics between cyber-criminality and state-sponsored cyber operation initiatives. Therefore, the author dedicates Chapter 4 to high-profile attacks that have been attributed to nation-state activities in order to understand the methods employed to realize their objectives.

CONCLUSION

In this chapter, the author has discussed a number of high-profile hacks from a technical exploitation perspective. The author has introduced different types of hacker groups who keep exploiting system weaknesses, whether it be legacy code, poor configuration, or flawed implementations (Konios, 2019):

- **Cyber-Criminals:** Use various techniques to acquire PII for resale on the Dark Web, undertake hacking-for-hire, or seek financial reward through electronic blackmail.
- **Opportunist Attackers:** May include experienced attackers at the high end of the skills scale to script-kiddies at the opposite end, who both use off-the-shelf tools to scan and extrapolate information for personal advantage.

Flaws or bugs in legacy software all have their part to play in presenting risk. So, the *status quo* is slightly more complicated than the original hypothesis stated earlier in this chapter. There is a wider breadth to the problem that has resulted in external attacker abuse. Recent events drawn from Chapter 2 have shown that accidental data exposure online is a particular problem through misconfigurations. The breaches that ensued in the main were from vulnerabilities or inadequate implementations that can be abused and enable accidental data exposures. The evidence shows that legacy vulnerabilities are indeed part of the challenge facing users and IT teams alike. This chapter has been a journey to identify legacy vulnerabilities that are continuing to work their way through successive iterations of software releases and have had their part to play in cyber security incidents. However, more worryingly, the evidence also suggests that flaws can persist and even increment over time, especially when there are measures to enhance best practice within the Software Development Lifecycle (SDLC) and regimes in place during system operations and through-life.

A TechRepublic article from 2019 highlights a number of issues within software development ranging from traditional and agile development approaches that cause design flaws. Each of these issues lead to security and reliability issues, which are not insurmountable and could have been remedied by agile approaches (Rayome, 2019). Additionally, the Forrester report found that implementing security at design-time cost 1/60th of the total expense to implement fixes in a retrospective manner (Wango, 2016). In 2016, Veracode were keen to point out that DevOps appeared to be turning back the tide by enabling bug remediations during sprints (Veracode, 2016b), and this was reiterated in the 2018 report singling out its successor – DevSecOps – as effectively shortening the period in which flaws persist during development (Veracode, 2018). Meanwhile, Java continues to be the most popular language of choice in web development. Veracode's reports provide evidence that 97% of Java application components had at least one vulnerability associated with each of them in 2016. By 2017, this had dropped to 88%, and in 2018, it was down marginally to 87.5% (Veracode, 2016a; Veracode, 2016b; Veracode, 2018). Thus, development regimes seem to be having some effect towards beneficial improvements, such as vetting libraries and conducting automated testing to search for syntax errors at one level and exploitable flaws on another (Lemos, n.d.). Potentially agile development practices with tight timelines could inadvertently seep errors in the code; however, a combination of the static analysis of code and repository enforced versioning could go some way to eliminate coding errors (Assembla, 2020).

Finally, the U.S. Department of Homeland Security stated that vulnerabilities in code account for 90% of security breaches (Assembla, 2020). The importance of rigor whilst undertaking software development or supporting systems during operation require security enabling properties. At minimum, these are comprised of: (a) verification of code / software integrity and validation of software provenance in the supply chain; (b) identification / detection of flaws, bugs and vulnerabilities; (c) patch and software update development; (d) test and deployment of software, patches and updates as necessary; (e)

Figure 1. Cyber security properties and dependencies

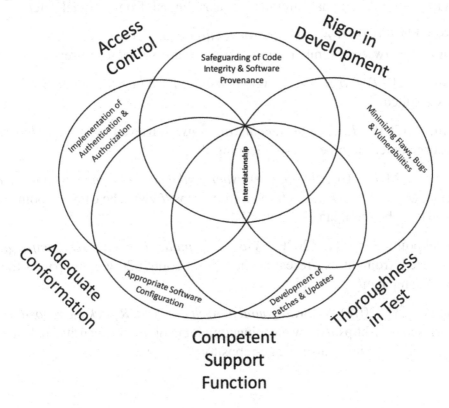

avoiding the misconfiguration of software; and (f) implementing relevant M2M, user and administrator authentication, and authorization mechanisms. Without this rigor, chinks can be left in the armor that are ripe for exploitation by adequately skilled attackers (Rossi, 2014). Figure 1 represents these key elements to enable better cyber security defense in the SDLC. This is particularly important since cyber-criminals are becoming more productive by organizing themselves into groups more akin to the structure of big business organizations (Palmer, 2016).

REFERENCES

Amnesty International. (2018). *When best practice isn't good enough: Large campaigns of phishing attacks in Middle East and North Africa target privacy-conscious users.* Retrieved from https://www.amnesty.org/en/latest/research/2018/12/when-best-practice-is-not-good-enough/

Anderson, T. (2016). *Linux Mint hacked: Malware-infected ISOs linked from official site.* Retrieved from https://www.theregister.co.uk/2016/02/21/linux_mint_hacked_malwareinfected_isos_linked_from_official_site/

Assembla. (2020). *How to secure your source code industry report.* Retrieved from https://www.assembla.com/security/secure-source-code-report

Bird, D. (2017). *Cybertalk: Prevent a menace from lurking within.* Software Box Limited.

Bird, D. (2018). *Beware of sleeping dragons.* Retrieved from https://www.bcs.org/content-hub/beware-of-sleeping-dragons/

Brewster, M. (2020). *All-volunteer cyber civil defence brigade assembles to fight COVID-19 hackers.* Retrieved from https://www.cbc.ca/news/politics/covid19-cyber-companies-1.5508570

Checkpoint Security. (2020). *Vicious panda: The COVID campaign.* Retrieved from https://research.checkpoint.com/2020/vicious-panda-the-covid-campaign/

Cimpanu, C. (2018). *Malware found in Arch Linux AUR package repository.* Retrieved from https://www.bleepingcomputer.com/news/security/malware-found-in-arch-linux-aur-package-repository/

Cimpanu, C. (2019a). *US company selling weaponized BlueKeep exploit.* Retrieved from https://www.zdnet.com/article/us-company-selling-weaponized-bluekeep-exploit/

Cimpanu, C. (2019b). *Microsoft warns of two new 'wormable' flaws in Windows Remote Desktop Services.* Retrieved from https://www.zdnet.com/article/microsoft-warns-of-two-new-wormable-flaws-in-windows-remote-desktop-services/

Clarke, L. (2020). *Cyber-attack on US health agency aimed to disrupt COVID-19 response.* Retrieved from https://tech.newstatesman.com/security/us-health-human-services-department-cyber-attack

Cohen, Z., & Marquardt, A. (2020). *Hackers hit US coronavirus response: 'They are trying to steal everything'.* Retrieved from https://www.msn.com/en-us/news/us/hackers-hit-us-coronavirus-response-they-are-trying-to-steal-everything/ar-BB13aGWh?ocid=sl2

Cox, J. (2018). *How hackers bypass Gmail 2FA at scale.* Retrieved from https://www.vice.com/en_us/article/bje3kw/how-hackers-bypass-gmail-two-factor-authentication-2fa-yahoo

Cyber Emergency Response Team UK. (n.d.). *Common cyber attacks: Reducing the impact* [PDF document]. Retrieved from https://assets.publishing.service.gov.uk/government/uploads/system/uploads/attachment_data/file/396124/common_cyber_attacks_infographic.pdf

CybersecAsias Editors. (2020). *'Lure and decoy' cyber-threats exploit COVID-19.* Retrieved from https://www.cybersecasia.net/news/lure-and-decoy-cyber-threats-exploit-covid-19

Danchev, D. (2011). *Yahoo! Mail introduces two factor authentication.* Retrieved from https://www.zdnet.com/article/yahoo-mail-introduces-two-factor-authentication/

Davis, J. (2020). *Hackers target WHO, COVID-19 research firm with cyberattacks.* Retrieved from https://healthitsecurity.com/news/hackers-target-who-covid-19-research-firm-with-cyberattacks

De Groot, J. (2019). *A history of ransomware attacks: The biggest and worst ransomware attacks of all time.* Retrieved from https://digitalguardian.com/blog/history-ransomware-attacks-biggest-and-worst-ransomware-attacks-all-time

Dellinger, A. (2019). *Capital one hit with class-action lawsuit following massive data breach*. Retrieved from https://www.forbes.com/sites/ajdellinger/2019/07/30/capital-one-hit-with-class-action-lawsuit-following-massive-data-breach/

Dey, B. (2016). *Linux Mint website breach leads to trojanised download and loss of personal data* [Weblog comment]. Retrieved from https://www.forcepoint.com/blog/x-labs/linux-mint-website-breach-leads-trojanised-download-and-loss-personal-data

Dignan, L. (2015). *Legacy vulnerabilities easy route for hackers*. Retrieved from https://www.zdnet.com/article/legacy-vulnerabilities-easy-route-for-hackers/

Eddy, N. (2020). *WHO, coronavirus testing lab hit by hackers as opportunistic attacks ramp up*. Retrieved from https://www.healthcareitnews.com/news/who-coronavirus-testing-lab-hit-hackers-opportunistic-attacks-ramp

Flitter, E., & Weise, K. (2019). *Capital One data breach compromises data of over 100 million*. Retrieved from https://www.nytimes.com/2019/07/29/business/capital-one-data-breach-hacked.html

Gatlan, S. (2020). *Coronavirus phishing attacks are actively targeting the US*. Retrieved from https://www.bleepingcomputer.com/news/security/coronavirus-phishing-attacks-are-actively-targeting-the-us/

Gibbs, S. (2018). *Yahoo fined £250,000 for hack that impacted 515,000 UK accounts*. Retrieved from https://www.theguardian.com/technology/2018/jun/12/yahoo-fined-hack-ico-uk-accounts-russia

Goldberg, D., & Greitser, R. (2017). *Sambacry, the seven year old Samba vulnerability is the next big threat (for now)*. Retrieved from https://www.guardicore.com/2017/05/samba/

Goodin, D. (2011). *Kernel.org Linux repo rooted in hack attack*. Retrieved from https://www.theregister.co.uk/2011/08/31/linux_kernel_security_breach/

Greenberg, A. (2019). *Mysterious iOS attack changes everything we know about iPhone hacking*. Retrieved from https://www.wired.com/story/ios-attack-watering-hole-project-zero/

Griffin, A. (2020). *Text scams use fears about coronavirus outbreak and to panic people and steal money.* Retrieved from https://www.independent.co.uk/life-style/gadgets-and-tech/news/coronavirus-outbreak-text-scams-owed-money-government-final-warning-link-a9428821.html

Gyles, S. (2020). *Cyberattacks hit hospitals and health departments amid COVID-19 coronavirus pandemic.* Retrieved from https://vpnoverview.com/news/cyberattacks-hit-hospitals-and-health-departments-amid-covid-19-coronavirus-pandemic/

Helpnet Security. (2019). *Multi-stage attack techniques are making network defense difficult.* Retrieved from https://www.helpnetsecurity.com/2019/07/15/multi-stage-attack-techniques/

Hern, A. (2016). *Yahoo faces questions after hack of half a billion accounts.* Retrieved from https://www.theguardian.com/technology/2016/sep/23/yahoo-questinos-hack-researchers

Herridge, C. (2020). *Cybercriminals are capitalizing on coronavirus fears, security firm warns.* Retrieved from https://www.cbsnews.com/news/coronavirus-cybercriminals-capitalize-on-fears-cyber-firm-crowdstrike-says/

Hoffman, C. (2016). *Ubuntu developers say Linux Mint is insecure. Are they right?* Retrieved from https://www.howtogeek.com/176495/ubuntu-developers-say-linux-mint-is-insecure-are-they-right/

Holmes, A. (2020). *Hackers attacked a US health agency's computer system in an attempt to slow down its COVID-19 response.* Retrieved from https://www.businessinsider.com/coronavirus-covid-19-cyberattack-hhs-health-human-services-hack-attempt-2020-3?r=US&IR=T

Islam, A., Oppenheim, N., & Thomas, W. (2017). *SMB exploited: WannaCry use of "EternalBlue".* Retrieved from https://www.fireeye.com/blog/threat-research/2017/05/smb-exploited-wannacry-use-of-eternalblue.html

Jay, J. (2020). *Amid COVID-19 outbreak, hackers target UK medical research firm.* Retrieved from https://www.teiss.co.uk/hackers-target-uk-medical-research-firm/

Kang, Y., Chen, Z., & Wei, R. (2015). *XcodeGhost S: A new breed hits the US.* Retrieved from https://www.fireeye.com/blog/threat-research/2015/11/xcodeghost_s_a_new.html

Kelly, B. (2019). *PayThink Operational holes cause breaches more than security glitches.* Retrieved from https://www.paymentssource.com/opinion/operational-holes-cause-breaches-more-than-security-glitches

Kerner, S. (2016). *Hackers breach Linux Mint distribution, forums.* Retrieved from https://www.eweek.com/security/hackers-breach-linux-mint-distribution-forums

Khandelwal, S. (2018). *Malicious software packages found on Arch Linux user repository.* Retrieved from https://thehackernews.com/2018/07/arch-linux-aur-malware.html

Khandelwal, S. (2019a). *Critical flaws found in VxWorks RTOS that powers over 2 billion devices.* Retrieved from https://thehackernews.com/2019/07/vxworks-rtos-vulnerability.html?m=1

Khandelwal, S. (2019b). *Capital One data breach affects 106 million customers; Hacker arrested.* Retrieved from https://thehackernews.com/2019/07/capital-one-data-breach.html?m=1

Konios, A. (2019). *Cyber security in the software and development life cycle.* Training course retrieved from https://www.futurelearn.com/courses/cyber-security-in-the-software-development-life-cycle/1/steps/444756

Krebs, B. (2016). *Yahoo: One billion more accounts hacked.* Retrieved from https://krebsonsecurity.com/2016/12/yahoo-one-billion-more-accounts-hacked

Kumar, M. (2018). *New Linux kernel bug affects Red Hat, CentOS, and Debian distributions.* Retrieved from https://thehackernews.com/2018/09/linux-kernel-vulnerability.html?m=1

Kumar, U. (2020). *Linux Mint vs Ubuntu – Which distro should you choose?* Retrieved from https://www.techlila.com/linux-mint-vs-ubuntu/

Lemos. R. (n.d.). *The best open-source DevOps security tools, and how to use them.* Retrieved from https://techbeacon.com/app-dev-testing/best-open-source-devops-security-tools-how-use-them

Leyden, J. (2016). *Linux Mint forums hacked: All users urged to reset passwords.* Retrieved from https://www.theregister.co.uk/2016/02/22/linux_mint_forums_hacked/

Lin, M., & Seltzer, L. (2014). *The shellshock FAQ: Here's what you need to know*. Retrieved from https://www.zdnet.com/article/the-shellshock-faq-heres-what-you-need-to-know/

Linux Mint. (2016). *Monthly news – February 2016*. Retrieved from https://blog.linuxmint.com/?p=3007

Lucian, C. (2014). *Hacker puts 'full redundancy' code hosting firm out of business*. Retrieved from https://www.pcworld.com/article/2365602/hacker-puts-full-redundancy-codehosting-firm-out-of-business.html

Lyngaas, S. (2020). *Czech Republic's second-biggest hospital is hit by cyberattack*. Retrieved from https://www.cyberscoop.com/czech-hospital-cyberattack-coronavirus/

Mačák, K., Gisel, L., & Rodenhäuser, T. (2020). *Cyber Attacks against Hospitals and the COVID-19 Pandemic: How Strong are International Law Protections?* Retrieved from https://www.justsecurity.org/69407/cyber-attacks-against-hospitals-and-the-covid-19-pandemic-how-strong-are-international-law-protections/

Man, J. (2015). *PCI SSC Announces the end of SSL usage for the payment card industry*. Retrieved from https://www.tenable.com/blog/pci-ssc-announces-the-end-of-ssl-usage-for-the-payment-card-industry

McLean, R. (2019). *A hacker gained access to 100 million Capital One credit card applications and accounts*. Retrieved from https://edition.cnn.com/2019/07/29/business/capital-one-data-breach/index.html

Meyers, A. (2019). *Meet the threat actors: List of APTs and adversary groups*. Retrieved from https://www.crowdstrike.com/blog/meet-the-adversaries/

Milmo, C. (2017). *Ex-GCHQ officer warns cyber crooks have same hacking tools as Western intelligence*. Retrieved from https://inews.co.uk/news/uk/cyber-crime-ex-gchq-officer-warns-bad-guys-capability-western-intelligence-leak/

Mimoso, M. (2014). *Hacker puts hosting service code spaces out of business*. Retrieved from https://threatpost.com/hacker-puts-hosting-service-code-spaces-out-of-business/106761/

Mitre. (2019). *CVE-2018-14634*. Retrieved from https://www.tenable.com/cve/CVE-2018-14634

National Cyber Security Centre. (2017). *Cyber crime - understanding the online business model.* Crown Copyright.

National Cyber Security Centre. (2020). *Advisory: COVID-19 exploited by malicious cyber actors* [PDF document]. Retrieved from https://www.ncsc.gov.uk/files/Joint%20Advisory%20COVID-19%20exploited%20by%20malicious%20cyber%20actors%20V1.pdf

Open Web Application Security Project. (2016). *Open software assurance maturity model* [PDF document]. Retrieved from http://www.opensamm.org/downloads/SAMM-1.0.pdf

Paganini, P. (2020a). *New cyber attack campaign leverages the COVID-19 infodemic.* Retrieved from https://securityaffairs.co/wordpress/98484/malware/covid-19-hacking-campaign.html

Paganini, P. (2020b). *One of the major COVID-19 testing laboratories in Czech hit by cyberattack.* Retrieved from https://securityaffairs.co/wordpress/99598/hacking/covid-19-czech-hospital-hit-cyberattack.html

Paganini, P. (2020c). *Interpol warns that crooks are increasingly targeting hospitals.* Retrieved from https://securityaffairs.co/wordpress/101178/cyber-crime/interpol-warns-hospitals-attacks.html

Pagliery, J. (2016). *Hackers selling 117 million LinkedIn passwords.* Retrieved from https://money.cnn.com/2016/05/19/technology/linkedin-hack/index.html

Palmer, D. (2016). *Cybercrime Inc: How hacking gangs are modeling themselves on big business.* Retrieved from https://www-zdnet-com.cdn.ampproject.org/c/s/www.zdnet.com/google-amp/article/cybercrime-inc-how-hacking-gangs-are-modeling-themselves-on-big-business/

Palmer, D. (2018). *Cybercrime: Ransomware attacks have more than doubled this year.* Retrieved from https://www.zdnet.com/article/cyber-crime-ransomware-attacks-have-more-than-doubled-this-year/

Palmer, D. (2020a). *Hackers are scanning for vulnerable VPNs in order to launch attacks against remote workers.* Retrieved from https://www-zdnet-com.cdn.ampproject.org/c/s/www.zdnet.com/google-amp/article/hackers-are-scanning-for-vulnerable-vpns-in-order-to-launch-attacks-against-remote-workers/

Palmer, D. (2020b). *Rogue IoT devices are putting your network at risk from hackers*. Retrieved from (https://www.zdnet.com/article/rogue-iot-devices-are-putting-your-network-at-risk-from-hackers/?ftag=TRE3e6936e&bh id=25938706913849853718443426927355

Palmer, D. (2020c). *Hackers are scanning for vulnerable VPNs in order to launch attacks against remote workers*. Retrieved from https://www-zdnet-com.cdn.ampproject.org/c/s/www.zdnet.com/google-amp/article/hackers-are-scanning-for-vulnerable-vpns-in-order-to-launch-attacks-against-remote-workers/

Prince, B. (2014). *Code hosting service shuts down after cyber attack*. Retrieved from https://www.darkreading.com/attacks-breaches/code-hosting-service-shuts-down-after-cyber-attack/d/d-id/1278743

Protalinski, E. (2013). *Yahoo Mail users hit by widespread hacking, XSS exploit seemingly to blame (Update: Fixed)*. Retrieved from https://thenextweb.com/insider/2013/01/07/yahoo-mail-users-hit-by-widespread-hacking-xss-exploit-seemingly-to-blame/#!t1aGP

Ranger, S. (2019). *One issue is probably to blame for your IT outages and data losses - and it's not hackers*. Retrieved from https://www-zdnet-com.cdn.ampproject.org/c/s/www.zdnet.com/google-amp/article/cybersecurity-broken-hardware-behind-many-outages-but-ransomware-threat-increases/

Rashid, F. (2016). *Lesson from Linux Mint breach: Trust is not enough*. Retrieved from https://www.infoworld.com/article/3036178/lesson-from-linux-mint-breach-trust-is-not-enough.html

Rayome, A. (2017). *Report: 2016 saw 8.5 million mobile malware attacks, ransomware and IoT threats on the rise*. Retrieved from https://www.techrepublic.com/article/report-2016-saw-8-5-million-mobile-malware-attacks-ransomware-and-iot-threats-on-the-rise/

Rayome, A. (2019). *Why your software project failed, and how to succeed next time*. Retrieved from https://www.techrepublic.com/article/why-your-software-project-failed-and-how-to-succeed-next-time/?ftag=TRE684d53 1&bhid=24734138609373909185025257836691

Reed, T. (2015). *XcodeGhost malware infiltrates App Store*. Retrieved from https://blog.malwarebytes.com/cybercrime/2015/09/xcodeghost-malware-infiltrates-app-store/

Reuters. (2020). *Coronavirus cyber-attacks: Elite hackers target WHO.* Retrieved from https://gadgets.ndtv.com/internet/news/coronavirus-cyber-attacks-who-hack-attempts-2199570

Rossi, B. (2014). *Catastrophe in the Cloud: What the AWS hacks mean for cloud providers.* Retrieved from https://www.information-age.com/catastrophe-cloud-what-aws-hacks-mean-cloud-providers-123458406/

Rossignol, J. (2015). *What you need to know about iOS malware XcodeGhost.* Retrieved from https://www.macrumors.com/2015/09/20/xcodeghost-chinese-malware-faq/

Rushe, D. (2017). *Yahoo says all of its 3bn accounts were affected by 2013 hacking.* Retrieved from https://www.theguardian.com/technology/2017/oct/03/yahoo-says-all-of-its-3bn-accounts-were-affected-by-2013-hacking

Sanders, J. (2016). *Why the Linux Mint hack is an indicator of a larger problem.* Retrieved from https://www.techrepublic.com/article/why-the-linux-mint-hack-is-an-indicator-of-a-larger-problem/

Sanger, D., Perlroth, N., & Rosenberg, M. (2020). *Hackers attack health and human services computer system.* Retrieved from https://www.nytimes.com/2020/03/16/us/politics/coronavirus-cyber.html?referringSource=articleShare

Santucci, J., Faulders, K., Margolin, J., Barr, L., & Levine, M. (2020). *Suspicious cyberactivity targeting HHS tied to coronavirus response, sources say.* Retrieved from https://abcnews.go.com/Politics/cyberattack-hhs-meant-slow-coronavirus-response-sources/story?id=69619094

Shekhar, A. (2020). *Top 10 common hacking techniques you should know about.* Retrieved from https://fossbytes.com/hacking-techniques/

Shu, C., & Conger, K. (2016). *Passwords for 32M Twitter accounts may have been hacked and leaked.* Retrieved from https://techcrunch.com/2016/06/08/twitter-hack/

Shukla, G. (2019). *Google reveals malicious websites have been secretly hacking into iPhones for years.* Retrieved from https://gadgets.ndtv.com/mobiles/news/iphone-hack-google-project-zero-day-websites-imessage-whatsapp-live-location-files-2092914

Smith, T. (2017). *Over 80% of breaches still result of poor patch management.* Retrieved from https://dzone.com/articles/80-of-breaches-still-result-of-poor-patch-manageme

Stransky, S. (2020). *Cyber attackers are exploiting coronavirus fears.* Retrieved from https://www.lawfareblog.com/cyber-attackers-are-exploiting-coronavirus-fears

Synopsys Inc. (2019). *The Heartbleed bug.* Retrieved from http://heartbleed.com

Thielman, S. (2016). *Yahoo hack: 1bn accounts compromised by biggest data breach in history.* Retrieved from https://www.theguardian.com/technology/2016/dec/14/yahoo-hack-security-of-one-billion-accounts-breached

Thorpe, E. (2019). *50% of cyber attacks now use island hopping.* Retrieved from https://www-itpro-co-uk.cdn.ampproject.org/c/s/www.itpro.co.uk/security/33946/50-of-cyber-attacks-now-use-island-hopping?amp

Tung, L. (2020). *Coronavirus: Microsoft directly warns hospitals, 'Fix your vulnerable VPN appliances'.* Retrieved from https://www-zdnet-com.cdn.ampproject.org/c/s/www.zdnet.com/google-amp/article/coronavirus-microsoft-directly-warns-hospitals-fix-your-vulnerable-vpn-appliances/

U.S. Department of Homeland Security. (2008). *Recommended practice for patch management of control systems* [PDF document]. Retrieved from https://www.us-cert.gov/sites/default/files/recommended_practices/RP_Patch_Management_S508C.pdf

Veracode. (2016a). *State of software security.* Burlington, MA: Veracode.

Veracode. (2016b). *Secure development survey: Developers respond to application security trends.* Burlington, MA: Veracode.

Veracode. (2018). *State of software security.* Burlington, MA: Veracode.

Wango, J. (2016). *Brief: App security can't happen without developers.* Forrester Research Inc.

Watson, J. (2016). *Linux Mint: The right way to react to a security breach.* Retrieved from https://www.zdnet.com/article/linux-mint-the-right-way-to-react-to-a-security-breach/

Wei, W. (2019). *Capital One hacker also accused of hacking 30 more companies and cryptojacking.* Retrieved from https://thehackernews.com/2019/08/paige-thompson-capital-one.html?m=1

Wheatley, M. (2013). *Yahoo Mail hacked again – Serious questions raised about its ability to protect users.* Retrieved from https://siliconangle.com/2013/04/30/yahoo-mail-hacked-again-serious-questions-raised-about-its-ability-to-protect-users/

Williams, G. (2014). *The attack that forced Code Spaces out of business – what went wrong?* Retrieved from https://www.itgovernance.co.uk/blog/the-attack-that-forced-code-spaces-out-of-business-what-went-wrong/

Williams, O. (2020). *"Phishing emails work better in a pandemic": How Covid-19 led to a surge in cybercrime.* Retrieved from https://www.newstatesman.com/science-tech/security/2020/03/phishing-emails-work-better-pandemic-how-covid-19-led-surge-cybercrime

Winder, D. (2020a). *COVID-19 vaccine test center hit by cyber attack, stolen data posted online.* Retrieved from https://www.forbes.com/sites/daveywinder/2020/03/23/covid-19-vaccine-test-center-hit-by-cyber-attack-stolen-data-posted-online/

Winder, D. (2020b). *CV19: Meet the volunteer COVID-19 cyber heroes helping healthcare fight the hackers.* Retrieved from https://www.forbes.com/sites/daveywinder/2020/03/23/meet-the-volunteer-covid-19-cyber-fighters-helping-healthcare-fight-the-hackers/#2f5244fa6d82

Wright, R. (2019). *FBI charges former AWS engineer in Capital One breach.* Retrieved from https://searchsecurity.techtarget.com/news/252467616/FBI-charges-former-AWS-engineer-in-Capital-One-breach

Zorz, Z. (2020). *Vulnerable VPN appliances at healthcare organizations open doors for ransomware gangs.* Retrieved from https://www.helpnetsecurity.com/2020/04/02/vpn-healthcare-ransomware/

ADDITIONAL READING

Bartlett, J. (2015). *The dark net.* Windmill Books.

Bowden, M. (2011). *Worm: The first digitak world war.* Grove Press UK.

Coleman, G. (2014). *Hacker hoaxer, whistleblower, spy: The many faces of anonymous*. Verso.

Mansfield, R. (2000). *Hacker attack! Shield your computer from Internet crim*. Sybex.

Mitnick, K., & Simon, W. (2002). *The art of deception: Controlling the human element of security*. Wiley Publishing Inc.

Olson, P. (2012). *We are anonymous*. William Heinemann.

Poulson, K. (2011). *Kingpin: How one hacker took over the billion dollar cybercrime underground*. Broadway Paperbacks.

KEY TERMS AND DEFINITIONS

Bourne Again Shell: A command line interface that administrators of Unix and Linux operating system distributions use heavily.

Development Operations (DevOps): DevOps is a sprint-based approach that can catch coding flaws during the development of code due to security reviews, rework on previous sprint cycles, and testing.

Island Hopping: This involves the subversion of web sites from one organization to redirect them to a malicious site hosting exploit kits used to find vulnerabilities in a bid to launch attacks against users of other organizations who visited the site; effectively, this acts as Watering Holes.

Linux: An open source operating system originally developed by Linus Torvalds that is based on a monolithic kernel which contains a number of different open source applications and different forms of graphic user interfaces.

Man-in-the-Middle Attack: A method used to interact with the user and/or the intended recipient of a communication, transaction or session in order to capture credentials, intercept traffic, and collect data to undertake further nefarious activities.

Two-Factor Authentication: An example is an SMS message to a user's registered cellular phone that forms part of a two-stage verification process.

Virtual Private Network: A security function that uses cryptographic key exchanges and encryption suites to encapsulate and tunnel traffic securely across insecure IP-based networks using TCP (SSL/TLS) or UDP (Internet Protocol Security) methods.

WannaCry: A ransomware worm that used the Eternal Blue exploit to abuse the unpatched Server Message Block protocol and propagate between Windows computers.

Watering Hole: The use of compromised web sites to infect computer hosts with malware or directly interact with them using subversion in order to springboard another phase of a cyber-attack to achieve an aim like acquire banking details.

Chapter 4
Attributed State Actors

ABSTRACT

Chapter 4 looks at the technical aspects and effects of some attributed and high-profile state-sponsored cyber-attacks that have been encountered through our interaction with the networked world. Coverage also includes a look at the approach of nation-states against commercial companies as well as government institutions to achieve various objectives. The author uses these scenarios to focus attention on the important pillars of cyber security that all have important interrelationships in safeguarding of data and information. Within the context of their implementation, a weakness or series of weaknesses within one or more pillars can be enough to facilitate a cyber-attack. These pillars are underpinned by important factors, and the impact of improper cyber security considerations can be directly and indirectly problematic to continued e-commerce and our constructive evolution of knowledge sharing across the internet.

INTRODUCTION

In this chapter, the author discusses a number of cyber-attacks by state actors colloquially known as the 'high threat club.' The author uses the analysis of these high-profile security breaches to outline how society may better defend itself during users' interaction with cyberspace. The author will build upon examples provided in Chapter 3 to discuss the following categories of attacker groups (Chinnaswamy & Milford, 2019):

DOI: 10.4018/978-1-7998-3979-8.ch004

- **Industrial Espionage Campaigns:** First, industrial espionage campaigns target users to deploy home grown exploits and zero-days in order to exfiltrate data over protracted periods of time. As the author alluded to in Chapter 1, some hacker groups can be affiliated or used by nation-states to avoid attribution, and therefore, they may achieve their own goals and those of the state, potentially at the same time.

- **State Actors:** State actors undertake state-sponsored activities using weaponized malware to perform economic, espionage, or politically influenced actions by infiltrating many different public and private organizations and institutions. Depending on the actor, this may involve seeking financial reward for the state or even in some cases, seeking out PII.

BACKGROUND

In 2019, a little-known hacker group called 0v1ru$, which was aligned with the Digital Revolution group, hacked the Russian company SyTech. This contractor has been involved in cyber capability development on behalf of the Russian state-actor *Federal'naya sluzhba bezopasnosti Rossiyskoy Federatsii* (FSB) and had already been targeted by Digital Revolution in the past. This was the largest cyber-attack against the FSB, revealing 7.5 Terabytes of leaked secret projects, including a number of interesting capabilities such as The Onion Router (TOR) network de-anonymization project linked to the Kvant Research Institute (Abrams, 2019; Doffman, 2019). This haul has been appended by another series of tools also attained by Digital Revolution after a cyber-attack against the Kvant Research Institute and provided evidence of state sponsored Mirai malware use in 2016. In addition, this breach reveals the Russian Government's intention of targeting and attacking IoT devices through capabilities developed under the Fronton Program (Asif, 2020). Researchers stipulated that the use of default passwords, or hard coded credentials for that matter, was the instigator that allowed the Mirai botnet to infiltrate Linux-based commodity IoT (Hellard, 2018). This is just a small taste of the efforts, deviousness, and capabilities that can be used by state-actors.

Historically, researchers have blamed Russia and China for cyber-espionage activities, but the weaponization of cyberspace that has been gradually building over the second decade of the new millennium includes others, such as Syria, Iran, and Vietnam. Even the U.S. Office of Tailored Access Operations, which came to light after the Edward Snowden revelations, has also been branded an APT (Leclare, 2015; Zetter, 2016; Geary, 2018). FireEye has published a list of prolific APT groups attributed as nation-state actors. State-sponsored groups do not necessarily have to carry the APT tag and may hail using pseudonyms or aliases (Stirparo, 2015; FireEye, 2020) just like hackers. This chapter investigates a variety of infamous state-sponsored cyber-attacks and lessons that can be learned from these attacks.

STATE-SPONSORED ATTACK VECTORS

Stuxnet

There has been speculation about Stuxnet pointing the finger at a U.S.-Israeli collaborative effort. Recent revelations have showed that Stuxnet was certainly built by a nation-state level actor and might have been developed partly from intelligence and information provided at an international level since the 1990s. Researchers have surmised that research activity was conducted against seized centrifuges, which an engineering black market had built from blueprints stolen by a Pakistani engineer who worked for a Dutch engineering firm in the 1970s and were illicitly *en route* to Libya (Paganini, 2019a). Researchers have associated an elite Israeli signals intelligence unit called Unit 8200 with this research activity (Zilber, 2018). Using the W32.Stuxnet malware family, a state-actor level threat actor performed the cyber-attack over a protracted period, using different variants between 2008 and 2010.

The first stage Stuxnet derivative was allegedly planted by an Iranian insider working for foreign intelligence services. According to Kaspersky Labs, early Stuxnet is known to have incorporated elements which are now known as Flame to undertake the cyber-surveillance activities (Kushner, 2013). The initial attack vector bridged an airgap using an insider's USB thumb drive, which contained Microsoft Windows Zero-day exploit, to abuse a design flaw in Windows. Stuxnet was subsequently launched using Window's automatic execution capability. Stuxnet evaded detection because it came armed with a valid signed certificate, fooling the Windows host into running it; subsequently, the malware hid itself on its host by using a rootkit. Once it had gained a foothold, the Stuxnet worm propagated by exploiting a Windows Remote Procedure Call Zero-day and a Windows Zero-day related to a print spooler remote code execution vulnerability to spread via network file shares that were usually protected by weak passwords. The worm then attempted to call home using two URLs, one in Malaysia and the other in Denmark, in order to set up C2. Any reconnaissance data extracted from the target network was communicated out and received back in encrypted format using XOR, and the format used different 31-bit keys (Symantec, 2010).

By 2009, hackers unleashed a Stage Two variant to conduct further reconnaissance that targeted engineering firms in Behpajooh. Researchers associated the Neda Industrial Group and CGJ with ICS design aspects linked to the new Iranian uranium conversion plant in Esfahan (Zetter, 2014a). Again, it appeared that the Stuxnet compromise path was the use of USB thumb drives in Natanz itself (Paganini, 2019a). This attack consisted of the worm that sought and targeted Windows hosts containing Siemens SIMANTEC Step7 software. The malware hooked into Kernel32 Dynamic Link Library (DLL) functions on the Windows host to hide malicious files (Thabet, 2011). The inference here is that if Natanz was not directly connected to the Internet, then there may have been some form of indirect network connection between third-party companies supporting the Iranian nuclear program for Stuxnet's C2.

In 2010, hackers then reportedly replaced Stuxnet with other variants, building upon the capabilities of the previous versions but with payloads to undertake the Stage Three attack. The main objective was the centrifuges at the Natanz Nuclear Processing Facility in Iran (Kelley, 2013). If the intended target could not be found on a host, then Stuxnet would do nothing. Where its target was found, Stuxnet had the ability to modify Step7 WinCC programming block constituents and deploy them onto S7-400 PLCs masked via a PLC rootkit to avoid detection by staff working on the device (Schneier, 2010; Thabet, 2011; Kushner, 2013). From this vantage point, Stuxnet was able to undertake the actual attack by stealthily sending commands from the PLCs using the Profibus protocol to the uranium enrichment centrifuges that they controlled. The malware used the PLCs to sabotage the centrifuges by commanding them to perform spin-up and slow-down functions over several months, causing at least 984 units to be degraded (Zetter, 2014a). Meanwhile, false values were returned to the HMI used by the centrifuge operators, controlling the centrifuges in order to avoid arousing suspicion.

This cyber operation resulted in serious damage that massively set the Iranian nuclear program back (Zetter, 2014a). Researchers discovered the malware after it had infected customers of at least five contractor companies. The first indications of Stuxnet were traces of malware related DLL files originally found and analyzed by a Belarus computer security company; their experts were responding to reports of computers continually crashing and rebooting in Iran (Zetter, 2014a). The Iranian regime confirmed that

30,000 computers had been affected by Stuxnet (Beaumont, 2010). This led to thousands of machines being infected globally, which is how Stuxnet was discovered outside of Iran and famously made public by Symantec Research Labs in 2010 (Irish Examiner Ltd, 2013).

Subsequently, researchers found the W32.Duqu malware 'in the wild' in 2011, before finding Duqu 2.0, which was prevalent around 2014 and 2015 and affected countries involved in the Iranian nuclear deal negotiations. The latter strain used three zero-days to operate, and Kaspersky Labs suspect that it was originally launched through a phishing attack. Unlike Stuxnet, Duqu was not designed to be destructive but was associated with cyber-espionage of ICS type systems and other interrelated information. Because of Duqu's apparent commonality with Stuxnet code development, researchers speculated that its presence preceded a future Stuxnet type cyber-attack (Bradley, 2011; Infosec Institute, 2019). Then, by 2018, researchers found that a newer, more prevalent, and destructive form of Stuxnet attacked Iranian systems, although specific details have not been forthcoming (Shepherd, 2018). Stuxnet is revered to be the first cyber-weapon used to undertake a cyber-physical attack against ICS.

Havex

As previously discussed in Chapter 1, Havex is also known as Energetic Bear and Dragonfly. Between 2013 and 2014, hackers conducted Stage One using spear phishing or Watering Hole attacks from ICS-orientated websites in at least Germany, Switzerland, and Belgium (Constantin, 2014). Attackers redirected victims to third-party sites hosting software embedded with a Remote Access Trojan (RAT) coded in PHP. Therefore, it appeared to be legitimate to ICS operators, but in effect, they were actively arbitrating the infection of critical national infrastructure. Hackers undertook this malware campaign between 2010 and 2014, and according to CrowdStrike, the Russian Intelligence Services architected it.

The state-actors infected target computers specifically with Backdoor. Oldrea, also known as Havex, Backdoor.Goodor, Backdoor.Dorshel, and Trojan.Karagany.B (Aboud, 2014; Khandelwal, 2014; Unknown, 2017). The malware would seek out and locate SCADA and ICS devices on the network, while reporting back to the C2 servers as part of the second stage. To do this, it used the Open Platform Communications (OPC) to conduct reconnaissance and propagation (New Jersey Cybersecurity and Communications Integration

Cell, 2017). OPC is a universal client/server model that enables SCADA software on Windows hosts to interoperate with PLCs (Wilhoit, 2017). Stage Three in this context was cyber-espionage undertaken using the Distributed Component Object Model to connect to OPC servers on the inside of a DCS to collect data. Examples of parameters sought by the attackers include the following:

- A globally unique identifier that identifies a Component Object Model class object in Windows Registry;
- Server name;
- Program ID;
- OPC version;
- Vendor information;
- Running state;
- Group count;
- Server bandwidth.

The attackers exfiltrated these parameters to C2 servers, and subsequent analysis has deemed them to be useful for further reprehensible purposes against the energy sector in the future (New Jersey Cybersecurity and Communications Integration Cell, 2017).

Sony Hack

Hackers conducted the Sony hack over the fall of 2014 and they called themselves the Guardians of Peace (GOP). The attackers performed Stage One using phishing emails that targeted executives in the company to verify their Apple account details, including passwords, via a spoof web site as well as utilizing social engineering through the Linkedin website. In effect, the attackers managed to acquire system administrator credentials, and they used them to infect Sony's networks by the December (Bort, 2014; Tripwire, 2014; Bisson, 2015).

The threat actor gained an initial foothold using a 'dropper' executable that was run on a single server within what academics have described as an inadequately segregated and questionably flat network architecture (Mazzarella, 2015). This executable was signed by a valid certificate used by Sony containing a forged MD5 hash. This enabled it to be run and in effect circumvent security enforcing functions. The malware deployment started as a backdoor Windows Service DLL complete with a web server that displayed a message from the attackers to the users. Either by a remote command or at a preset time, hackers performed a number of Stage Two actions:

- **Stage Two:** Actions that the attackers undertook:
    - ◦ Replicate itself four times to run different command-line arguments.
    - ◦ Set up a file share accessible to the network for staging.
    - ◦ Beacon out to the C2 servers via proxies located in Italy, Singapore, Poland, the United States, Thailand, Bolivia, and Cyprus.
    - ◦ Set up a VPN to the proxies in order to hide egressed traffic and inbound commands.
    - ◦ Spread to other Windows servers using the Server Message Block (SMB) protocol by using logs to guess passwords for network file share connections.
    - ◦ Shut down Microsoft Exchange Information Store service, making e-mail inaccessible from the host (Gallagher, 2014; GReAT, 2014).

Before enacting its destructive capabilities on each contaminated host in order to perform data erasure of the hard disk, hackers exfiltrated the following as part of Stage Three: (a) employee salaries and bonuses; (b) Social Security numbers and birth dates, (c) HR employee performance reviews; (d) criminal background checks and termination records; (e) passport and visa information; (f) correspondence regarding staff medical conditions (g) source code; (h) Oracle and Structured Query Language database passwords; (i) movie schedules; (j) emails; and (k) the films themselves making this information mostly public (Bort, 2014; Zetter, 2014b). Under Stage Three, Wiper malware used drivers to evade the Windows NT File System security permissions and proceeded to erase data on the hard disk sector by sector and further infected each disk's MBR. The threat actor then forced the host to reboot, at which point malware in the MBR erased the rest of the disk space (Baumgartner, 2014; Gallagher, 2014; Lennon, 2014).

Stage Four was not successful to remove traces of hacker activity, which helped the FBI investigation (Peterson, 2014). Retrospectively, it transpired that the malware contained 10,000 hard-coded host names, which revealed the extensive and unprecedented research undertaken by the attackers over several months. It also contained code used to attack some Unix/Linux systems used by Sony (Strom, 2018). The whole episode was very damaging to Sony's reputation, costing them millions of dollars and resulting in an estimated 100 terabytes of data being taken from their networks (Zetter, 2014b). Shortly after the attack, the FBI attributed the attack to North Korean associated IPs that the hackers accidentally revealed (Nakashima, 2015). Furthermore, the U.S. Department of Justice subsequently indicted Park Jin Hyok, who works at a North Korean government front-company called 'Chosun Expo,' which is based out of China. In the end, the U.S. FBI attributed the GOP to APT 37 - the Lazarus Group, known as Bureau 121 in North Korea (LeClare, 2015; Strom, 2018).

Office of Personnel Management Attack

The U.S. Office of Personnel Management (OPM) is a federal organization that holds the Human Resources data of U.S. government employees. In 2015, an OPM security engineer detected a beacon that was using SSL to communicate with a spurious URL called 'opmsecurity.org.' This was emanating from a malicious file masquerading as a McAfee Antivirus DLL, which was not used by OPM. Within 24 hours, the U.S. Cyber Emergency Response Team of the Department of Homeland Security arrived to start an investigation. They found that a credential issued to a contractor had been compromised, and coincidentally, the contractor company KeyPoint had been hacked between late 2013 and early 2014. KeyPoint and another contractor, USIS, also subjected to a security breach before KeyPoint, were both involved in conducting background checks on behalf of their client using OPM's network (Krebs, 2015; Koerner, 2016; Fruhlinger, 2018). The threat actors had breached OPM's network and extracted stolen information on the OPM's network design during that period. The U.S. CERT detected them in the first quarter of 2014, and OPM decided to contain the attackers on the network and monitor their activity for counterintelligence purposes. Likely to have occurred over the Fourth of July weekend, the attackers using the KeyPoint sourced credential installed an undetected backdoor. Even though the U.S. CERT alerted OPM to the first cyber-attack, unfortunately, up to two attackers maintained a covert foothold on the OPM network and continued to pursue their objectives into 2015 (Higgins, 2015; Fruhlinger, 2018a).

After the event the U.S. CERT team found 2,000 pieces of unrelated malware on the OPM network, which is not surprising because the OPM had been subjected to 10 million attempted cyber intrusions per month as it was deemed a soft target. Specialists uncloaked the offending DLL file and found it to be PlugX malware. This was a known tool used by APTs from the

Far East, and it resided on only 10 jump boxes (Koerner, 2016; Fruhlinger, 2018a). In effect, the attackers had been exfiltrating sensitive PII using the Roshal Compressed file format known as RAR pertaining to: 19.7 million federal employees' security clearance records, the social security numbers of more than 22 million people, and the biometric data artefacts of 1.1 million personnel (Higgins, 2015; Krebs, 2015; Fisher, 2019). In this case, the OPM had implemented 2FA, but it was too late to stop the PlugX infestation. By 2016, none of the PII had been found in use by the Blackhat Hacker underground, which certainly seemed to point the finger at a state-sponsored APT. The attackers' use of Marvel characters for domain registrations was a hallmark of Unit 61398 of the Peoples Liberation Army of China (Koerner, 2016) known as APT 1, although independent researchers also attributed APT 19 to this attack (Leclare, 2015; Stirparo et al., 2015).

Subsequently, the agency's director and Chief Information Officer (CIO) both elected to take early retirement, and lawsuits ensued against the OPM (Koerner, 2016; Fruhlinger, 2018a). As a result, the OPM notified employees of the hack and provided advice and guidance on how to avoid becoming a victim of crime (US Office of Personnel Management, 2015a). The U.S. House Oversight and Reform Committee conducted an investigation into the OPM's failings (Adams, 2016), resulting in a paper being issued by the OPM on the improvements that the organization would be making in light of the cyber-attack (US Office of Personnel Management, 2015b). Additionally, the OPM tendered a 133 million USD contract to undertake credit monitoring services for three years on behalf of the millions of victims affected by the breach (Krebs, 2016). It transpired that the Federal Accreditation Authority approved only 75% of OPM systems to operate under the Federal Information Security Management Act due to poor governance and oversight at program level (Gallagher, 2015). Immediately after the event, the U.S. Federal CIO initiated an immediate program of work for security improvements focusing on better cyber hygiene across U.S. government departments and agencies. Two years after this reputation damaging breach, there was still an outcry for more to be done to update the IT systems of federal organizations (Moore, 2017).

WannaCry

Between 2017 and 2018, the Wanna Decryptor 2.0 (WannaCry) worm attacked the U.K. National Health Service (NHS) and other corporations, including a Boeing aircraft factory (Gates, 2018), Fedex, Spanish Telefonica, the French car manufacturer Renault, the Russian Interior Ministry, Chinese universities, and more (National Health Service England, 2017). In the case of the NHS, 80 out of 236 trusts were infected in May, causing 34% disruption that degraded the NHS's nationwide capability. The U.K. National Audit Office anticipated the initial attack vector to be an exposed Internet-facing SMB port rather than traditional means, such as phishing emails (Symantec Security Response, 2017; Controller & Editor General, 2018). Hackers landed the malware onto each infected host in the form of a 'dropper,' which contained the ransomware component consisting of: (a) an application to encrypt and decrypt data; (b) files containing encryption key; and (c) a client for TOR network.

Once Stage One was complete, the malware transitioned to the Second Stage by first attempting to access a hard-coded URL. If the URL was not contactable, then a search was commenced for target files to be encrypted and then proceeded onto Stage Three. Here, it would deny access to the data by encrypting 176 different files types and holding the data to ransom. WannaCry spread by making use of the EternalBlue exploit, which used SMB version 1 to propagate and exploit a contaminated system without any user/attacker intervention (Bhat, 2017).

This malware strain primarily affected Windows 7 and Windows Server 2008, rather than Windows XP, causing each host to reboot. In the case of Windows XP, many of these systems crashed, stopping the infection in its tracks (National Health Service England, 2017; Controller & Editor General, 2018). The ransom demand associated with WannaCry was 300 USD worth of Bitcoin that doubled after three days, and after seven days, the threat actor threatened to delete the encrypted files – although Symantec Research Labs retrospectively found there was no such capability within the malware (Symantec Security Response, 2018).

Within days, the U.K. cyber security researcher Marcus Hutchins sacrificed his annual leave to look into the WannaCry malware. He soon discovered the so called 'kill switch,' which was the URL's domain name that had not been assigned. He quickly registered the domain for 10.96 USD to set up a web site and effectively created a sinkhole, which, by making the URL active, halted the encryption function of the worm. This provided the researcher with unwanted notoriety. Subsequently, an FBI investigation revealed that he had previously been a poacher in the murky world of Blackhat Hackers. However, he had turned over a new leaf and became a committed Whitehat (Fruhlinger, 2018b; Krebs, 2019) gamekeeper, and is a hero to many. It also became evident from the WannaCry attack that Chinese hackers attempted to steal the domain by transferring it to another registrar; however, this failed.

Researchers do not think that this was the attackers themselves, but another group trying to acquire some kudos (Fruhlinger, 2018b; Krebs, 2019).

In the same year as the WannaCry strain, hackers unleashed the unrelated NotPetya copycat worm, which also used EternalBlue to disseminate itself (Whittaker, 2019a). Google attributed the Sandworm APT to this campaign working for the Russian State. The *Wired* journalist Andy Greenberg has linked fallout from NotPetya to a cyber-carpet bombing of commercial, financial, municipal, and governmental institutions in Ukraine that then went global (Brumfield, 2019). Other affected organizations consisted of FedEx, Pharmaceutical Merck, software vendor Nuance Communications, and food and beverage company Mondelez International. NotPetya, also had a 'kill switch' in the form of a file that effectively vaccinated the malware. The cyber security researcher Amit Serper identified this immobilizing technique (Asher-Dottan, 2017). In both cases, recipients of the cyber-attack could have prevented the sustained cyber-attack if Windows 7 had been patched with a security update released by Microsoft in March 2017 (Microsoft, 2017).

The WannaCry episode cost the NHS 92 million Pounds Stirling, and NotPetya is thought to have cost global revenues one billion USD by the end of 2017 alone (Asher-Dottan, 2017; Field, 2018). Although Windows XP is end of life and support, Microsoft still released a security update to fix the SMB version 1 vulnerability at the time. Subsequently, the NHS decreed that it will invest up to 150 million Pounds Stirling to augment cyber security controls within their business (Balsamo, Tucker, & Satter, 2018). Security firms McAfee and Intezer blamed the North Korean Lazarus Group for WannaCry not only for commonality to the Sony hack but also for similarity in malware payload *modus operandi* and attribution of online aliases associated with the group. It was not that unusual for this threat actor group, in which attack tool code re-use was a common occurrence (Palmer, 2018). Again, unsurprisingly, the United States indicted Park Jin Hyok for this attack (Balsamo, 2017; Sommerlad, 2018). Since 2017, the fear of prolific wormable exploits, like the more recent Windows BlueKeep and Exim Mail vulnerability for Linux, are being more readily reported (Cimpanu, 2019a; O'Donnell, 2019; Paganini, 2019b).

TRITON

Between late 2016 and early 2017, a threat actor group conducted two cyber-attacks against several Schneider Electric Triconex SIS at the petrochemical plant in Petro Rabigh, Saudi Arabia (Reyner, 2019). The attack was revealed when the SIS was triggered to instigate a safety feature that shutdown the plant's actuators. The petrochemical company called in Mandiant, a part of the FireEye group, after incident responders found suspicious files that transpired to be residual digital traces of a malware framework on the SIS workstation (Sobczak, 2019). Luckily, this was an unintended consequence of the hacker's actions from the attack that failed and inadvertently raised the alarm averting a potential catastrophe; however, FireEye experts suspected the original intent to have been the instigation of an unsafe condition or state reprogramming the Triconex SIS. Hackers initially perpetuated the attack by subverting the DCS layer from at least 2014 before targeting the workstation used to operate the Triconex system (Giles, 2019). Originally, architects designed the SIS to be a separate network that directly interfaced with the actuators, but over time, the Triconex workstation had been 'dual homed' to the DCS, providing the hackers access for Stage One. FireEye speculates that the attackers spent a year remoting reconnoitering the SIS and testing their exploits on a local Triconex SIS in their possession before undertaking the Stage Two cyber-attack. Undoubtedly, their TTP consisted of reverse engineering the proprietary TriStation protocol because its code constituents were not publicly disclosed.

For the third stage, the hackers used a RAT to land a crafted executable onto the Windows workstation, comprising: (a) a compiled python script and a zip file containing Python libraries; (b) open source libraries; and (c) what is now known as the TRITON framework to interact with the Triconex controller modules. The pre-built TRITON framework itself also consisted of secure tunneling techniques, reconnaissance functions, and a firmware zero-day exploit to deploy two malicious binary files into memory and initiate a direct attack (Johnson et al., 2017). After escalating privileges, the attackers were able to subvert the first of three controller modules within the Triconex system. While attempting to hack the second controller with buggy code, the Triconex controller defaulted to its safe-mode and safely shutdown the actuators. Mandiant found that a final payload was absent, revealing that it was an incomplete attack. A particularly important and poignant aspect to the hackers was the fact that Triconex had a built in physical key enabled failsafe switching system that was left in the Program state rather than Run – thus enabling the aggressors to pursue their cyber-attack. If a user had switched it to Run, then the attackers would not have been able to perform the suspected re-programming of the SIS in their attempt to cause an unsafe condition (Lough & Caban, 2019; Whittaker, 2019b). Inevitably, because the threat actor had not achieved stage four clean-up, this evidence unveiled their *modus operandi* to incident responders.

According to the U.S. ICS CERT, TRITON is the first malware family specifically designed to target a safety system within industrial systems with the intent to do physical harm (Heller, 2018). The Saudis initially thought the attackers to be Iranian, but FireEye subsequently attributed the source to the Central Scientific Research Institute of Chemistry and Mechanics in Moscow that has a research focus linked to CNI and industrial safety (Computing, 2019). FireEye thereby affiliated the group to a Russian state-sponsored activity. The attackers had even crafted the malware to avoid being detected by antivirus software, although this occurred the antivirus did detect the incursion. Yet the victim organization's staff failed to raise the alarm (Giles, 2019). The threat actor group behind TRITON, named Xenotime by cyber security firm Dragos, is now targeting electricity utility companies in the United States and within the Asia-Pacific region (Dragos Inc, 2019).

Equifax Breach

In the summer of 2017, Equifax, the consumer credit assessment company, was operating a vulnerable Java Open Source Framework Apache Struts project on an Internet facing web server. A hacker was able to craft and upload an exploit onto the web server using the Jakarta-based plugin (Sahu, 2017). The result of this attack was that the threat actor absconded with PII between 143 and 148 million people.

- **Compromised PII data amounted to the following**:
    - Social security numbers, birth dates, addresses, and some driving license numbers for people in the United States.
    - Names, dates of birth, email addresses, and telephone numbers of U.K. citizens.

PII belonged to customers from the United States and Canada (Robinson, 2017; Safe Harbor on Cyber, 2020), including nearly half a million records belonging to U.K. consumers. This breach was contrary to the Privacy Shield agreement that enforces the protection of EU citizens personal data outside the European economic zone. The penetration test (pentest) community decreed that this breach would have been particularly trivial for the hacker to conduct remotely. The irony is that it was preventable if the vulnerability had been mitigated by deploying the available patch (Whittaker, 2018). Equifax had two months grace from notification of the Common Vulnerabilities and Exposures up to May 2017 when the attack occurred (Sharwood, 2017). The U.S. Security and Exchange Commission estimated that Equifax incurred a cost of at least 1.4 billion USD (Olenick, 2019) to recover their reputation and position within the market over successive years since the breach. This number includes approximately 700 million USD as a settlement for people who had been affected, which the U.S. Consumer Financial Protection Bureau and the Federal Trade Commission arbitrated (Associated Press, 2019; Colby, 2020). Ironically, a second security breach occurred shortly after the first attack, which expounded the company's already infamous reputation. Equifax began serving fraudulent Adobe Flash Player updates in the October. A malware researcher originally assessed it to potentially be part of an adware campaign, but it swiftly turned into another furor when an independent cyber security researcher suspected malvertizing (Goodin, 2017). The cyber security researcher subsequently identified that there was another unpatched flaw that enabled malicious links to be embedded via a third-party vendor that had legitimate hooks into the Equifax website. This situation was even more unforgivable since the U.S. CERT had previously notified the company of the vulnerability, and this incident subsequently impacted the company's share price (Guynn, 2019).

More recently, the results of a DevSecOps Community survey indicated that 26% of companies have reported, confirmed, or have suspected a web application breach in the past 12 months (Weeks, 2019). Thus, Equifax is not alone. The company Sonotype established that during the past year, over 10,000 organizations have continued to download the flawed Java web-component that caused the Equifax breach (Fazzini, n.d.). Following the Equifax cyber-attack, the FBI conducted an investigation that culminated in a grand jury declaration by the U.S. Justice Department; revealing that the attack had been conducted by at least four serving members of the 54th Research Institute of the People's Liberation Army of China and attributed as being APT 10. After running 9,000 queries to accumulate the relevant data that they wanted, the attackers split an archive containing 49 directories into more manageable 600-megabyte chunks for exfiltration purposes (Barrett, 2020; Kanell, 2020; Kumar, 2020). The threat actor tried to anonymize themselves by hiding their tracks bouncing between 34 servers and across 20 countries. This entire episode affected Equifax's reputation and stock value to some degree (Brewster, 2020). The company reaffirmed their commitment to bolster their incremental spending in security and technical measures as part of their cloud technology transformation, totaling 1.25 billion USD between 2018 and 2020 (Equifax, 2020).

US Navy Undersea Warfare Center Contractor Hack

An undisclosed contractor at the U.S. Navy Undersea Warfare Center in Newport, Rhode Island was hacked between January and February of 2018. Hackers exfiltrated 614 Gigabytes of UNCLASSIFIED data from the company's network, which contained data relating to the new U.S. Navy Sea Dragon weapon system. This project had been under development since 2015 and was scheduled for sea trials by late 2018. Also, details of submarine cryptographic systems, signals, and sensor data are thought to have been taken, and U.S. officials deemed the aggregation effect of all this data by its association to be quite sensitive (Osbourne, 2018; Morris, 2018). This incident occurred at a time when the United States was modifying and upgrading its offensive weapons systems (Larter, 2018). The timing of this cyber-attack was coincidental with a resurgence of Chinese state-sponsored hacking. The finger has firmly been pointed at the Chinese Ministry of State Security, even though China denies being a party to this cyber-attack (GoLocalProv News Team, 2018; Mazza, 2018).

While the FBI was investigating the details of the hack (Nakashima & Sonne, 2018), industry experts reported that contractors are constantly in the crosshairs of foreign state actors (Lynch, 2018). The cyber security community in the United States speculated that the data exfiltration may have been conducted very cautiously to avoid detection by the contractor's network defenses. Cyber security representatives also agreed that standards need to be tightened. Contractors are 'self-attesting' their compliance to the NIST-800-171 standard and are meeting the Defense Federal Acquisition Regulation Supplement security controls as a starting point for handling, storing, and processing Controlled Unclassified Information as part of Department of Defense contracts (National Institute of Standards and Technology, 2017).

State-actors target contractors because they perceive their company systems to be weaker than the government's systems. Therefore, it would make sense for state actors to target the 'low hanging fruit' rather than government organizations directly (Fryer-Biggs, 2018). Thus, industry C-Suite representatives have speculated that conforming to standards has become akin to a compliance mapping exercise against the 14 control-set groups of NIST 800-171 (Taylor, 2018) and does not necessarily or adequately drill down into the appropriateness of control implementation for a particular purpose or the defined risk profile allocated by the DoD.

Citrix Hacks

In 2018, hackers attacked Citrix and exfiltrated six Terabytes of documents that related to the National Aeronautics and Space Administration, the FBI, aerospace contractors and a Saudi Arabian oil company (The Inquirer, 2019). Citrix thinks that the attackers gained access by using password spraying against employee accounts (Cluley, 2019). The actors undertook the attack in a way that minimized account lockouts (Ikeda, 2019) over the Christmas period. Cyber security firm Resecurity stated that the attackers also used techniques to bypass two-factor authentication in order to gain access to Citrix's internal network. According to a Citrix spokesperson, once a foothold had been established, the threat actor then circumvented additional layers of security to pursue their attack (Cimpanu, 2019b). Resecurity blamed the attack on the Iranian state-sponsored group Iridium, even though the FBI was not as specific. Iridium was attributed to hacks against financial institutions, CNI, and government resources based in the United States, the United Kingdom, Canada, Australia, and the Middle East. Resecurity attributed Iridium by monitoring the Dark Web and correlating attacks undertaken between 2014 and 2017 (O'Flaherty, 2019).

This cyber-attack follows the Citrix GoToMyPC hack of 2016, but Citrix soon realized that attackers gained access and blamed it on password re-use. Another article stipulates that the Russian threat actor group W0rm gained a foothold by guessing a weak password and then exploited a series of security vulnerabilities or weaknesses in order to access the company's administrative system and the remote assistance system (Rossi, 2016). In this circumstance, Citrix identified the hacks and reset users' passwords to negate the attackers' utilization of the acquired credentials (Whitney, 2016). Before the 2018 Christmas attack, Citrix again reset passwords for some users after Citrix ShareFile services experienced a credential stuffing attack targeting customer accounts on a completely different and unrelated network to the Iridium cyber-attack (Cimpanu, 2019b).

SOLUTIONS AND RECOMMENDATIONS

The author draws upon the lessons learned from the examples specified in this chapter to list key takeaways are listed in Table 1. Furthermore, by analyzing the points drawn out from these cyber incursions, it is possible to define the main pillars of cyber security, as shown in Figure 1.

Figure 1. The cyber security pillars

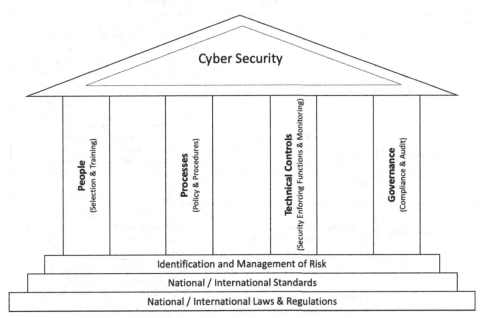

FUTURE RESEARCH DIRECTION

There is a worrisome escalation in cyber operations between the United States and Russia that is leading to a dangerous tit-for-tat approach to hacking CNI within each other's borders. Thus, this could potentially lead to a declared state of perpetual cyber warfare between the two countries (Vijayan, 2017; Goodin, 2019; Ranger, 2019). The attack vectors used by state-sponsored actors are similar in approach to cyber-criminals but are expected to use a higher degree of competency with regards to the exploits used (MSS Global Threat Response, 2014). However, a means of avoiding attribution to state-sponsored actors is to use hacker tools and techniques to disguise one's activities, providing some element of plausible deniability (Walton, 1996)

Table 1. Highlighted security controls and lessons learned

Security Control	Cyber Security Risk	Lesson Learned
System design	• Making modifications to system architectures without understanding the full context of consequences.	• One should not modify valid and approved architecture designs for the sake of convenience. • One should have configuration and change control regimes in place.
Manage removable media	• Organizations can no longer think of isolated networks as a defensive posture in their own right by relying on an airgap.	• One should have robust controls to detect the insertion of USB media into hosts using monitoring agents. • One should block or prevent auto-execution from removable media. • One should antivirus sweep removable media on data transfer to systems. • Encrypted removable media is a ideal measure for protecting data-at-rest, but if decryption has not been undertaken prior to an antivirus engine scan, then undetectable malware can be hidden on the volume.
Passwords and password constitution	• Inadequate access control mechanisms. • Weak passwords or re-used passwords, which may have already been compromised, can be easily guessable using dictionary lists (Be'ery, 2014).	• One should employ 2FA when possible, but one should not use 2FA with weak passwords or, even worse, default passwords. • Robust password constitution should be used, and passwords should be protected, using salts that make attempts to use offline brute force guessing very drawn out and untenable. • One should not reuse passwords.
Software authenticity	• Malicious code or fake software could end up being incorporated into baseline builds or deployed operationally thereby affecting system integrity.	• Code should not be trusted by default. • Downloads should be verified by associated certificates or hashes as a form of provenance verification.
Audit	• Ineffective identification of crucial technical weaknesses using documentary-based compliance audits.	• One should identify gaps in policy and processes against standards like ISO27001:2013 to identify vulnerabilities, such as ineffective patching and weak Business Continuity regimes. • One should use active pentest findings cross referenced against control criteria to identify control-measure gaps.
Monitoring	• One should investigate antivirus alerts.	• One should deploy antivirus onto system hosts and regularly update engines and signatures. • One should implement active and passive security enforcing functions that form preventative and detective controls.
Procedural controls	• Humans tend to be nonchalant towards procedures or may actively seek to take short-cuts or circumvent process-based controls if they are presented with the opportunity.	• Procedures and processes that enforce organizational security policy cannot be solely relied upon without some form of technical control to augment it. • Users must not bypass policy, procedures, or processes.
User training	• Computers left screen-locked and unnecessarily left on overnight are prime candidates to be subverted and used as staging servers for data exfiltration purposes.	• One should undertake user training to enhance user competency, so that security mechanisms are used properly in line with security policy.

during cyber operations (Greene, 2016). The author will further explore examples of effective cyber-warfare outcomes transcending the digital and real worlds in Chapter 5.

CONCLUSION

The cyber aggressiveness in this chapter has drawn out a number of key areas that can elaborate on three commonly defined mainstays used in the community, namely: people, processes, and technology (Dutton, 2017). This is in contrast to the CIA triad itself, which is sometimes mis-defined in this way when they are in fact really key attributes of cyber security. Figure 1 shows the pillar categories that the author has discerned from the case-studies explored in this chapter. The pillars are supported by the foundations, consisting of national and international laws, regulations, and standards identified in Chapter 1; and risk, which has been inferred throughout the first three chapters. There is no keystone in this model because each individual pillar is as important as the other. Risk management approaches ensure that relevant and salient security controls within each pillar are deployed in the right context to mitigate the risks. From the undertow in Chapters 1 and 2 and the attack profiles from Chapters 3 and 4, readers have seen the consequences of inadequacies, oversights, or failings associated with computerized system security. That is the depth and breadth of controls deployed in a salient context is particularly relevant. Furthermore, this is why compliance audits reside in the Governance pillar as a contributary and influential factor of cyber security, but it is not the basis of cyber security itself (Hagerman, 2016), as the author discussed in Chapter 2.

REFERENCES

Aboud, J. (2014). *HAVEX proves (again) that the Airgap is a myth: Time for real cybersecurity in ICS environments*. Retrieved from https://blogs.cisco.com/digital/havex-proves-again-that-the-airgap-is-a-myth-time-for-real-cybersecurity-in-ics-environments?dtid=osscdc000283

Abrahams, L. (2019). *Russian FSB intel agency contractor hacked, secret projects exposed*. Retrieved from https://www.bleepingcomputer.com/news/security/russian-fsb-intel-agency-contractor-hacked-secret-projects-exposed/

Adams, M. (2016). *Why the OPM hack is far worse than you imagine*. Retrieved from https://www.lawfareblog.com/why-opm-hack-far-worse-you-imagine

Asher-Dottan, L. (2017). *Notpetya vaccine discovered by cyberreason*. Retrieved from https://www.cybereason.com/blog/cybereason-discovers-notpetya-kill-switch

Asif, S. (2020). *Russian Intel Agency FSB's contractor hacked; Sensitive data leaked online*. Retrieved from https://www.hackread.com/russian-intel-agency-fsb-contractor-hacked/?utm_content=buffer6439a&utm_medium=social&utm_source=twitter.com&utm_campaign=buffer

Associated Press. (2019). *Equifax to pay $700m over breach that exposed data of 150m people*. Retrieved from https://www.theguardian.com/us-news/2019/jul/22/equifax-data-breach-security-ftc-settlement

Balsamo, M., Tucker, E., & Satter, R. (2018). *North Korean programmer charged in Sony hack, WannaCry attack*. Retrieved from https://www.pbs.org/newshour/nation/north-korean-programmer-charged-in-sony-hack-wannacry-attack

Barrett, B. (2020). *How 4 Chinese hackers allegedly took down Equifax*. Retrieved from https://www.wired.com/story/equifax-hack-china/amp

Baumgartner, K. (2014). *Sony/Destover: Mystery North Korean actor's destructive and past network activity*. Retrieved from https://securelist.com/destover/67985/

Be'ery, T. (2014). *Brute-force attacks: Crossing the online-offline password chasm*. Retrieved from https://www.securityweek.com/brute-force-attacks-crossing-online-offline-password-chasm

Beaumont, P. (2010). *Stuxnet worm heralds new era of global cyberwar*. Retrieved from https://www.theguardian.com/technology/2010/sep/30/stuxnet-worm-new-era-global-cyberwar

Bhat, S. (2017). *DoublePulsar – A very sophisticated payload for Windows*. Retrieved from https://www.secpod.com/blog/doublepulsar-a-very-sophisticated-payload-for-windows/

Bisson, D. (2015). *Sony hackers used phishing emails to breach company networks*. Retrieved from https://www.tripwire.com/state-of-security/latest-security-news/sony-hackers-used-phishing-emails-to-breach-company-networks/

Bort, J. (2014). *How the hackers broke into Sony and why it could happen to any company*. Retrieved from https://www.businessinsider.com/how-the-hackers-broke-into-sony-2014-12?r=US&IR=T

Bradly, T. (2011). *Duqu: New malware is Stuxnet 2.0*. Retrieved from https://www.pcworld.com/article/242114/duqu_new_malware_is_stuxnet_2.html

Brewster, T. (2020). *Chinese government hackers charged with massive Equifax hack*. Retrieved from https://www.forbes.com/sites/thomasbrewster/2020/02/10/chinese-government-hackers-charged-with-massive-equifax-hack/#6f786b3561d6

Brumfield, C. (2019). *Russia's Sandworm hacking group heralds new era of cyber warfare*. Retrieved from https://www.csoonline.com/article/3455172/a-new-era-of-cyber-warfare-russias-sandworm-shows-we-are-all-ukraine-on-the-internet.html

Chinnaswamy, A., & Milford, B. (2019). *The cyber security landscape*. Training course retrieved from https://www.futurelearn.com/courses/cyber-security-landscape/1/steps/600019

Cimpanu, C. (2019a). *Microsoft warns of two new 'wormable' flaws in Windows Remote Desktop Services*. Retrieved from https://www.zdnet.com/article/microsoft-warns-of-two-new-wormable-flaws-in-windows-remote-desktop-services/?ftag=TRE49e8aa0&bhid=25938706913849853718443426927355

Cimpanu, C. (2019b). *Citrix discloses security breach of internal network*. Retrieved from https://www.zdnet.com/article/citrix-discloses-security-breach-of-internal-network/

Cluley, G. (2019). *Citrix hackers may have stolen six terabytes worth of files* [Weblog comment]. Retrieved from https://www.grahamcluley.com/citrix-hack/

Colby, C. (2020). *You're running out of time to submit your Equifax data breach claim -- Here's how*. Retrieved from https://www.cnet.com/how-to/equifax-settlement-see-if-you-are-eligible-file-an-ftc-claim-find-out-what-you-may-get/

Computing. (2019). *Hackers behind the world's deadliest code are probing US power firms*. Retrieved from https://www.technologyreview.com/f/613775/hackers-behind-the-worlds-deadliest-code-are-probing-us-power-firms/

Constantin, L. (2014). *New Havex malware variants target industrial control system and SCADA users.* Retrieved from https://www.pcworld.com/article/2367240/new-havex-malware-variants-target-industrial-control-system-and-scada-users.html

Controller & Editor General. (2018). *Investigation: WannaCry cyber attack and the NHS* [PDF document]. Retrieved from https://www.nao.org.uk/wp-content/uploads/2017/10/Investigation-WannaCry-cyber-attack-and-the-NHS.pdf

Doffman, Z. (2019). *Russia's secret intelligence agency hacked: 'Largest data breach in its history'.* Retrieved from https://www.forbes.com/sites/zakdoffman/2019/07/20/russian-intelligence-has-been-hacked-with-social-media-and-tor-projects-exposed/

Dragos Inc. (2019). *Threat proliferation in ICS cybersecurity: XENOTIME now targeting electric sector, in addition to oil and gas* [Weblog comment]. Retrieved from https://dragos.com/blog/industry-news/threat-proliferation-in-ics-cybersecurity-xenotime-now-targeting-electric-sector-in-addition-to-oil-and-gas/

Dutton, J. (2017). *Three pillars of cyber security.* Retrieved from https://www.itgovernance.co.uk/blog/three-pillars-of-cyber-security

Equifax. (2020). *Statement of Mark W. Begor, Chief Executive Officer of Equifax, on the U.S. Department of Justice indictment alleging China carried out 2017 cyber attack.* Retrieved from https://investor.equifax.com/news-and-events/news/2020/02-10-2020-160714269

Fazzini, K. (n.d.). *Companies still downloading flaw that led to Equifax breach.* Retrieved from https://de.sonatype.com/hubfs/WSJ%20-%20Companies%20Still%20Downloading%20Flaw%20that%20Led%20to%20Equifax%20Breach.pdf?t=1528728914577

Field, M. (2018). *WannaCry cyber attack cost the NHS £92m as 19,000 appointments cancelled.* Retrieved from https://www.telegraph.co.uk/technology/2018/10/11/wannacry-cyber-attack-cost-nhs-92m-19000-appointments-cancelled/

FireEye. (2020). *Advanced persistent threat groups Who's who of cyber threat actors.* Retrieved from https://www.fireeye.com/current-threats/apt-groups.html

Fisher, T. (2019). *What is a RAR file?* Retrieved from https://www.lifewire.com/rar-file-2622216

Fruhlinger, J. (2018a). *The OPM hack explained: Bad security practices meet China's Captain America. Retrieved from* https://www.csoonline.com/article/3318238/the-opm-hack-explained-bad-security-practices-meet-chinas-captain-america.html

Fruhlinger, J. (2018b). *What is WannaCry ransomware, how does it infect, and who was responsible?* Retrieved from https://www.csoonline.com/article/3227906/what-is-wannacry-ransomware-how-does-it-infect-and-who-was-responsible.html

Fryer-Biggs, Z. (2018). *Latest theft of Navy data another sign of China targeting defense companies.* Retrieved from https://news.usni.org/2018/06/11/latest-theft-navy-data-another-sign-china-targeting-defense-companies

Gallagher, S. (2014). *Inside the "wiper" malware that brought Sony Pictures to its knees [Update].* Retrieved from https://arstechnica.com/information-technology/2014/12/inside-the-wiper-malware-that-brought-sony-pictures-to-its-knees/

Gallagher, S. (2015). *Why the "biggest government hack ever" got past the feds.* Retrieved from https://arstechnica.com/information-technology/2015/06/why-the-biggest-government-hack-ever-got-past-opm-dhs-and-nsa/

Gates, D. (2018). *Boeing hit by WannaCry virus, but says attack caused little damage.* Retrieved from https://www.seattletimes.com/business/boeing-aerospace/boeing-hit-by-wannacry-virus-fears-it-could-cripple-some-jet-production/

Geary, S. (2018). *Rise of the rest: APT groups no longer from just China and Russia.* Retrieve from https://www.fireeye.com/blog/executive-perspective/2018/04/rise-of-the-rest-apt-groups-no-longer-from-just-china-and-russia.html

Giles, M. (2019). *Triton is the world's most murderous malware, and it's spreading.* Retrieved from https://www.technologyreview.com/s/613054/cybersecurity-critical-infrastructure-triton-malware/

Global Threat Response, M. S. S. (2014). *Emerging threat: Dragonfly / energetic bear – APT group.* Retrieved from https://www.symantec.com/connect/blogs/emerging-threat-dragonfly-energetic-bear-apt-group

GoLocalProv News Team. (2018). *Flanders calls for "stiff sanctions" on China following hack at NUWC*. Retrieved from https://www.golocalprov.com/politics/sen.-candidate-flanders-calls-for-stiff-sanctions-on-china-following-hack

Goodin, D. (2017). *Equifax website borked again, this time to redirect to fake Flash update*. Retrieved from https://arstechnica.com/information-technology/2017/10/equifax-website-hacked-again-this-time-to-redirect-to-fake-flash-update/

Goodin, D. (2019). *Russia warns of "cyberwar" following report the US attacked its power grid*. Retrieved from https://arstechnica.com/information-technology/2019/06/russia-warns-that-reported-us-attacks-on-its-power-grid-could-trigger-cyberwar/?amp=1

GReAT. (2014). *'Destover' malware now digitally signed by Sony certificates (updated)*. Retrieved from https://securelist.com/destover-malware-now-digitally-signed-by-sony-certificates/68073/

Greene, T. (2016). *U.S. cyberwar against ISIS could use methods and tactics criminals use against enterprises*. Retrieved from https://www.cio.com/article/3062700/us-cyberwar-against-isis-could-use-methods-and-tactics-criminals-use-against-enterprises.html#tk%2Erss_all

Guynn, J. (2019). *Equifax says it was not breached again, but vendor on site served 'malicious content'*. Retrieved from https://eu.usatoday.com/story/tech/news/2017/10/12/equifax-may-have-been-breached-again/758734001/

Hagerman, K. (2016). *Security vs. compliance* [Weblog comment]. Retrieved from https://www.armor.com/blog/security-vs-compliance/

Hellard, B. (2018). *IoT vendors urged to ditch devices' default passwords and improve security*. Retrieved from http://www.itpro.co.uk/internet-of-things-iot/30707/iot-vendors-urged-to-ditch-devices-default-passwords-and-improve

Heller, M. (2018). *FireEye ties Russia to Triton malware attack in Saudi Arabia*. Retrieved from https://searchsecurity.techtarget.com/news/252451307/FireEye-ties-Russia-to-Triton-malware-attack-in-Saudi-Arabia?track=NL-1820&ad=923979&src=923979&asrc=EM_NLN_102813624&utm_medium=EM&utm_source=NLN&utm_campaign=20181101_Triton%20ICS%20malware%20attack%20on%20Saudi%20Arabia%20linked%20to%20Russia

Higgins, K. (2015). *OPM breach: Two waves Of attacks likely connected, congressional probe concludes.* Retrieved from https://www.darkreading.com/endpoint/opm-breach-two-waves-of-attacks-likely-connected-congressional-probe-concludes/d/d-id/1326834

Ikeda, S. (2019). *Massive Citrix data breach thought to be the work of Iranian hackers.* Retrieved from https://www.cpomagazine.com/cyber-security/massive-citrix-data-breach-thought-to-be-the-work-of-iranian-hackers/

Infosec Institute. (2019). *Duqu 2.0: The most sophisticated malware ever seen.* Retrieved from https://resources.infosecinstitute.com/duqu-2-0-the-most-sophisticated-malware-ever-seen/

Irish Examiner Ltd. (2013). *Symantec, Snowden and the Stuxnet virus - all in a day's work for Liam O' Murchu.* Retrieved from https://www.irishexaminer.com/lifestyle/features/symantec-snowden-and-the-stuxnet-virus--all-in-a-days-work-for-liam-o-murchu-249373.html

Johnson, B., Caban, D., Krotofil, M., Scali, D., Brubaker, N., & Glyer, C. (2017). *Attackers deploy new ICS attack framework "TRITON" and cause operational disruption to critical infrastructure.* Retrieved from https://www.fireeye.com/blog/threat-research/2017/12/attackers-deploy-new-ics-attack-framework-triton.html

Kanell, M. (2020). *Chinese army hackers charged in huge Equifax cyber attack.* Retrieved from https://www.ajc.com/news/breaking-news/chinese-army-hackers-charged-huge-equifax-cyber-attack/C5n1MYTzzC6q8mgKA25j9I/

Kelley, M. (2013). *The Stuxnet attack on Iran's nuclear plant was 'far more dangerous' than previously thought.* Retrieved from https://www.businessinsider.com/stuxnet-was-far-more-dangerous-than-previous-thought-2013-11?r=US&IR=T

Khandelwal, S. (2014). *Dragonfly Russian hackers target 1000 western energy firms* [Web log comment]. Retrieved from https://thehackernews.com/2014/07/dragonfly-russian-hackers-scada-havex.html

Koerner, B. (2016). *Inside the cyberattack that shocked the US government.* Retrieved from https://www.wired.com/2016/10/inside-cyberattack-shocked-us-government/

Krebs, B. (2015). *Catching up on the OPM breach.* Retrieved from https://krebsonsecurity.com/2015/06/catching-up-on-the-opm-breach/

Krebs, B. (2016). *Congressional report slams OPM on data breach*. Retrieved from https://krebsonsecurity.com/tag/opm-breach/

Krebs, B. (2019). *No jail time for "WannaCry hero"*. Retrieved from https://krebsonsecurity.com/2019/07/no-jail-time-for-wannacry-hero/

Kumar, M. (2020). *U.S. charges 4 Chinese military hackers over Equifax data breach*. Retrieved from https://thehackernews.com/2020/02/equifax-chinese-military-hackers.html?m=1

Kushner, D. (2013). *The real story of Stuxnet*. Retrieved from https://spectrum.ieee.org/telecom/security/the-real-story-of-stuxnet

Larter, D. (2018). *US Navy pushes ahead with bid to extend the range of its sub-killer torpedo*. Retrieved from https://www.defensenews.com/naval/2018/06/13/us-navy-pushing-ahead-with-bid-to-extend-the-range-of-its-sub-killer-torpedo/?utm_campaign=Socialflow&utm_source=Linkedin&utm_medium=social

Leclare, L. (2015). *10 ominous state-sponsored hacker groups*. Retrieved from https://listverse.com/2015/01/08/10-ominous-state-sponsored-hacker-groups/

Lennon, M. (2014). *Hackers used sophisticated SMB worm tool to attack Sony*. Retrieved from https://www.securityweek.com/hackers-used-sophisticated-smb-worm-tool-attack-sony

Lough, V., & Caban, D. (2019). *Triton malware case-study: FireEye, Schneider Electric*. Paper presented at CyberUK Conference, Glasgow, UK.

Lynch, J. (2018). *Chinese attacks on contractors 'a phenomenon' on the rise*. Retrieved from https://www.fifthdomain.com/critical-infrastructure/2018/06/12/chinese-attacks-on-contractors-a-phenomenon-on-the-rise/

Mazza, C. (2018). *Chinese hackers steal U.S. Navy secrets, exposing plans for underwater warfare*. Retrieved from https://www.newsweek.com/chinese-hackers-steal-us-navy-secrets-exposing-plans-underwater-warfare-967697

Mazzarella, J. (2015). *The Sony hack – What happened, how did it happen… What did we learn?* Retrieved from http://blogs.umb.edu/itnews/2015/01/06/the-sony-hack/

Microsoft. (2017). *Microsoft security bulletin MS17-010 – Critical.* Retrieved from https://docs.microsoft.com/en-us/security-updates/SecurityBulletins/2017/ms17-010

Moore, L. (2017). *Two years after OPM cyberattack, more must be done.* Retrieved from https://morningconsult.com/opinions/two-years-opm-cyberattack-must-done/

Morris, D. (2018). *Chinese hackers steal sensitive data on U.S. subs and missiles from military contractor, report says.* Retrieved from https://fortune.com/2018/06/10/chinese-hackers-steal-sensitive-data-us-military/

Nakashima, E. (2015). *FBI director offers new evidence to back claim North Korea hacked Sony.* Retrieved from http://www.washingtonpost.com/world/national-security/fbi-director-offers-new-evidence-to-back-claim-north-korea-hacked-sony/2015/01/07/ce667980-969a-11e4-8005-1924ede3e54a_story.html

Nakashima, E., & Sonne, P. (2018). *FBI investigate claims Chinese hackers stole plans for US 'supersonic anti-ship missile' from navy contractor.* Retrieved from https://www.independent.co.uk/news/world/americas/china-government-hackers-us-navy-contractor-fbi-investigation-a8390831.html

National Health Service England. (2017). *Lessons learned review of the WannaCry Ransomware Cyber Attack* [PDF document]. Retrieved from https://www.england.nhs.uk/wp-content/uploads/2018/02/lessons-learned-review-wannacry-ransomware-cyber-attack-cio-review.pdf

National Institute of Standards and Technology. (2017). *How do I know if I need to be DFARS compliant?* Retrieve from https://www.nist.gov/mep/cybersecurity-resources-manufacturers/dfars800-171-compliance

New Jersey Cybersecurity and Communications Integration Cell. (2017). *Havex.* Retrieved from https://www.cyber.nj.gov/threat-profiles/ics-malware-variants/havex

O'Donnell, L. (2019). *Millions of Linux servers under worm attack via Exim flaw.* Retrieved from https://threatpost.com/linux-servers-worm-exim-flaw/145698/

O'Flaherty, K. (2019). *Who is resecurity, The mysterious firm that blamed Iran for the Citrix hack?* Retrieved from https://www.forbes.com/sites/kateoflahertyuk/2019/03/15/who-is-resecurity-the-mysterious-firm-that-blamed-iran-for-the-citrix-hack/#7e6bc4cb80e9

Olenick, D. (2019). *Equifax data breach recovery costs pass $1 billion.* Retrieved from https://www.scmagazine.com/home/security-news/data-breach/equifax-data-breach-recovery-costs-pass-1-billion/

Osborne, C. (2018). *China blamed for data theft from US Navy contractor.* Retrieved form https://www.zdnet.com/article/china-blamed-for-data-theft-from-us-navy-contractor/

Paganini, P. (2019a). *The role of a secret Dutch mole in the US-Israeli Stuxnet attack on Iran.* Retrieved from https://securityaffairs.co/wordpress/90698/cyber-warfare-2/dutch-mole-stuxnet-attack.html

Paganini, P. (2019b). *CVE-2019-15846 Exim mail server flaw allows Remote Code Execution.* Retrieved from https://securityaffairs.co/wordpress/90893/hacking/exim-mail-server-flaw.html

Palmer, D. (2018). *North Korea's hackers are re-using old code to build new attacks.* Retrieved from https://www-zdnet-com.cdn.ampproject.org/c/s/www.zdnet.com/google-amp/article/north-koreas-hackers-are-re-using-old-code-to-build-new-attacks/

Peterson, A. (2014). *The Sony Pictures hack, explained.* Retrieved from https://www.washingtonpost.com/news/the-switch/wp/2014/12/18/the-sony-pictures-hack-explained/

Ranger, S. (2019). *Cyberwarfare escalation just took a new and dangerous turn.* Retrieved from https://www.zdnet.com/article/cyberwarfare-escalation-just-took-a-new-and-dangerous-turn/?ftag=TRE3e6936e&bh id=2593870691384985371844342692735

Reyner, S. (2019). *Report: Russian hackers' Triton malware targets 2nd facility.* Retrieved from https://www.newsmax.com/newsfront/hackers-triton-malware-infrastructure/2019/04/11/id/911376/

Robinson, T. (2017). *Web App vulnerability enables Equifax breach affecting up to 143m in US.* Retrieved from https://www.scmagazineuk.com/web-app-vulnerability-enables-equifax-breach-affecting-143m-us/article/1474134

Rossi, B. (2016). *Hackers could've gained access to every Citrix customer's computer – and Citrix didn't notice a thing.* Retrieved from https://www.information-age.com/hackers-couldve-gained-access-every-citrix-customers-computer-and-citrix-didnt-notice-thing-123460763/

Safe Harbor on Cyber. (2020). *Safe harbor on cyber.* Retrieved from https://www.safeharboroncyber.com/2018/02/12/equifax-data-breach-may-exposed-critical-personal-data-first-reported/

Sahu, S. (2017). *CVE-2017-5638: Apache struts 2 vulnerability leads to remote code execution.* Retrieved from https://blog.trendmicro.com/trendlabs-security-intelligence/cve-2017-5638-apache-struts-vulnerability-remote-code-execution/

Schneier, B. (2010). *The story behind the Stuxnet virus.* Retrieved from https://www.forbes.com/2010/10/06/iran-nuclear-computer-technology-security-stuxnet-worm.html#3ea502df51e8

Sharwood, S. (2017). *Missed patch caused Equifax data breach.* Retrieved from https://www.theregister.co.uk/2017/09/14/missed_patch_caused_equifax_data_breach/

Shepherd, A. (2018). *Stuxnet is back, Iran admits.* Retrieved from https://www.itpro.co.uk/security/32264/stuxnet-is-back-iran-admits

Sobczak, B. (2019). *The inside story of the world's most dangerous malware.* Retrieved from https://www.eenews.net/stories/1060123327

Sommerlad, J. (2018). *North Korea poses a greater cyber-attack threat than Russia, security expert warns.* Retrieved from https://www.independent.co.uk/life-style/gadgets-and-tech/news/north-korea-cyber-security-threat-russia-wannacry-ransomware-hack-crowdstrike-a8234906.html

Stirparo, B., Bizeul, D., Bell, B., Chang, Z., & Esler, J. … Egloff, F. (2015). *APT groups and operations* [Data file]. Retrieved from https://docs.google.com/spreadsheets/u/1/d/1H9_xaxQHpWaa4O_Son4Gx0YOIzlcBWMsdvePFX68EKU/pubhtml# Strom, D. (2018). *The Sony hacker indictment: 5 lessons for IT security.* Retrieved from https://www.csoonline.com/article/3305144/the-sony-hacker-indictment-5-lessons-for-it-security.html

Symantec. (2010). *W32.Stuxnet.* Retrieved from https://www.symantec.com/security-center/writeup/2010-071400-3123-99

Symantec Security Response. (2017). *What you need to know about the WannaCry Ransomware*. Retrieved from https://www.symantec.com/blogs/threat-intelligence/wannacry-ransomware-attack

Taylor, H. (2018). *DFARS, NIST 800 171 and the Chinese hack of American submarine technology*. Retrieved from https://journalofcyberpolicy.com/2018/07/24/dfars-nist-800-171-chinese-hack-american-submarine-technology/

Thabet, A. (2011). *Stuxnet malware analysis paper*. Retrieved from https://www.codeproject.com/Articles/246545/Stuxnet-Malware-Analysis-Paper

The Inquirer. (2019). *Citrix hack*. Retrieved from https://www.theinquirer.net/inquirer/news/3072335/citrix-hack

Tripwire. (2014). *Wiper malware behind Sony hack illustrates the importance of risk management*. Retrieved from https://www.tripwire.com/state-of-security/latest-security-news/wiper-malware-behind-sony-hack-illustrates-the-importance-of-risk-management/

Unknown. (2017). *Dragonfly 2.0: Hacking group infiltrated European and US power facilities*. Retrieved from https://thehackernews.com/2017/09/dragonfly-energy-hacking.html

US Office of Personnel Management. (2015a). *OPM to notify employees of cybersecurity incident*. Retrieved from https://www.opm.gov/news/releases/2015/06/opm-to-notify-employees-of-cybersecurity-incident/

US Office of Personnel Management. (2015b). *Actions to strengthen cybersecurity and protect critical IT systems* [PDF document]. Retrieved from https://www.opm.gov/cybersecurity/cybersecurity-incidents/opm-cybersecurity-action-report.pdf

Vijayan, J. (2017). *US critical infrastructure target of Russia-linked cyberattacks*. Retrieved from https://www.darkreading.com/attacks-breaches/us-critical-infrastructure-target-of-russia-linked-cyberattacks/d/d-id/1330196

Walton, D. (1996). Plausible deniability and evasion of burden of proof. In Augmentation, 10, 47-58. doi. doi:10.1007/BF00126158

Weeks, D. (2019). *26 percent acknowledge a Web application breach in 2019*. Retrieved from https://dzone.com/articles/26-acknowledge-a-web-application-breach-in-2019

Whitney, L. (2016). *Citrix's GoToMyPC user passwords compromised after hack attack*. Retrieved from https://www.cnet.com/news/citrix-gotomypc-user-passwords-hack/

Whittaker, Z. (2018). *Equifax breach was 'entirely preventable' had it used basic security measures, says House report*. Retrieved from https://techcrunch.com/2018/12/10/equifax-breach-preventable-house-oversight-report/

Whittaker, Z. (2019a). *Two years after Wanna-Cry, a million computers remain at risk*. Retrieved from https://techcrunch.com/2019/05/12/wannacry-two-years-on/

Whittaker, Z. (2019b). *The hacker group behind the Triton malware strikes again*. Retrieved from https://techcrunch.com/2019/04/09/triton-malware-strike/

Wilhoit, K. (2017). *Havex, it's down with OPC*. Retrieved from https://www.fireeye.com/blog/threat-research/2014/07/havex-its-down-with-opc.html

Zetter, K. (2014a). *An unprecedented look at Stuxnet, the world's first digital weapon*. Retrieved from https://www.wired.com/2014/11/countdown-to-zero-day-stuxnet/

Zetter, K. (2014b). *Sony got hacked hard: What we know and don't know so far*. Retrieved from https://www.wired.com/2014/12/sony-hack-what-we-know/

Zetter, K. (2016). *NSA hacker chief explains how to keep him out of your system*. Retrieved from https://www.wired.com/2016/01/nsa-hacker-chief-explains-how-to-keep-him-out-of-your-system/

Zilber, N. (2018). *The rise of the cyber-mercenaries*. Retrieved from http://fp-reg.onecount.net/onecount/redirects/index.php?action=get-tokens&js=1&sid=&return=https%3A%2F%2Fforeignpolicy.com%2F2018%2F08%2F31%2Fthe-rise-of-the-cyber-mercenaries-israel-nso%2F&sid=7f5k0rfbukvhh8afm7ajvi5gg4

ADDITIONAL READING

Clarke, R. (2010). *Cyber war: The next threat to national security and what to do about it*. Harper-Collins.

Griffiths, J. (2019). *The great firewall of China: How to build and control an alternative version of the Internet.* Zed Books Ltd.

Harris, S. (2014). @war: The rise of cyber warfare. London: Headline Publishing Group.

Lucas, E. (2015). *Cyberphobia: Identify, trust, security and the Internet.* Bloomsberry.

Schneier, B. (2018). *Click here to kill everybody: Security and survival in a hyper-connected world.* Norton and Company Inc.

Soldatov, A., & Borogan, I. (2015). *The red web.* PublicAffairs.

KEY TERMS AND DEFINITIONS

Credential Stuffing: An unauthorized authentication attempt reusing a limited number of guessed or compromised passwords from a previous breach.

Cyber Operations: A sequence of actions that are conducted through cyberspace to achieve an objective which may inflict harm to technology or potentially upon human beings.

Dropper: A trojan horse that is used to download further malicious software payloads and tools in order to conduct further stages of a cyber-attack.

Federal'naya sluzhba bezopasnosti Rossiyskoy Federatsii: Known by the acronym FSB, this organization is the Russian internal security service, akin to the legacy KGB, whose mission is to protect the interests of the homeland, but this group can operate outside Russia's borders.

GoToMyPC: A Citrix service that enables signed up users to remotely access their own computers.

Hash: A digital digest that represents inputted data as unique values after being passed through a one-way cryptographic function. Some hashes, like MD5, are susceptible to a collision state that enables more than one copy of a value to be created.

Jump Boxes: Used as an additional authentication barrier for administrators to log in to other assets on the network such as servers in a different security zone.

Onion Router: An obfuscation network of proxies used to encrypt traffic between TOR entry and exit nodes that is synonymous with the Dark Web, although it is not explicitly used by cyber-crime.

Password Spraying: A more refined variant of credential stuffing but across a large number of accounts.

Server Message Block: Used to share files between file shares over a network.

Social Engineering: Uses various real-world and electronic methods to coerce users into unknowingly facilitate a compromise whether it be revealing credentials or trying to persuade them to click on a malicious URL link or malware laden file.

Wormable: A term used to highlight worms that can propagate without a need to conduct authentication on a system.

Chapter 5
A Geo–Political Analysis

ABSTRACT

Chapter 5 examines issues currently being encountered in the Middle East that demonstrate a cross-over between electronic warfare and cyber-warfare activities, affecting not only typical targets over the internet but also ships, aircraft, and unmanned aerial vehicles during the second decade of the new millennium. This overview provides examples of how cyber-warfare techniques are now being used in the battle space domain to affect geo-political situations within regions. The evidence shows how the cyber domain can influence real-life situations, taking its capabilities progressively just that one step further to hacker and state-sponsored cyber-attacks already witnessed against ICS cyber-physical assets. The viewpoint here draws upon historical stimuli and escalating political tensions now being encountered by opposing nations that could have a wider reaching impact.

INTRODUCTION

Over the past seven years, there have been escalating tensions in the Middle East especially since the United States pulled out of the nuclear deal with Iran (Whittaker, 2018). This action resulted in speculation over Iranian cyber-borne reprisals but left Russia, China, the United Kingdom, France, and Germany still committed to the original 2015 agreement (Efimchik, 2019). The main belligerent in the region is Iran, who has recently been disrupting global shipping lanes in the vicinity of the Strait of Hormuz. As a regional antagonist and littoral nation, the Iranians would seek to use the UN

DOI: 10.4018/978-1-7998-3979-8.ch005

Convention on Law of the Sea as a pretext to board merchant ships. This area can be up to 24 miles from their coastline instead of the traditional 12-mile limit (Dyer, 2019). In addition, the Iranian Republican Guard Corps (IRGC) based on Abu Musa island are suspected of using Electronic Warfare (EW) measures to jam and spoof Global Positioning System (GPS) Position, and Navigation and Tracking (PNT) data being received by tankers. This coerces merchantmen to deviate from their actual course into Iranian territorial waters (Crowe, 2019).

In the summer of 2019, Unmanned Aerial Vehicles (UAV) conducted strikes and alleged cruise missiles (Law, 2019a) attacks against the Saudi Arabian Aramco company's Abqaiq oil facility and Khurais oil field. The resultant shutdown of these facilities interrupted five percent of the world's oil supply (McKay & Tomlinson, 2019). Iranian-backed Houthi rebels in Yemen claimed responsibility as retaliation against the Saudi Arabian intervention in their civil war (CBS News & Associated Press, 2019; Cunningham & Noack, 2019). However, from a U.S. perspective, the *New York Times* provides a compelling case (Hubbard, Karasz & Reed, 2019) showing that there appears to be no evidence of the attacks originating from Yemen (Valero & Hamid, 2019). Analysis of delta-wing UAV debris indicates that the origins of this aerial asset was Iran (Turak, 2019), and the Iranians had actively been training their allies in the use of UAVs in the region (Hubbard et al., 2019). Therefore, the inferred finger of blame has been firmly wagging in Iran's direction, and this is not surprising since the Iranians have been early adopters of UAV technology over many years. Iran has even purportedly been using front companies to acquire foreign aero engines for their unmanned aircraft. As a result, the Iranians have many variants of UAV, including the Shahed 129 type that the United States has spotted participating in the conflict in Syria (Michel, 2013; Rawnsley, 2014).

There is also evidence of the Iranians using UAVs to undertake reconnaissance against U.S. naval warships in the Persian Gulf (CBS News & Associated Press, 2019b). This brings a new threat to U.S. forces because UAVs and drones have progressed from reconnaissance and intelligence purposes into dual homed weapons delivery platforms (Allen, 2013). This is certainly the case with regards to the US RQ-170 that the Iranians acquired and reverse engineered in 2011. Thereafter, the IRGC aerospace division copied and converted it for an unmanned combatant role to drop precision-guided bombs (Cenciotti, 2016). The European Council has already stated their concern about the reliability of remotely controlled aircraft and argued a need to legislate acceptable uses for such vehicles (Dworkin, 2013).

Then tensions were heightened with the shooting down of a U.S. Northrop Grumman RQ-4 Global Hawk UAV, which the Americans proclaimed to be operating in international aerospace. However, the Iranians declared that this was not the case, leading them to shoot down the aerial vehicle (Law, 2019b). As a result, the United States were on the verge of military retaliation that would have probably culminated in surface launched cruise missile strikes and airborne targeted ordinance (Gallagher, 2019a). Yet on reflection, the United States took the decision to utilize cyber-warfare techniques against assets from Iran, which had been causing mayhem in the region (Nettitude, 2019; Paganini, 2019a). For their part, the Iranians have decreed that any military conflagration against them will be met with force (Karimi & Cambrell, 2019). The U.S. Cyber Command has confirmed to *The Times* that the U.S. military had targeted Iranian computing infrastructure allegedly used to plan attacks against oil tankers in the Persian Gulf (Gallagher, 2019b). Coincidently, the chief radio communications regulator in Iran admitted that GPS interference was experienced in the country (Radio Farda, 2019). This chapter investigates the combined use of EW and cyber-warfare measures to produce geo-politically motivated outcomes against cyber-physical systems by using the Middle East as a case-study.

BACKGROUND

GPS typically comprises at least 30 or more Navstar satellites arranged in a Medium Earth Orbit (MEO) Global Navigation Satellite System (GNSS) constellation (Howell, 2018) in order to three-dimensionally fix an asset's position. At least three satellites are needed to enable the GPS receivers to perform geolocational computations called trilateration (Geographic Information Systems, 2017; GIS Geography, 2019). Unfortunately, GPS receivers lock onto the strongest signal strength and thereby can ignore legitimate satellite signals of lower signal strength. Alternatively, radio spectrum denial can be achieved by jamming laterally across the frequency bands used by the GPS spread spectrum system (Divis, 2018; Rashid et al., 2019). Nevertheless, GPS spoofing is a different cyber-attack method to those conducted by rogue WiFi Access Points (WAP) and should not be confused as the same *modus operandi*. Such an attack uses an evil-twin WAP to broadcast the same service set identifier by using a stronger radio signal than a legitimate WAP. This approach abuses the physical layer pertaining to the modulated wireless signal and data link layer comprising the logical link control and media access control (Parekh, n.d.; Tektronix, n.d.). It also requires a two-way handshake to interact with the network layer provided by the WAP's router in order to acquire an IP address (Professor Messer, 2017). Hackers can use an evil twin either to acquire WiFi credentials, such as the PSKs related to WiFi Protected Access data link encryption, or to conduct a man-in-the-middle attack in order to intercept data transiting through the rogue WAP *en route* the Internet. GPS spoofing is dissimilar to the scenario described above. Rather, GPS spoofing is categorized as a physical layer attack (Rashid et al., 2019) that is simply achieved by replaying unencrypted broadcast data streams carried by channelized signals of the Navstar system to fool the receiving GPS device into processing fake data.

With a background in Cyber and Electromagnetic Activities, the author felt it was important to justify the statement that asymmetric measures are being used as a full spectrum approach to achieve a desired cyber outcome by the Iranians and other countries (Ministry of Defence, 2018). According to the Tallinn Manual on International Law applicable to Cyber Warfare (Jensen, 2018) that was released in the post-Stuxnet era (Wikipedia, 2019; Baumann, 2019), an atypical definition of cyberspace is, "The environment formed by physical and non-physical components, characterized by the use of computers and the electro-magnetic spectrum, to store, modify, and exchange data using computer-networks" (Baumann, 2019).

Another valid characterization from the North Atlantic Treaty Organization (NATO) Cooperative Cyber Defense Centre of Excellence is, "Cyberspace is a time-dependent set of interconnected information systems and the human users that interact with these systems" (The NATO Cooperative Cyber Defense Centre of Excellence, n.d.).

There is a differentiation between EW and cyber-warfare techniques; the former uses associated equipment to jam frequencies of the radio spectrum to deny an adversary the ability to communicate with their resources or assets, while the latter uses cyber means to manipulate or interfere with computer equipment to achieve a particular purpose. Historically, cyber operations have all been about using the Internet to impede an adversary, but the tools, techniques, and tactics have evolved in today's diversely interconnected world. Traditional thinking by experts has been that cyber-warfare could be used to impede an enemy as a prelude to the use of kinetic warfare armaments. However, the dimensions and divisions between the virtual realm of computing and the real-world of mechanized assets are blurring as the cyber-physical domain advances. Hence, these aspects have been acknowledged by cybersecurity and GPS experts, who recognize the convergence of EW and cyber-warfare methods as a cyber operations capability to interfere with radio dependent systems implied in the earlier definitions. More specifically, jamming is followed by spoofing of unprotected commercial GPS data, in which an attacker transmits specially crafted radio signals that are identical to the authentic satellite broadcast but with minor delays to the signal's time synchronization (Zangvil, 2019).

EVIDENCE OF IRANIAN INTERFERENCE OPERATIONS

Since its encounter with Stuxnet, the Iranian state has built up its own homegrown cyber capabilities drawn from state institutions, academia, and industry. Iran has adopted defensive and offensive postures with oversight provided by the Supreme Cyberspace Council established in 2012. Iran's *modus operandi* in the use of cyber-warfare measures is based on its value as part of an asymmetric strategy to complement irregular methods of warfare. In tandem with this thinking, there is a link between the IRGC and hacker groups that enable the regime to refute any foreign accusations of nation-state cyber-warfare activities. In 2010, such a deniable capability had already been used through the state affiliated Iranian Cyber Army attack against the Chinese Baidu search engine website. Experts thought it was in response to calls for reforms by Chinese Twitter users during the 2009 Iranian election protests. The attackers redirected users by abusing the dependent DNS located in the United States for up to four hours, inciting Chinese hackers to respond (Branigan, 2010), and predictably, the Iranian State denied any involvement (Jie & Limin, 2010). Subsequently, the Iranian approach to build cyber operations capabilities culminated in cyber-attacks by the Izz-Din-al-Quassam Cyberspace fighters against the Bank of America and the New York Stock Exchange as revenge for disrespect towards the prophet Muhammed by the American movie industry in 2012.

Yet more importantly, that August, hackers unleashed Shamoon malware against at least 30,000 office-based computers of the Saudi oil company Aramco. The virus also targeted IT systems of the Qatar-based company ResGas. The hacker group, called The Cutting Sword of Justice, claimed responsibility for the cyber-attack, but cyber security specialists have attributed it to APT 34, also called OilRig. The U.S. anti-virus company Symantec analyzed the virus and concluded that its primary purpose was data destruction rather than having any cyber-espionage origins. Further attacks targeted oil and gas companies around the Persian Gulf led the United States to conclude that it was an Iranian campaign with possible Hizbollah connections (Fisher, 2012; Siboni & Kronenfeld, 2012; Sobczak, 2019). Following this, in 2015, the Press have claimed the cyber-attack against Turkish CNI to the Iranians and thought to be in retaliation to Turkey's support of Saudi Arabia in their stance against Houthi rebels in Yemen (Hoggins & Chowdhury, 2019). In the months leading up to 2020, APT 33 used password spraying techniques to intrude into U.S. CNI company systems (Whitcomb, 2020).

Another Iranian state-sponsored group is APT 39, which conducts cyber-espionage against targeted individuals by planting SEAWEED, CACHEMONEY, AND POWBAT backdoors before exfiltrating credentials and data using a combination of bespoke and off-the-shelf tools (Paganini, 2019b). According to the firm ClearSky, both APTs 33 and 34 as well as APT 39, also known as Charfer, have been targeting vulnerable VPN servers pertaining to Pulse Secure, Palo Alto Networks, Fortinet, and Citrix. The intention is to surveil the targets, plant backdoors, and potentially deploy data-wiping tools, such as ZeroCleare and Dustman, which the firm ClearSky has attributed to Iran (Cimpanu, 2020).

Iran's ability to deviate their efforts and combine EW and cyber-warfare measures against the electromagnetic spectrum has come from a simple pedigree. Satellite television signals have been jammed for many years as part of the Islamist State's agenda to censor foreign media and foreign influence (Small Meda, n.d.). In addition, in 2011, Iran showed off their EW jamming capability that reportedly had been built by the Iranian military (Simon, 2016), and the Iranian Authorities suspected the IRGC of conducting tests in Iran that consequently interfered with mobile phone GPS receivers. These activities preceded the controlled landing of a Lockheed Martin RQ-170 Sentinel UAV within the Northern Iranian Afghan border region in the same year. Experts surmised that the UAV's military-level encrypted GPS P(Y) code used on L1 and L2 frequency bands could have been jammed. As a protective measure, the UAV would have potentially defaulted to the unencrypted GPS C/A code on L1 (Renfro et al., 2015), making it susceptible to spoofing and deceiving it into landing in Iran (Rawsley, 2011) instead of a U.S. base in Afghanistan. Researchers at the University of Toledo and a ViaSat researcher conducted studies on similar simulated GPS jamming methods in an artificial environment (Javaid et al., 2017), adding credence to these claims. However, researchers suspect that the regime had some foreign assistance to execute such an impressive and cavalier tactic.

On the maritime front, according to the Lloyds List Intelligence of the 1,250 vessels that transit the Strait of Hormuz each month, approximately 600 merchantmen are tankers. A Lloyds List analyst alleged that the track of the British flagged merchant vessel Stena Impero, which is sourced from spurious Automatic Identification System (AIS) messages emanating from the ship, is indicative of the ship's position data being misled through spoofed GPS. In addition, the timestamp of the messages and the latitude and longitude co-ordinates were also erroneous, and they were potentially the reason why the vessel veered off its intended course (Bockmann, 2019). On their part, the Iranians have stipulated that the Stena Impero was involved in a collision with an Iranian flagged fishing vessel because their AIS had been turned off. The U.S. media has gone one step further, alleging that the IRGC are not only using GPS jamming and spoofing techniques, but rather they were falsely representing themselves as U.S. Naval forces on bridge-to-bridge communications (Mikelionis & Tomlinson, 2019). Their assumed intent was to redirect ships into Iranian territorial waters so that they could be seized. However, not everyone is convinced that GPS spoofing was to blame for the Stena Impero incident, and one reporter has implied that the reason may just be bullying tactics by the IRGC (Loftus, 2019). Undoubtedly, the geo-political situation in the Persian Gulf is a truly global problem with Iran harassing vessels transiting international shipping lanes (Cozzens, 2019). Perhaps there is some truth in both the sides of this story. More acrimoniously but conceivably, it could be a combination of GPS spoofing and IRGC verbal agitation over maritime radio bands used for inter-ship communications. Since the culmination of suspected Iranian spoofing efforts, the United States has implemented Operation Sentinel to preserve the international community's freedom of navigation in the Persian Gulf (Koudsy & Al-Awsat, 2019).

RUSSIA'S SPECULATIVE INVOLVEMENT

The Tech Press has started to draw conclusions about Russia assisting the Iranians with EW and cyber-warfare measures to jam and interfere with GPS in the Persian Gulf. They are making distinctions that the Iranians are targeting shipping whilst the Russians are concentrating on airspace interference operations (Halpern, 2019). However, there is no clear evidence to substantiate these claims apart from newsworthy items in the British Press (Warrell & Foy, 2019). Previous academic analysis concluded that cyber warfare is an ideal tool for the Iranians' to antagonize the United States but in a way that is supposedly below the military response threshold. In fact, academics stated in a paper that Iran is increasingly more aligned with Russia and China, and this will springboard knowledge sharing as well as opportunities to jointly conspire on cyber matters (Disegi, 2016). Interestingly, in 2018, the director of the Russian *Sluzhba Vneshney Razvedki* (SVR) met with director-level intelligence representatives from China, Iran, and Pakistan to discuss regional collaboration in order to combat the Islamic State in Afghanistan (Fitsanakis, 2019). This meeting perhaps potentially formalized pre-existing relationships between Russia and Iran at this level.

Russia's Cyber Capabilities in the Middle East

On the one hand, a Kremlin spokesman presented the stance that Russia is opposed to any sanctions imposed by the United States against Tehran in retaliation to the shooting down of the RQ-4 UAV (Gillespie, 2019). On the other hand, the British and U.S. security agencies have made accusations that recent cyber-attacks purportedly by Iranian hackers were in fact performed by a Russian nation-state affiliated APT group called Turla (Stirparo, 2015); this group is linked to the FSB (Malcrawler, 2019). The United Kingdom's NCSC and the National Security Agency of the United States reported that the Russian attackers infiltrated an Iranian hacker's cyber-attack infrastructure assumed to be through a compromised account and then utilized Iranian Neuron and Nautilus implants after deploying the Iranian Snake rootkit (Oates, 2019). Turla has also been active in the Middle East since November 2017, compromising the infrastructure of the Iranian cyberespionage group OilRig APT 34 group (Ilascu, 2019). Additionally, Turla conducted a 'false flag' activity supposedly unbeknownst to the Iranian hosts by using their Neptun dropper to conduct post-exploitation password stealing with the Mimikatz toolkit (Barth, 2019).

Furthermore, as previously discussed in Chapter 4, there was the TRITON cyber-attack in Saudi Arabia in which at least six Triconex SIS were affected during Ramedan of 2017. Mandiant, part of FireEye, has attributed this attack to the Russian government-owned Central Scientific Research Institute of Chemistry and Mechanics in Moscow (FireEye Intelligence, 2018). However, as FireEye specialists assisted in reconstituting the affected Tricon 3008 v10 controllers, there was proof of APT 34 probing the networks at Petro Rabigh. Around the same timeframe, Crowdstrike reported a spear phishing campaign by APT 34 against an undisclosed petrochemical plant in the Middle East during the summer of 2017. Is this evidence of another false flag incident? Or could this be a collaborated operation to enable Russia to pursue its objectives of disrupting the West's supply of oil and gas facilities at source and fulfil Iran's aim of continuing attacks against a rival oil producing country (Sobczak, 2019)?

Interference operations conducted by Russia in Syria is a good starting point to understand Russian military EW and cyber-warfare capabilities (Axe, 2019a). Certainly, the German Institute for International and Security Affairs has gone on the record saying that Russia has been using Syria to provide combat experience to its pilots and aircrews as well as using the conflict as a testing ground for their weapons systems, such as the 3M54-1 Kalibr cruise missiles. The net effect has been an improvement in Russia's military concept of operations (Kasapoğlu, 2019). Purported to be a defensive system to protect Russian troops in Syria, Russian GPS interference has been causing havoc with Israeli and U.S. GPS devices in the region. This is notwithstanding the fact that the Iranians also have a presence in Syria, and therefore, Russia may be protecting Iranian UAV operations. The signal strength used by the Russians is allegedly 500 times more powerful than the original GPS satellite signal itself. The Israelis have said that this might be a side effect, but because Russia has continued to use it, it is perceived to be more than a coincidence (Axe, 2019b). NBC news reported that the Russians have been deliberately jamming U.S. UAV operations to avoid U.S. retaliatory strikes against forces of the Assad regime targeting Syrian rebels (Kube, 2018).

Furthermore, Bendett concluded that the range of the Krasukha-2 truck-mounted heavy jammer is 150 miles, but more advanced interference equipment used by the Russian Northern Fleet can reach 3,000 miles. He also questioned why Jordan has not reported similar interference in the vicinity of their national airport. This leads to a hypothesis that the Russians are deliberately targeting the Israelis, notably an ally of the United States, in order to finely tune their electromagnetic interference equipment. Speculation has also arisen over these activities being conducted in retribution for the mistaken shooting down of a Russian Ilyushin-20 Maritime Intelligence Reconnaissance and Surveillance (ISR) aircraft by the Syrian regime in 2018. The Russian ISR plane was targeted instead of an Israeli F-16 combat air patrol, and the 15 Russian aircrew all perished in the encounter (British Broadcasting Corporation, 2018). Other experts estimate that such sporadic interference might be coming from airborne assets, like Russian aircraft fitted with EW equipment.

According to Iasiello (2017), Russia has a strong cyber operations pedigree that tends to focus on information-technical and information-psychological disciplines; these are hallmarks of Russia's past cyber initiated activities that have subsequently resulted in kinetic conflicts with Georgia and the Ukrainians on the Crimean Peninsula. The author's point here is that denial of GNSS services can be attributed to both of these aspects. Israel has decreed that the Russians have been jamming GPS signals using their 1RL257 Krasukha-4 ground-based electronic warfare system (Clarke, 2017) from the Khmeimim airbase in Syria. This has caused a denial of airliners' radio reception of legitimate global positioning in the vicinity of the Israeli Ben Gurion International airport. Ground-based GPS systems were reportedly unaffected during the 3-week episode, which has raised the specter that the jamming is specifically EW measures aimed at airplanes flying at altitude by radiating interference more powerfully than the satellite GPS bands operating in the lower 1.1, 1.2, and 1.5 GHz frequency ranges (Gabor, M, n.d). In addition, the Israelis reported that GPS spoofing is causing airplane receivers to report false positions to aircrew. This is similar to an over-the-air man-in-the-middle attack, in which perpetrators intercept GPS signals. The positioning and timing data can then be altered and replayed using a stronger signal that has the effect of blotting out the legitimate GPS broadcast (Javaid et al., 2017; Cameron, 2019).

GPS Disorientation Prowess

In 2018, both Norway and Finland lodged complaints about Russia's GPS jamming exploits in northern Scandinavia, stating that they were posing a danger to both military and civil aircraft. The timing of these accusations overlaps with the large-scale NATO Trident Juncture exercise, which is the largest military maneuvers since the end of the Cold War (Jozwiak, 2018). In effect, GPS interference was encountered by NATO forces during this drill (Axe, 2019c; RF Wireless World, n.d.) and a backdrop of accusations followed about Russian GPS jamming exploits in the Black Sea in 2017. In that year, the master of a vessel alerted the U.S. Coast Guard Navigation Center of discrepancies affecting at least 20 ships on the basis that the U.S. Coast Guard monitors GPS service reliability globally (Goward, 2017). Also, during the Russian conflict with the Ukraine, there have been heightened EW and cyber warfare activities, in which, without a doubt, the Ukrainians have lost at least 100 drones due to GPS spoofing attacks (Snow, 2019).

Additionally, in the same year there were reports in Moscow of smartphone GPS receivers being affected by displaying false coordinates and geo-locating devices up to 32km away. Experts stated that this is potentially a defensive measure vis-à-vis a cyber-weapon developed to counter NATO weapons systems that use GPS PNT. This cyber capability includes suspected GPS countermeasures placed on masts in prominent areas in Russia (Burgess, 2019; Hambling, 2019). According to a C4ADS report, over the past three years, Russian interference of U.S. GNSS broadcast channels has been identified in the following areas of Russia: Gelendzhik, Sochi, Vladivostok, Saint Petersburg, Arkhangelsk, and Moscow; and Olyva, Kerch, and Sevastopol in Crimea. The report also intimated that GPS interference incidents in Arkhangelsk, Vladivostok, and Kerch were coincidentally active during high-profile visits by the Russian president (Burgess, 2019; Cimpanu, 2019).

Summation

The evidence is inconclusive about direct Russian cyber operations involvement with Iran. The political backdrop is misleading with misinformation, but what is clear is that there are Russian clandestine 'smoke and mirrors' activities at play. While the Russian state publicly provides political backing to Iran, it is not a stretch by any means to surmise that they may also privately support the Iranians with technology and techniques practiced in other areas of the world, like Syria. Russia has exported clandestine equipment to Iran in the past. These exports include the Kilo-class submarines that are operated by the Islamic Republic of Iran Navy as the Tareq-class (Nuclear Threat Initiative, 2019). Perhaps there is a relationship of convenience that knowingly or unknowingly also helps disavow Russian Internet-based cyber operations in the Middle East by covering their tracks masquerading as Iranian hackers. Thus, it is a possibility that there may be some element of truth behind accusations of Russian involvement with Iranian GPS interference. Coincidentally, GPS disturbances affecting the Ben Gurion airport certainly racketed up shortly before the Iranian activities in the Persian Gulf (Egozi & Freedberg, 2019).

SOLUTIONS AND RECOMMENDATIONS

The U.S. Department of Homeland Security has provided guidance on how to defend against spoofing, which also includes efforts to persuade manufacturers to implement anti-spoofing technology. This technology recognizes, rejects, and reports spoofed signals, including simpler approaches, such as encouraging ship operators to install antennas in different locations on their vessels in order to try to detect GPS timing discrepancies (Editor, 2018). Unfortunately, in urban areas, interfering with GPS signals can be achieved quite simply by using continuous waves radiated from easily available light-weight commercial-off-the-shelf (COTS) jammers (Malenkovich, 2019). Technology miniaturization and mass production has also reduced the cost enabling GPS jammers to be purchased by hackers, albeit the use of GPS jamming is illegal under U.K. and U.S. law (Arthur, 2013; Hill, 2017).

As a result of the geopolitical situation arising in the Persian Gulf and the recent GPS interference episodes globally, the author articulates a series of remediation methods in this section. These are based on current thinking of how to overcome GNSS electromagnetic obstructions and cyber interloping. Solutions range from: (a) enhancements to GPS signals; (b) modifications to GPS terminal equipment; (c) techniques to geo-locate jammers and spoofing emitters; or (d) the use of alternative terrestrial radio signals as a tertiary PNT solution.

GPS Signal Remedial Measures

The Finns declared that there has been a noticeable increase in the transmission strength of P(Y) traffic from GPS satellites where the power from unencrypted C/A channels has been marginally decreased. Additionally, Steigenberger et al. (2019) concluded that this is an anti-jam measure being undertaken by the GPS satellites to compensate for interference (Javaid et al., 2017; Cameron, 2019) in the Nordics. Anti-jam antennae can complement GPS equipment with filters to reduce in-band and out-of-band interference (Milne, 2018). Additionally, it is possible to effectively use COTS multiantenna receiver configurations and beamforming technology to detect spoof GPS signals. There are also third-party devices that can independently verify discrepancies between the actual location and the one perceived by the potentially spoofed GPS (Taylor, 2018). Some advanced GPS signal generators are capable of recording and replaying signals, but this is not necessarily possible in real-time. However, the Russian military interference systems are more responsive timewise. Researchers have also raised the specter of denial of service attacks against GPS receiver interfaces in user platforms (Javaid et al., 2017; Rashid et al., 2019).

The Pentagon is particularly incensed by GPS interference operations and contracted defense corporation Lockheed Martin to introduce M-code emanators for their third generation of Navstar satellites. Launches of these spacecrafts into orbit commenced in 2018. These spacecrafts provide resilience to military GPS users in order to counter GPS-related attacks. Furthermore, they provide eight times the resistance to jamming than the previous generation (Strout, 2019a). The EU Galileo GNSS program has learned from the GPS experience and implemented wideband Public Related Service using cryptographic means to assist civil authorities. This means that the data cannot be reproduced by someone interfering with the signal. In addition, for the current constellation of at least 11 active satellites (Visser, Lapucha, Tegedor, Ørpen, & Memarzadeh, 2018), the Galileo E1 Open Service for safety of life uses Navigation Message Authentication that cannot be replicated by a rogue GPS signal. Similar principles apply to spread spectrum and encryption techniques planned for the Galileo Commercial Service in order to counter jamming (GPS World Staff, 2011; Dutton, 2018; Heue, 2018).

Time, Velocity, and Position Measurements

Academia has been working on practicable techniques to geolocate GPS spoofing or jamming emitters using Time Difference of Arrival (TDOA), Frequency Difference of Arrival (FDOA), and Angle of Arrival (AOA). According to the Chinese representatives of the International Telecommunications Union, it is feasible to geolocate ground-based interferers based on satellite velocity and position. Yet such an approach would require two satellites and a reference ground station to achieve an accuracy of 20 km using TDOA/FDOA. It is even possible to use TDOA alone combined with noise cancelling methods between the satellites to establish line intersections and thereby reveal the emitter's approximate position (Hao, n.d.; Lui, Yang, & Mihaylova, 2017). The RAND corporation argues that the versatility and maneuverability of UAVs makes them ideal for locating ground emitters even where the transmitter side-lobes are masked by buildings in urban areas, for instance. This approach still uses TDOA/FDOA and AOA measurements through an array of various antennae on the airframe and a reference position to establish the azimuth and elevation of the radio frequency interference (Hale, 2012; Canizan et al., 2017).

Separate Terrestrial Radio Navigation Systems

An alternative technology to GNSS is Long-range Navigation (LORAN), which is a legacy terrestrial Radio Navigation System (RNS). The United States developed LORAN-A during the Second World War, and during the post-war period, the U.S. Navy produced LORAN-B and the U.S. Airforce further developed LORAN-C. The former had an accuracy of tens of feet with the latter being less precise with an accuracy of hundreds of feet. The U.S. Coastguard took over the operation of the LORAN system in the late 1950s. Even though it was eventually a backup to GPS, including a function to transmit GPS corrections, the United States gradually phased it out between 1994 and 2009. LORAN was operational around the continental United States, and it used groups of stations - a minimum of a primary and two secondaries - located approximately 600 miles apart. Additionally, it had a range of up to 800 miles. LORAN functioned by transmitting pulses on four frequency ranges across 1.75, 1.85, 1.9, or 1.95 MHz (Lo & Peterson, 2009; Wikipedia, 2020).

In more recent times, the United Kingdom was not so reconciled with an 'all eggs in one basket' approach provided by GPS and tested a further advancement of the technology called enhanced LORAN (eLORAN). This advancement was intended to be a navigational backup for the Europe. This eLORAN system required continued participation by France, Norway, and Denmark. Yet the Europeans were more committed to the Galileo GNSS system as an alternative to GPS. A disadvantage of eLORAN was its the lack of altitudinal data, that contrastingly is provided by satellite PNT. Thus, in 2016, the Europeans shut down their transmitters, leaving only a British one based in Cumbria remaining operational. Now, the U.S. Congress is calling for a successor system based on eLORAN beacons to transmit low frequency signals that are 1.3 million times stronger than GPS or Galileo and less susceptible to jamming or spoofing. The Russians have recognized the vulnerability of satellite-based navigation systems like their own GLObal NAvigation Satellite System (GLONASS) that has been operational since the early 1980s. Thus, as a result, Russia has further enhanced their own RNS, called Chayka, and adopted eLORAN principles to produce Sprut-N1, which is also known as eChayka as a backup for GLONASS (Clarke, 2017; Goward, 2019).

Diversification With Other GNSS Providers

In addition to GPS, Galileo, and GLONASS, there are alternative GNSS systems that may experience similar symptoms to GPS. An example is the Chinese Beidou PNT constellations in both geosynchronous earth orbit and MEO. China made Beidou available to Asian users in 2012, and there will be 35 satellites in orbit providing global coverage in 2020 (Jakhar, 2019). Although it has been touted as being more resistant to interference with an inbuilt jamming suppression system (Zhang, Yang, Pan, & Zheng, 2019) and potentially more accurate in some cases than GPS (Zhou, 2016), other sources say that Beidou has been experiencing interference from the complex electromagnetic environment (China Daily, 2013). In addition, the Chinese system has an Achilles heel: the functionality of this GNSS necessitates a two-way interaction between satellite, the receiving device, and back again. This can affect its accuracy, and any radio interference could degrade its performance and reliability (Jakhar, 2018). Notwithstanding, the United States has accused China, and North Korea of being perpetrators of GPS jamming in the South China Sea (Editor, 2016).

Since 2010, the United States has been seeking to collaborate with China and other countries, including countries in the EU, in order to ensure compatibility and interoperability with GPS (Gps.gov, n.d.). The apparition of jamming has encouraged collaboration between GNSS providers in order to increase interoperability and resilience for their customers (Visser et al., 2018). This is particularly useful since it has been reported that interference has degraded the serviceable GPS satellites in the Navstar constellation to far fewer than the total number of 31 in 2018. This has occurred even with the Navstar II generation of satellites increasing the L2 signal decibels as part of an anti-jamming measure. This problem has prompted calls for regulation and better collaboration in the future (Heue, 2018).

Modifications to GPS Equipment

The threats against GPS is so prevalent that the U.S. Army Program Office is developing a Mounted Assured Positioning, Navigation, and Timing system for its mechanized units based on chip-scale atomic clock with anti-jamming antenna. This is being followed by Dismounted Assured Positioning, Navigation, and Time system in a miniaturized form factor for ground troops (Gould, 2019). The Radio Industry is also developing Controlled Reception

Pattern Antennas as part of their response for better anti-jamming measures and anti-spoofing solutions. The U.S. military is testing these concepts via simulation for both mounted and dismounted systems (Strout, 2019b). At a more strategic level, the U.S. Department of Defense (DoD) intends to embed Selective Availability Anti-Spoofing Modules (SAASM) for synchronizing military mission critical electronics systems and instrumentation to ensure satellite communications and defense infrastructure is unaffected by GPS spoofing. This technology ensures accurate timing distribution and the implementation of the M-code, which provides authentication of military navigation messages, unlike the messages across legacy L1 and L2 bands (Mil & Aero Staff, 2017). Initially, the DoD will use SAASM to support existing legacy Defense Advanced GPS Receiver (DAGR) equipment. Effectively, at present if DAGRs lose their key-fill for the military P(Y) code, they automatically resort back to the C/A codes – in the same manner as the suspected RQ-170 UAV incident in 2011. U.S. land-based assets can use SAASM to prevent spoofing under such conditions by performing over-the-air re-keying of DAGRs or other compatible GPS equipment with military grade encryption keys. This can be undertaken across existing encrypted military links or unprotected links using encrypted key distribution mechanisms. Either way, military grade keys can be redeployed to re-program DAGR terminals and avoid the precursory dependency on the unprotected C/A code messages that can be spoofed (Solis, 2016).

Taking a non-military view beyond maritime and air travel, the Israeli company Regulus has ignited a conversation about CAV dependence on GPS. The company has been able to reportedly deviate Tesla Model S and Model 3 non-autonomous vehicles from their intended course while in Autopilot mode. Admittedly, the Regulus cyber researchers manipulated the results slightly by changing the antenna used by the Tesla test vehicles to achieve these results; however, it highlights the risks to mobile COTS equipment in the future (Helpnet Security, 2019; Petri, 2019). This is especially true when CAV users will be utilizing the unencrypted GPS broadcast segment. Regulus states that although GPS spoofing is difficult to thwart, it is detectable, and on the back of their experiment, they are advertising a system that can detect anomalies and thereby prevent a GPS system accepting false data from GPS spoofing. The system acts like a filter, where the processing is conducted using an online cloud-based connection. However, this does not alter the risk that legitimate GPS PNT can still be denied, and under such circumstances, it would mean that in order to avoid dangers, the CAV system would have to rely on other onboard motion sensors or even a 5G connection (Salter,

2019). Therefore, one can argue that modifications to GPS equipment can be justified for safety reasons, or one can argue that users should consider options for retrofitting protective measures to at least detect GPS spoofing even if this risk cannot be remediated completely.

FUTURE RESEARCH DIRECTION

The potential connection between Russia and Iran conducting joint cooperative GPS, EW, and cyber warfare is not entirely proven – albeit collaboration between them is a distinct probability. However, what is clear is that there are risks to GPS systems exploitation through spectrum denial and GPS broadcast spoofing that stretches across most use-cases. Elaborating on this threat, the EU has been conducting research into the effects of emulating GPS spoofing against simulated flights by using real pilots. These tests prove that cyber-attacks can cause confusion within the flight crews, and the effect of spoofing against PNT is not immediately apparent. With this in mind, the United States-based Southwest Research Institute has developed a system to test CAV PNT systems that rely on GNSS as part of a cyber resilience validation program (Hayward, 2019). While this process will evaluate the susceptibility of equipment under test, it also raises the need for more research into GPS receiver vulnerabilities and approaches to mitigate them (European Aviation Safety Agency, 2018) prior to testing. GPS adds to the issues discussed in Chapter 1. Additionally, researchers certainly need to further investigate the threats against CAVs with the advent of autonomous transportation.

CONCLUSION

GPS is a multiple use GNSS system that is available to non-military users through their smart devices and to the military using encrypted links. The common threat throughout this chapter has been the concept of disruption and disturbance or the counterfeiting of GPS PNT data, which the author represents conceptually in Figure 1. Unlike emanations that could cause accidental and inadvertent interference with GNSS services (Milne, 2018), the International Telecommunications Union decrees that deliberate jamming and spoofing could qualify as harmful interference if there is performance degradation, misinterpretation, or loss of information from systems. Baumann (2019) argues that under international law, jamming and spoofing of PNT

Figure 1. Conceptual diagram of GPS jamming and spoofing

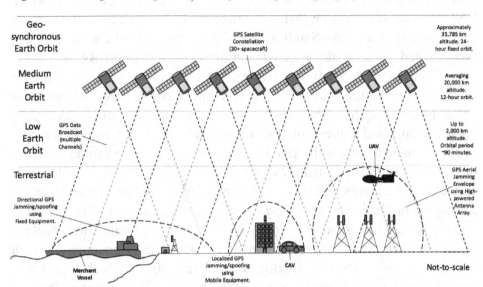

signals does not constitute an act of aggression, such as an armed attack, unless destructive damage is inflicted either directly or indirectly. Subsequently, if a hostile cyber operation has not crossed the threshold of an armed attack, then any retaliatory action by affected states must employ countermeasures that do not amount to the use of force unless the UN Security Council intervenes.

In Chapter 4, the author explored state-sponsored cyber operations that have been conducted against host nation governmental organizations as well as commercial companies contrary to international law. Taşdemir and Albayrak (2017) articulate that the Tallinn Manual decrees that states have sovereignty over their own cyber infrastructures and activities within their own territories. Physical damage or injury to people could constitute a breach of sovereignty. This is already occurring in the ICS world, where U.S. leaders are blaming the Russians for intrusions into its CNI via the attribution of the threat actor to the Russian State (Chirgwin, 2018; Greenberg, 2019). This has thus resulted in an alleged reciprocal cyber incursion into Russia's power grid by the United States (Sanger & Perlroth, 2019), sparking fear of a full-scale cyber-war between the two nations (Nechepurenko, 2019). Notwithstanding, Iran also has aspirations to pursue attacks against U.S. civil installations, which the author also discussed in Chapter 4. This is in line with their 2011 warning of reprisals against U.S. national infrastructure (Siboni & Kronenfeld, 2012). Iran could achieve this directly against CNI using Internet-based cyber-attacks or indirectly by affecting the PNT, which CNI relies upon for timing (Mills & Owens, 2019), albeit the latter is more likely against an ally like Saudi Arabia. Therefore, if cyber interference can be attributed to a state, the affected nation may attempt to invoke 'necessity' under international law to justify a forced military response where any damage is inflicted upon critical infrastructure (Baumann, 2019). However, care must be taken because aggressors can inflict unforeseen secondary effects especially upon essential and non-essential services linked to civilian infrastructure.

A case in point here is the kinetic use of force against the Saudi petroleum plants allegedly by the Yemeni Houthi non-state militia. International law only applies to state actors, but by association, it applies to the Iranian state. As a proxy-actor, the International community may not only consider the act to be an act of terrorism, but they may also consider it an indirect unlawful act of aggression by Iran. The use of non-state proxy forces is inconsistent with traditional conflict ethos (Taşdemir & Albayrak, 2017), which is probably why Iran supports militia groups to do their bidding. To this end, in January 2020, the U.S. government killed the IRGC Quds Force Major General Qassim Suleimani using an armed MQ-9 Reaper UAV (Lee, 2020). The general was suspected of coordinating attacks against U.S. interests through Shiite militia groups in Iraq. At approximately the same time, the United States also made an attempt to neutralize another Iranian Quds Force official Abdul Reza Shahlai in Yemen by the same method – but this was unsuccessful (Schmitt, Wong, & Barnes, 2020). There appears to be a connection here to aforementioned events covered in this chapter in the way which the White House responded in the manner that it did. Following the Iranian intermediate ballistic missile attacks against U.S. bases in Iraq a few days later, the alert state increased due to the threat of follow-up armed Iranian UAV strikes (Star, 2020). As a result, it may even be conceivable that a coalition of forces under a UN Security Council resolution could be mobilized to protect international waterways in this area.

The White House has certainly been keen to pursue some form of alliance to protect the shipping lanes and the global economy (Kheel, 2019), and the Iranians have met this with disquiet (CBS News, 2019). As a result, Operation Sentinel is now under way to escort merchant tankers, container ships, liquid gas carriers, and cruise liners entering or leaving the Persian Gulf. Participating nations include the United States, the United Kingdom, Australia, Bahrain, Saudi Arabia, the United Arab Emirates, and Albania (Ministry of Defence, 2019). In response Iran, Russia, and notably, China conducted their own 4-day long joint naval exercise as an expression of solidarity in the Indian

Ocean and in the Gulf of Oman during late December 2019 (Agence France Presse, 2019). The United States has met this with concern about Iran's future intent and their provocative actions over the summer of 2019 (Star, 2020). There has also been an isolated incident in January 2020, when a Russian combatant maneuvered aggressively and almost caused a collision with a U.S. destroyer in the Arabian Gulf (United States Navy, 2020). Therefore, the Strait of Hormuz could conceivably become a flash point, potentially returning the world to a new generation of the 'tanker wars' that occurred during the 1980s, when the shipping routes associated with the world's oil supply were disrupted (Peck, 2019). Since the 1990s, NATO has been active in a number of humanitarian intervention missions and peacekeeping operations in central Europe, North Africa, and the Middle East. The importance of shipping lanes for the transportation of goods is a dependency for trade and the global economy (Trevithick, 2020). Therefore, it is not too far-fetched to speculate that NATO could act as arbiter and coordinating authority, or it could operate with partners in an endeavor (North Atlantic Treaty Organization, 2019a) to protect global trade in the area.

Experts hold a view that the Iranian regime cannot rely on any overt action from Russia or China to support them (Small Media, n.d.). In addition, Iran is assessed as not being at the same level of proficiency as China and Russia in the cyber realm, but they are still quite a proficient threat; especially if there is discrete collaboration between Iran and Russia, whether it be in cahoots during Iran's overt cyber operations or Russia working independently through a nondescript covert cyber strategy (Heller, 2020). This is particularly worrying if Russia continues to actively conduct false flag cyber operations as Iran. Furthermore, there are concerns as to whether this may mistakenly lead to conflict. Undoubtedly, the deliberate act of interference of GNSS is not only aggravating but is also a menace to navigation at sea, on land, and in the air. Interference with GNSS, which disastrously affects both combatant and non-combatant maritime assets through kinetic damage or loss of life, could stray terribly close to qualifying as an act of aggression if it is caused through Iranian provocation (Ali, 2019). Under NATO's doctrine, allies can conduct cyber operations to retain freedom of maneuver in cyberspace, utilization of nodes, and links in the physical domain to perform functions in cyberspace and deny the freedom of action by adversaries (North Atlantic Treaty Organization, 2019b). Academic analysis indicates that pre-emptive or accidental conflict between NATO and Russia is more likely to be spurred on from regional circumstances than premeditated aggression by either party (Michaels, 2019). The tinderbox of complex geo-political agendas fueled by

Iran in the Middle East has all the hallmarks of paving a pathway towards unintended consequences. Following on from this, Chapter 6 explores the use of cyber operations for political purposes.

REFERENCES

Agence France Presse. (2019). *Iran, China, Russia start joint naval drills.* Retrieved from https://news.yahoo.com/iran-china-russia-start-joint-naval-drills-164013033.html

Ali, A. (2019). *Iran could take 'provocative actions' in Middle East - Top U.S. Navy official.* Retrieved from https://news.yahoo.com/iran-could-provocative-actions-middle-202736804.html

Allen, R. (2013). The Drone Debate: Sudden Bullet or Slow Boomerang? Centre for Strategic Studies Victoria University, New Zealand Victoria University of Wellington.

Arthur, C. (2013). *Thousands using GPS jammers on UK roads pose risks, say experts.* Retrieved from https://www.theguardian.com/technology/2013/feb/13/gps-jammers-uk-roads-risks

Axe, D. (2019a). *As U.S. forces gather near Iran (Think F-22s and F-35s), Russia jams their GPS* [Weblog comment]. Retrieved from https://nationalinterest.org/blog/buzz/us-forces-gather-near-iran-think-f-22s-and-f-35s-russia-jams-their-gps-65196

Axe, D. (2019b). *Russia is jamming the Air Force's F-35s and F-22s near Iran* [Weblog comment]. Retrieved from https://nationalinterest.org/blog/buzz/russia-jamming-air-forces-f-35s-and-f-22s-near-iran-68512

Axe, D. (2019c). *Russia vs. stealth F-35s: Is Moscow jamming F-35 GPS systems near Iran?* [Weblog comment]. Retrieved from https://nationalinterest.org/blog/buzz/russia-vs-stealth-f-35s-moscow-jamming-f-35-gps-systems-near-iran-72891

Barth, B. (2019). *Russian cyber spies likely hijacked Iranian APT group's infrastructure to deliver backdoor.* Retrieved from https://www.scmagazine.com/home/security-news/russian-cyber-spies-likely-hijacked-iranian-apt-groups-infrastructure-to-deliver-backdoor/

British Broadcasting Corporation. (2018). *Russia blames Israel after military plane shot down off Syria*. Retrieved from https://www.bbc.co.uk/news/world-europe-45556290

Baumann, I. (2019). *GNSS cybersecurity threats: An international law perspective*. Retrieved from https://insidegnss.com/gnss-cybersecurity-threats-an-international-law-perspective/

Bockmann, M. (2019). *Seized UK tanker likely 'spoofed' by Iran*. Retrieved from https://lloydslist.maritimeintelligence.informa.com/LL1128820/Seized-UK-tanker-likely-spoofed-by-Iran

Branigan, T. (2010). *'Iranian' hackers paralyse Chinese search engine Baidu*. Retrieved from https://www.theguardian.com/technology/2010/jan/12/iranian-hackers-chinese-search-engine

Burgess, M. (2019). *To protect Putin, Russia is spoofing GPS signals on a massive scale*. Retrieved from https://www.wired.co.uk/article/russia-gps-spoofing

Cameron, A. (2019). *Israel accuses Russia of spoofing in its airspace*. Retrieved from https://www.gpsworld.com/israel-accuses-russia-of-spoofing-in-its-airspace/

Canizan, L., Ciccotosto, S., Fantinato, S., Chiara, A., Gamba, G., & Pozzobon, O. (2017). *Interference localization from space* [PDF document]. Retrieved from https://insidegnss.com/wp-content/uploads/2018/01/janfeb17-WORKINGPAPERS.pdf

CBS News. (2019). *Iran warns that small but growing U.S. naval coalition in Strait of Hormuz raises the "risk of combustion"*. Retrieved from https://www.cbsnews.com/news/iran-us-naval-coalition-israel-united-kingdom-strait-of-hormuz-risk-of-combustion-persian-gulf-2019-08-13/

CBS News & Associated Press. (2019a). *Iran shoots down American drone in "clear message" to U.S.* Retrieved from https://www.cbsnews.com/news/iran-us-drone-shot-down-today-in-gulf-after-houthi-missile-strike-on-saudi-arabia-live-updates-2019-06-20/

CBS News & Associated Press. (2019b). *Video reportedly shows Iran guard drone spying on U.S. warships in Persian Gulf*. Retrieved from https://www.cbsnews.com/news/iran-revolutionary-guard-monitors-uss-dwight-d-eisenhower-with-drone-report-today-2019-04-27/

Cenciotti, D. (2016). *Iran unveils new UCAV modeled on captured U.S. RQ-170 stealth drone.* Retrieved from https://theaviationist.com/2016/10/02/iran-unveils-new-ucav-modeled-on-captured-u-s-rq-170-stealth-drone/

China Daily. (2013). *Beidou experienced past interference.* Retrieved from http://www.chinadaily.com.cn/china/2013-06/17/content_16630776.htm

Chirgwin, R. (2018). *No big deal... Kremlin hackers 'jumped air-gapped networks' to pwn US power utilities.* Retrieved from https://www-theregister-co-uk.cdn.ampproject.org/c/s/www.theregister.co.uk/AMP/2018/07/24/russia_us_energy_grid_hackers/

Cimpanu, C. (2019). *Report deems Russia a pioneer in GPS spoofing attacks.* Retrieved from https://www.zdnet.com/article/report-deems-russia-a-pioneer-in-gps-spoofing-attacks/

Cimpanu, C. (2020). *Iranian hackers have been hacking VPN servers to plant backdoors in companies around the world.* Retrieved from https://www.zdnet.com/article/iranian-hackers-have-been-hacking-vpn-servers-to-plant-backdoors-in-companies-around-the-world/#ftag=CAD-00-10aag7e

Clarke, H. (2017). *Is Russia really rigging GPS signals?* Retrieved from https://eandt.theiet.org/content/articles/2017/10/is-russia-really-rigging-gps-signals/

Cozzens, T. (2019). *Iran jams GPS on ships in Strait of Hormuz.* Retrieved from https://www.gpsworld.com/iran-jams-gps-on-ships-in-strait-of-hormuz/

Crowe, J. (2019). *Iran jamming ships' GPS to get them to wander into Iranian waters.* Retrieved from https://moneyandmarkets.com/iran-jamming-ship-gps/

Cunningham, E., & Noack, R. (2019). *Iran's strategic use of drones and missiles rattles Middle East rivals.* Retrieved from https://www.washingtonpost.com/world/irans-strategic-use-of-drones-and-missiles-rattles-middle-east-rivals/2019/09/16/64bb8894-d886-11e9-a1a5-162b8a9c9ca2_story.html

Disegi, J. (2016). *The evolution of Iranian cyber warfare, dynamics of cyber conflict course* [PDF document]. Retrieved from https://www.academia.edu/30359761/The_Evolution_of_Iranian_Cyber_Warfare

Divis, D. (2018). *Security and SatNav experts agree: GPS is a cybersecurity issue.* Retrieved from https://insidegnss.com/security-and-satnav-experts-agree-gps-is-a-cybersecurity-issue/

Dutton, J. (2018). *Galileo signals and services.* Retrieved from https://www.e-education.psu.edu/geog862/node/1877

Dworkin, A. (2013). *Drones and targeted killing: Defining a European decision* [PDF document]. Retrieved from https://www.ecfr.eu/page/-/ECFR84_DRONES_BRIEF.pdf

Dyer, J. (2019). *And the tanker and drone 'engagements' continue with Iran.* Retrieved from https://libertyunyielding.com/2019/07/20/and-the-tanker-and-drone-engagements-continue-with-iran/

(Ed.). (2016). *China jamming US forces' GPS* [Weblog comment]. Retrieved from https://rntfnd.org/2016/09/26/china-jamming-us-forces-gps/

(Ed.). (2018). *How to defend against GPS spoofing attacks – Wall Street Journal* [Weblog comment]. Retrieved from https://rntfnd.org/2018/09/20/how-to-defend-against-gps-spoofing-attacks-wall-street-journal/

Efimchik, E. (2019). *Pentagon claims Iran uses GPS jamming in the Gulf so it can lure and seize foreign ships – Report.* Retrieved from https://sputniknews.com/middleeast/201908081076499989-pentagon-claims-iran-uses-gps-jamming-in-the-gulf-so-it-can-lure-and-seize-foreign-ships--report/

Egozi, A., & Freedberg, S. (2019). *Why would Russia spoof Israeli GPS? F-35 & Iran.* Retrieved from https://breakingdefense.com/2019/06/if-russia-is-spoofing-israeli-gps-then-why-iran-f-35/

European Aviation Safety Agency. (2018). *Research project: Impact assessment of cybersecurity threats* [PDF document]. Retrieved from https://www.easa.europa.eu/sites/default/files/dfu/EASA-REP-RESEA-2016-1-v0.2-cln.pdf

FireEye Intelligence. (2018). *TRITON attribution: Russian government-owned lab most likely built custom intrusion tools for TRITON attackers.* Retrieved from https://www.fireeye.com/blog/threat-research/2018/10/triton-attribution-russian-government-owned-lab-most-likely-built-tools.html

Fisher, M. (2012). *The movie so offensive that Egyptians just stormed the U.S. embassy over it.* Retrieved from https://www.theatlantic.com/international/archive/2012/09/the-movie-so-offensive-that-egyptians-just-stormed-the-us-embassy-over-it/262225/

Fitsanakis, J. (2019). *Russian security services honor members of the Cambridge spy ring with plaque.* Retrieved from https://intelnews.org/tag/svr-russia/

Gabor, M. (n.d.). *GPS overview*. Retrieved from http://www.csr.utexas.edu/texas_pwv/midterm/gabor/gps.html

Gallagher, S. (2019a). *Missiles and drones that hit Saudi oil fields: Made in Iran, but fired by whom?* Retrieved from https://arstechnica.com/tech-policy/2019/09/missiles-and-drones-that-hit-saudi-oil-fields-made-in-iran-but-fired-by-whom/

Gallagher, S. (2019b). *US claims cyber strike on Iran after attack on Saudi oil facility*. Retrieved from https://arstechnica-com.cdn.ampproject.org/c/s/arstechnica.com/information-technology/2019/10/us-claims-cyber-strike-on-iran-after-attack-on-saudi-oil-facility/?amp=1

Geographic Information Systems. (2017). *Why does GPS positioning require four satellites?* [Weblog comment]. Retrieved from https://gis.stackexchange.com/questions/12866/why-does-gps-positioning-require-four-satellites /

Gillespie, T. (2019). *Iran tensions: Russia says it will counter 'illegal' US sanctions on Tehran*. Retrieved from https://news.sky.com/story/iran-tensions-russia-says-it-will-counter-illegal-us-sanctions-on-tehran-11747974

Geography, G. I. S. (2019). *Trilateration vs triangulation – How GPS receivers work*. Retrieved from https://gisgeography.com/trilateration-triangulation-gps/

Gps.gov. (n.d.). *International cooperation*. Retrieved from https://www.gps.gov/policy/cooperation/

World Staff, G. P. S. (2011). *The system: Test data predicts disastrous GPS jamming by FCC-authorized broadcaster*. Retrieved from https://www.gpsworld.com/the-system-test-data-predicts-disastrous-gps-jamming-by-fcc-authorized-broadcaster/

Gould, J. (2019). *Russia keeps jamming and spoofing US military operations, so the Army is testing jam-resistant GPS in Europe*. Retrieved from https://www.businessinsider.com/us-army-jam-resistant-gps-europe-amid-russia-hacking-spoofing-2019-6

Goward, D. (2017). *Mass GPS spoofing attack in Black Sea?* Retrieved from https://maritime-executive.com/editorials/mass-gps-spoofing-attack-in-black-sea

Goward, D. (2019). *Report: Russian Navy gets new precision terrestrial system to backup GPS/GLONASS*. Retrieved from https://insidegnss.com/report-russian-navy-gets-new-precision-terrestrial-system-to-backup-gps-glonass/

Greenberg, A. (2019). *How not to prevent a cyberwar with Russia.* Retrieved from https://www.wired.com/story/russia-cyberwar-escalation-power-grid/

Hale, K. (2012). *Expanding the use of time/frequency difference of arrival geolocation in the department of defense* (Doctoral dissertation). Retrieved from https://www.rand.org/content/dam/rand/pubs/rgs_dissertations/2012/RAND_RGSD308.pdf

Halpern, M. (2019). *Iran plays a dangerous hi-tech game.* Retrieved from https://www.newsmax.com/micahhalpern/strait-of-hormuz-jamming-centcom/2019/08/08/id/927875/

Hambling, D. (2019). *Ships fooled in GPS spoofing attack suggest Russian cyberweapon.* Retrieved from https://www.newscientist.com/article/2143499-ships-fooled-in-gps-spoofing-attack-suggest-russian-cyberweapon/

Hao. C. (n.d). *Advanced satellite interference geolocation techniques* [PDF document]. Lecture Notes Online Website. Retrieved from https://www.itu.int/en/ITU-D/Regional-Presence/AsiaPacific/Documents/Events/2018/SMWE-China/Presentations/Day2-1500-1600-Advanced%20Satellite%20Interference%20Geolocation%20Techniques-HaoCaiyong.pdf

Hayward, B. (2019). *GPS spoofing: tech researchers take aim at a self-driving car hazard that you've probably never thought about.* Retrieved from https://autonewsblaster.com/2019/05/gps-spoofing-tech-researchers-take-aim-at-a-self-driving-car-hazard-that-youve-probably-never-thought-about.html

Heller, M. (2020). Experts weigh in on risk of Iranian cyberattacks against U.S. Retrieved from https://searchsecurity.techtarget.com/news/252476469/Experts-weigh-in-on-risk-of-Iranian-cyberattacks-against-US

Helpnet Security. (2019). *Research shows Tesla Model 3 and Model S are vulnerable to GPS spoofing attacks.* Retrieved from https://www.helpnetsecurity.com/2019/06/19/tesla-gps-spoofing-attacks/

Heue, R. (2018). *GNSS jamming and spoofing: Hazard or hype?* Retrieved from https://www.space-of-innovation.com/gnss-jamming-and-spoofing-hazard-or-hype/

Hill, K. (2017). *Jamming GPS signals is illegal, dangerous, cheap, and easy.* Retrieved from https://gizmodo.com/jamming-gps-signals-is-illegal-dangerous-cheap-and-e-1796778955

Hoggins, T., & Chowdhury, H. (2019). *Qassim Soleimani: What are Iran's cyber warfare capabilities?* Retrieved from https://www-telegraph-co-uk.cdn.ampproject.org/c/s/www.telegraph.co.uk/technology/2020/01/03/qassim-soleimani-irans-cyber-warfare-capabilities/amp/

Howell, E. (2018). *Navstar: GPS satellite network.* Retrieved from https://www.space.com/19794-navstar.html

Hubbard, B., Karasz, P., & Reed, S. (2019). *Two major Saudi oil installations hit by drone strike, and U.S. blames Iran.* Retrieved from https://www.nytimes.com/2019/09/14/world/middleeast/saudi-arabia-refineries-drone-attack.html

Iasiello, E. (2017). Russia's improved information operations: From Georgia to Crimea. *Parameters, 42*(2), 51–63.

Ilascu, I. (2019). *Turla espionage group hacks OilRig APT infrastructure.* Retrieved from https://www.bleepingcomputer.com/news/security/turla-espionage-group-hacks-oilrig-apt-infrastructure/

Jakhar, P. (2018). *How China's GPS 'rival' Beidou is plotting to go global.* Retrieved from https://www.bbc.co.uk/news/technology-45471959

Javaid, A., Jahan, F., & Sun, W. (2017). Analysis of global positioning system-based attacks and a novel global positioning system spoofing detection/mitigation algorithm for unmanned aerial vehicle simulation. *Simulation: Transactions of the Society for Modeling and Simulation International, 93*(5), 427–441. doi:10.1177/0037549716685874

Jensen, E. (2018). *The Tallinn manual 2.0: Highlights and insights* [PDF document]. Retrieved from https://www.law.georgetown.edu/international-law-journal/wp-content/uploads/sites/21/2018/05/48-3-The-Tallinn-Manual-2.0.pdf

Jie, Y., & Limin, C. (2010). *Hackers attack Baidu; Iran govt denies connection.* Retrieved from http://www.chinadaily.com.cn/china/2010-01/13/content_9310376.htm

Jozwiak, R. (2018). *NATO Launches 'biggest military exercise since the end of the Cold War'.* Retrieved from https://www.rferl.org/a/nato-set-to-start-biggest-military-exercise-since-the-end-of-the-cold-war-/29561371.html

Karimi, N., & Cambrell, J. (2019). *Iran warns US of response to any action over attack on Saudi Arabia.* Retrieved from https://www.timesofisrael.com/iran-warns-us-of-response-to-any-action-over-attack-on-saudi-arabia/

Kasapoğlu, C. (2019). Why and how NATO should adapt to a new Mediterranean security environment. *Stiftung Wissenschaft und Politik, 1-4.* Advance online publication. doi:10.18449/2019C15

Kheel, R. (2019). *Bahrain joins US-led coalition to protect Gulf shipping.* Retrieved from https://thehill.com/policy/defense/457983-bahrain-joins-us-led-coalition-to-protect-gulf-shipping

Koudsy, H., & Al-Awsat, A. (2019). *US warns commercial ships from trap of Iran's communications jamming.* Retrieved from https://aawsat.com/english/home/article/1850491/us-warns-commercial-ships-trap-iran's-communications-jamming

Kube, C. (2018). *Russia has figured out how to jam U.S. drones in Syria, officials say.* Retrieved from https://www.nbcnews.com/news/military/russia-has-figured-out-how-jam-u-s-drones-syria-n863931

Law, T. (2019a). *'Locked and loaded,' the U.S. blames Iran for a drone attack against Saudi Arabia. Here's what to know.* Retrieved from https://time.com/5678242/saudi-arabia-oil-iran-drone-attacks/

Law, T. (2019b). *Iran shot down a $176 million U.S. drone. Here's what to know about the RQ-4 global hawk.* Retrieved from https://time.com/5611222/rq-4-global-hawk-iran-shot-down/

Lee, P. (2020). *Iran attack: How Reaper drones really carry out airstrikes.* Retrieved from http://theconversation.com/iran-attack-how-reaper-drones-really-carry-out-airstrikes-129411

Liu, C., Yang, L., & Mihaylova, L. S. (2017). Dual-satellite source geolocation with time and frequency offsets and satellite location errors. In *Proceedings of 20th International Conference on Information Fusion (Fusion).* Xi'an, China: IEEE. 10.23919/ICIF.2017.8009716

Lo, S., & Peterson, B. (2009). *Enhanced loran* [PDF document]. Retrieved from http://web.stanford.edu/group/scpnt/jse_website/documents/Enhanced_Loran_rv2-short.pdf

Loftus, J. (2019). *Russia's proof of the spoof // Russia plays the race card and fiddles with satellites while Iran returns to piracy on the high seas.* Retrieved from https://www.amimagazine.org/2019/08/07/russias-proof-of-the-spoof/

Malcrawler. (2019). *Turla group hacks APT34 (OilRig) infrastructure and puts malware on exchange server and YARA rule* [Weblog comment]. Retrieved from https://www.malcrawler.com/turla-group-hacks-apt34-oilrig-infrastructure-and-puts-malware-on-exchange-server-and-yara-rule/

Malenkovich, S. (2019). *Is it possible to guard against GPS attacks?* [Weblog comment]. Retrieved from https://www.kaspersky.com/blog/gps-spoofing-protection/26837

McKay, H., & Tomlinson, L. (2019). *Iranian cruise missiles and drones used in Saudi oil facilities, US officials say*. Retrieved from https://www.foxnews.com/world/iranian-cruise-missiles-drones-saudi-oil

Michaels, J. (2019). War with NATO: Essence of a Russian decision. Changing Character of War, Pembroke College, University of Oxford, 1-49.

Michel, A. (2013). *Iran's many drones*. Retrieved from https://dronecenter.bard.edu/irans-drones/

Mikelionis, M., & Tomlinson, L. (2019). *Iran using GPS jammers, pretend to be American warships to trick vessels, US says*. Retrieved from https://www.foxnews.com/world/iran-gps-jammers-warships-trick-vessels

Mil & Aero Staff. (2017). *Anti-spoofing SAASM server for synchronizing military electronics like SATCOM introduced by Microsemi*. Retrieved from https://www.militaryaerospace.com/unmanned/article/16726003/antispoofing-saasm-server-for-synchronizing-military-electronics-like-satcom-introduced-by-microsemi

Mills, E., & Owens, R. (2019). *The strategic drivers for a national space operations capability*. Paper presented at the U.K. Space Conference, Newport, UK.

Milne, E. (2018). *GNSS: Mitigating the threats of interference, jamming & spoofing* [PDF document], Lecture Notes Online Website. Retrieved from https://www.ths.org.uk/documents/ths.org.uk/downloads/thsis_-_gnss_mitigating_the_threats_of_interference_jamming_and_spoofing_(veripos_-_may_2018).pdf

Ministry of Defence. (2018). *Cyber and electromagnetic activities (JDN 1/18)* [PDF document]. Retrieved from https://www.gov.uk/government/publications/cyber-and-electromagnetic-activities-jdn-118

Ministry of Defence. (2019). *Royal Navy 'Bobbies' safeguard Gulf shipping over Christmas.* Retrieved from https://www.royalnavy.mod.uk/news-and-latest-activity/news/2019/december/17/191217-bobbies-in-the-gulf

Nechepurenko, I. (2019). *Kremlin warns of cyberwar after report of U.S. hacking into Russian power grid.* Retrieved from https://www.nytimes.com/2019/06/17/world/europe/russia-us-cyberwar-grid.html

Nettitude. (2019). *Tanker cyber attacks taking place in the Gulf* [Weblog comment]. Retrieved from https://blog.nettitude.com/tanker-cyber-attacks

North Atlantic Treaty Organization. (2019a). *Partners.* Retrieved from https://www.nato.int/cps/en/natohq/51288.htm

North Atlantic Treaty Organization. (2019b). *Allied joint doctrine for the conduct of operations 3 edition C version 1.* NATO Standardization Office.

Nuclear Threat Initiative. (2019). *Iran Submarine Capabilities.* Retrieved from https://www.nti.org/analysis/articles/iran-submarine-capabilities/

Oates, J. (2019). *Iran? More like Ivan: Brit and US spies say they can see through Turla hacking group's façade.* Retrieved from https://www.theregister.co.uk/2019/10/21/british_spies_russia_faking_iranian_hack/

Paganini, P. (2019a). *Trump secretly ordered cyber attacks against Iran missile systems.* Retrieved from https://securityaffairs.co/wordpress/87479/cyber-warfare-2/us-cyberattacks-against-iran.html

Paganini, P. (2019b). *Iran-Linked APT39 group use off-the-shelf tools to steal data.* Retrieved from https://securityaffairs.co/wordpress/80450/apt/iran-apt39-cyberespionage.html

Parekh, S. (n.d.). *IEEE 802.11 Wireless LANs* [PDF document]. Retrieved from Lecture Notes Online Web site https://inst.eecs.berkeley.edu/~ee122/sp07/80211.pdf

Peck, M. (2019). *Head-to-head: Could Iran take on the British Navy and survive?* Retrieved from https://nationalinterest.org/blog/buzz/head-head-could-iran-take-british-navy-and-survive-105846

Petri, J. (2019). *How hackers can take over your car's GPS.* Retrieved from https://www.bloomberg.com/news/articles/2019-06-19/threat-of-gps-spoofing-for-autonomous-cars-seen-as-overblown

Professor Messer. (2017). *Rogue access points and evil twins – CompTIA security+ SY0-501 – 1.2.* Retrieved from https://www.professormesser.com/security-plus/sy0-501/rogue-access-points/

Radio Farda. (2019). *Suspicions fall on IRGC for dangerous interference with GPS in Iran.* Retrieved from https://en.radiofarda.com/a/suspicions-fall-on-irgc-for-dangerous-interference-with-gps-in-iran/30033153.html

Rashid, A., Chivers, H., Danezis, G., Lupu, E., & Martin, A. (Eds.). (2019). *The cyber security body of knowledge version 1.0* [PDF document]. Retrieved from https://www.cybok.org/media/downloads/CyBOK-version_1.0.pdf

Rawsley, A. (2011). *Iran's alleged drone hack: Tough, but possible.* Retrieved from https://www.wired.com/2011/12/iran-drone-hack-gps/

Rawnsley, A. (2014). *Like it or not, Iran is a drone power.* Retrieved from https://warisboring.com/like-it-or-not-iran-is-a-drone-power/

Renfro, B., King, J., Terry, A., Kammerman, J., Munton, D., & York, J. (2015). *An analysis of global positioning system (GPS) standard positioning system (SPS) performance for 2013* [PDF document]. Retrieved from https://www.gps.gov/systems/gps/performance/2013-GPS-SPS-performance-analysis.pdf

Wireless World, R. F. (n.d.). *GNSS frequency band | GPS frequency band-GPS L1, GPS L2.* Retrieved from https://www.rfwireless-world.com/Terminology/GPS-Frequency-Band-and-GNSS-Frequency-Band.html

Salter, J. (2019). *Preventing GPS spoofing is hard—But you can at least detect it.* Retrieved from https://arstechnica.com/gadgets/2019/09/regulus-cybers-pyramid-gnss-software-detects-gps-spoofing/

Sanger, D., & Perlroth, N. (2019). *How not to prevent a cyberwar with Russia.* Retrieved from https://www.independent.co.uk/news/world/americas/us-politics/us-russia-cyber-attacks-trump-power-grid-putin-kremlin-a8960681.html

Schmitt, E., Wong, E., & Barnes, J. (2020). *U. S. unsuccessfully tried killing a second Iranian military official.* Retrieved from https://www.nytimes.com/2020/01/10/world/middleeast/trump-iran-yemen.html

Siboni, G., & Kronenfeld, S. (2012). Iran and cyberspace warfare. Military and Strategic Affairs, The Institute for National Security Studies, 4(3).

Simon, D. (2016). *EW, jamming GPS by IRGC vs. U.S. Navy.* Retrieved from https://founderscode.com/ew-gps-by-iranian-revolutionary-guard-corp-vs-navy/

Small Media. (n.d.). *Satellite jamming in Iran: A war over airwaves.* Retrieved from https://www-cache.pbs.org/wgbh/pages/frontline/tehranbureau/SatelliteJammingInIranSmallMedia.pdf

Snow, S. (2019). *US forces could learn from intense electronic war battle in Ukraine.* Retrieved from https://www.militarytimes.com/flashpoints/2019/10/30/us-forces-could-learn-from-intense-electronic-war-battle-in-ukraine/

Sobczak, B. (2019). *The inside story of the world's most dangerous malware.* Retrieved from https://www.eenews.net/stories/1060123327

Solis, N. (2016). *GPS spoofing: How Iran tricked U.S. patrol boats into capture.* Retrieved from https://sofrep.com/news/gps-spoofing-how-iran-tricked-us-patrol-boats-into-capture/

Starr, B. (2020). *U.S. forces on high alert for possible Iranian drone attacks, and intelligence shows Iran moving military equipment.* Retrieved from https://amp-cnn-com.cdn.ampproject.org/c/s/amp.cnn.com/cnn/2020/01/07/politics/us-iran-high-alert-drone-attacks/index.html

Steigenberger, P., Thölert, S., & Montenbruck, O. (2019). Flex power on GPS Block IIR-M and IIF. *GPS Solutions, 23*(1), 8. Advance online publication. doi:10.100710291-018-0797-8

Stirparo, B., Bizeul, D., Bell, B., Chang, Z., & Esler, J. ... Egloff, F. (2015). *APT groups and operations* [Data file]. Retrieved from https://docs.google.com/spreadsheets/u/1/d/1H9_xaxQHpWaa4O_Son4Gx0YOIzlcBWMsdvePFX68EKU/pubhtml#

Strout, N. (2019a). *Government leaders worry about GPS spoofing, hacking.* Retrieved from https://www.c4isrnet.com/c2-comms/satellites/2019/05/17/government-leaders-worry-about-gps-spoofing-hacking/

Strout, N. (2019b). *How does the Army know its new anti-spoofing antennas work?* Retrieved from https://www.c4isrnet.com/show-reporter/ausa/2019/10/14/how-does-the-army-know-its-new-anti-spoofing-antennas-work/

Taşdemir, F., & Albayrak, G. (2017). The law of cyber warfare in terms of Jus Ad Bellum and Jus in Bello: Application of international law to the unknown? *E-Journal of Law*, 1–16. doi:10.2139srn.3092654

Taylor, H. (2018). *Defending against GPS spoofing.* Retrieved from https:// journalofcyberpolicy.com/2018/07/04/defending-gps-spoofing/

Tektronix. (n.d.). *Wi-Fi: Overview of the 802.11 physical layer and transmitter measurements* [PDF document]. Retrieved from Lecture Notes Online Web site https://www.cnrood.com/en/media/solutions/Wi-Fi_Overview_of_ the_802.11_Physical_Layer.pdf

The NATO Cooperative Cyber Defense Centre of Excellence. (n.d.). *Cyberspace: Definition and implications.* Retrieved from https://ccdcoe.org/ library/publications/cyberspace-definition-and-implications/

Trevithick, J. (2020). *New pentagon map shows huge scale of worrisome Russian and Chinese naval operations.* Retrieved from https://www. thedrive.com/the-war-zone/32145/new-pentagon-map-shows-huge-scale-of- worrisome-russian-and-chinese-naval-operations

Turak, N. (2019). *Drone and missile debris proves Iranian role in Aramco attack, Saudi defense ministry claims.* Retrieved from https://www.cnbc. com/2019/09/18/saudi-arabia-drone-and-missile-debris-proves-iranian-role- in-attack.html

United States Navy. (2020). *Russian and US warships almost collide in Arabian Sea.* Retrieved from https://www.bbc.co.uk/news/av/world-middle- east-51071720/russian-and-us-warships-almost-collide-in-arabian-sea

Valero, J., & Hamid, N. (2019). *Pompeo blames Iran for drone attack on Saudi oil industry.* Retrieved from https://www.bloomberg.com/news/ articles/2019-09-14/pompeo-says-no-evidence-drone-attacks-on-saudi-came- from-yemen

Warrell, H., & Foy, H. (2019). *Russian cyberattack unit 'masqueraded' as Iranian hackers, UK says.* Retrieved from https://www.ft.com/content/ b947b46a-f342-11e9-a79c-bc9acae3b654

Visser, H., Lapucha, D., Tegedor, J., Ørpen, O., & Memarzadeh, Y. (2018). *Precise point positioning from combined GNSS.* Retrieved from https:// www.gim-international.com/content/article/precise-point-positioning-from- combined-gnss

Wikipedia. (2019). *Tallinn manual*. Retrieved from https://en.wikipedia.org/wiki/Tallinn_Manual

Wikipedia. (2020). *Loran*. Retrieved from https://en.wikipedia.org/wiki/LORAN

Whitcomb, A. (2020). *Iran-linked APT39 group use off-the-shelf tools to steal data*. Retrieved from https://www.wired.com/story/iran-hackers-us-electric-grid-border-social-media-surveillance/

Whittaker, Z. (2018). *Iran likely to retaliate with cyberattacks after nuclear deal collapse*. Retrieved from https://www.zdnet.com/article/iran-poised-to-launch-cyberattacks-after-nuclear-deal-collapses/?ftag=TRE49e8aa0&bhid=25938706913849853718443426927355

Zhang, J., Yang, Z., Pan, W., & Zheng, J. (2017). Design and implementation of interference suppression algorithm for BeiDou and GPS dual-frequency receiver. *Journal of Chinese Space Science and Technology, 37*, 117–123. doi:10.16708/j.cnki.1000-758X.2017.0007

Zangvil, Y. (2019). *Research on GPS resiliency & spoofing mitigation techniques across applications* [PDF document], Lecture Notes Online Website. Retrieved from https://www.gps.gov/governance/advisory/meetings/2019-06/zangvil.pdf

Zhou, V. (2016). *China's version of GPS 'is now just as accurate'*. Retrieved from https://www.scmp.com/news/china/diplomacy-defence/article/2022462/chinas-version-gps-now-just-accurate

ADDITIONAL READING

Aid, M. (2012). *Intel wars: The secret history of the fight against terror*. Bloomsbury Press.

Comunello, F., & Anzera, G. (2012). Will the revolution be tweeted? A conceptual framework for understanding the social media and the Arab Spring. *Islam & Christian-Muslim Relations, 23*(4), 453–470. doi:10.1080/09596410.2012.712435

Ghonim, W. (2012). *Revolution 2.0: The power of the people is greater than the people in power*. Harper Collins Publishers.

Healy, J. (2013). *A Fierce domain: Conflict in cyberspace, 1986 to 2012.* Cyber Conflict Studies Association Publication. Atlantic Council Publishers.

Libicki, M. (2007). *Conquest in cyberspace: National security and information warfare.* Cambridge University Press. doi:10.1017/CBO9780511804250

KEY TERMS AND DEFINITIONS

Asymmetric Measures: The utilization of more than one tactic or technique in the battlespace to reduce or deny the warfighting capabilities of a foe.

Cyber Warfare: Use of sophisticated tools, techniques and tactics to actively interfere with or deliver a desired effect against computerized systems by abusing the electromagnetic spectrum or computer networks in order to manipulate or deny an opponent's use of digital data capabilities.

Electronic Warfare: The use of passive or active capabilities to interfere, deflect, or deny the enemy's use of electromagnetic spectrum segments in order to impede an aggressor's use of energy emitters or signal emanations.

False Flag: A cyber-attack strategy to mask the activities of the true attacker by taking over cyber-attack infrastructure of another group and deflect blame upon the latter.

Galileo: A European GNSS program to deploy a position, navigation, and tracking satellite constellation independent to GPS and GLONASS.

Kinetic Warfare: Practice of deploying conventional ordnance and explosives to engage and inflict destructive physical damage upon opposition resources, assets, and forces.

Sluzhba Vneshney Razvedki: The Russian Foreign Intelligence Service that operates overseas to fulfil the national espionage agenda with a similar profile to the overseas contingent of the KGB during the Cold War.

Tallinn Manual: An academic study of applicable international law related to cyber conflicts and cyber warfare arbitrated by the NATO Cooperative Cyber Defense Center of Excellence.

Unmanned Aerial Vehicles: A technological progression from piloted aerial photographic reconnaissance and laser guided targeting capabilities towards remotely controlled dual homed weapons delivery platforms.

Chapter 6
Paradigm Shift for the Future

ABSTRACT

Through case studies of incidents around the world where the social media platforms have been used and abused for ulterior purposes, Chapter 6 highlights the lessons that can be learned. For good or for ill, the author elaborates on the way social media has been used as an arbiter to inflict various forms of political influence and how we may have become desensitized due to the popularity of the social media platforms themselves. A searching view is provided that there is now a propensity by foreign states to use social media to influence the user base of sovereign countries during key political events. This type of activity now justifies a paradigm shift in relation to our perception and utilization of computerized devices for the future.

INTRODUCTION

In previous years, the impact of technology upon society has been a focus of debate between the people who have the infrastructure and the financial means to gain access to it and those who do not. To some degree, social media platforms blur the discussion around the technology assets themselves due to their nature of being web-hosted platforms. As highly popular applications for communications and interaction, they transcend borders providing ubiquitous connectivity for the masses. In this chapter, the author examines Facebook. This particular social media platform's declared mission is to facilitate democratized connectivity to all. It is arguably the most popular

DOI: 10.4018/978-1-7998-3979-8.ch006

social media platform in the western world, and as a consequence, it is the biggest anthropological experiment in human history (Bird, 2017).

Presently, one third of the human race is connected to Facebook, and effectively, the company sells anonymized data from our online interactions to advertising companies. Users are all in effect the 'product' of this social network, in which their online activity is used to directly target us with advertising (Newton, 2019). However, some have started to use the Facebook social media platform for an unintended and unforeseen purpose (Sputnik News, 2019). Cambridge Analytica and subtle propagandist interference by Russia have blurred the intersection between freedom of speech and fake news to sway the U.S. democratic process. This chapter looks at the lessons that need to be learned and how cyber consciousness within society needs to be more attuned to informed facts. Without it misinformation provides contradiction, feeds personal bias, and undermines society as users have known it.

BACKGROUND

The Arab Spring of 2011 is an example of the use of social media messaging in unexpected ways (Al-Abdin & Costello, 2015). The epicenter was Tunisia after a street seller torched himself whilst protesting against the authorities who had seized his vegetable stand because he did not possess a permit (Huang, 2011; Wolfsfeld et al., 2013). Consequently, pro-democracy activists seized the opportunity to further protest in Tunis and this action ultimately caused the Tunisian dictator to abdicate and escape to Saudi Arabia (Wolfsfeld et al., 2013; Markham, 2014). Other countries followed with demonstrations at Tahrir Square in Cairo, Egypt as well as uprisings in Libya, Syria, and Yemen, igniting civil wars (Howard et al., 2011). Academics have listed Facebook, Twitter, and YouTube as key platforms that were used during the Arab Spring revolutions across North Africa and the Middle East (Wolfsfeld et al., 2013). Some believe that the use of social media in the Tunisian and Egyptian cases encouraged their tyrants to be deposed over a very short period of time. Protesters used these platforms to organize themselves and communicate with the outside world. People are still using social media today in Syria for communication and for keeping abreast of the news (Gire, n.d.). Researcher Gerbaudo (Coretti & Maha, 2013) provided a convincing argument that in the case of Egypt's disturbances when the government isolated Internet Service Providers to quell the disturbances, it had the opposite effect of driving more people onto the streets to demonstrate – thus escalating the problem. Another academic Moussa believes that online platforms like social media can facilitate the organization of protests where offline communities may not exist, and the message of the protest movement can percolate across borders using the Internet (Coretti & Maha, 2013).

The recent highly publicized accusations of Russian involvement in the 2016 U.S. presidential elections and the 2017 European democratic elections are a step change in the use of social media for geo-political purposes. Without the need to undertake traditional or novel cyber-attacks, the Russians used Facebook's legitimate functions to abuse the system in an attempt to influence U.S. voters (Paganini, 2019a). This took cyber means to the next level by misusing online platforms to achieve political ends. However, it does not stop there, and a problem that has been brewing for several years has been hiding in plain sight. Cambridge Analytica found a means to misappropriate Facebook data through the illicit use of an API hook into the Facebook system, and a third-party extrapolated data from which Cambridge Analytica effectively developed ML algorithms (Strong, 2018) to sway amenable voters into changing their votes. Cambridge Analytica had designs to use both approaches on the social media platform in a manner that had not been intended; that is, to conduct pointed political advertising against targeted people in the electorate that psychological assessments identified as being persuadable (Kenigsberg, 2019).

Kosiniski (Wang Lakkaraju, Kosinski, & Leskove, n.d.) does not see the use of profiling psycho-demographic traits as a threat to society, albeit he published a paper on how it can be used for social activism through the utilization of Facebook data. He likened psychological targeting as being similar to psychological grouping methods used by advertisers (McKeran, 2019). In this context, high street and online retailers draw upon our fear of missing out in order to hook us into things we might like through sales, offers, and special reductions based on our browsing history (Mathieson, 2017). However, in the U.S. 2016 elections, an inverse approach was true. In this case, Cambridge Analytica used psychology against targeted individuals, stoking a fear of things that they might dislike or might disapprove of in order to influence the way that they would vote (Dreyfous & Korin, 2019).

INTERFERENCE IN DEMOCRATIC PROCESSES

State Actor Influence

After the U.S. presidential elections in November 2016, the U.S. Intelligence community stated its suspicions of Russian interference in the election progress. At least three groups were involved associated with either the Russian FSB or SVR and the *Glavnoye upravleniye General'nogo shtaba Vooruzhonnykh Sil Rossiyskoy Federatsii*. These state-actor groups correlate to APT 29, also known as Cozy bear, APT 28, also called Fancy Bear (Paganini, 2019b), and the Sandworm (Greenberg, 2019) respectively. Initially, the White House rejected claims that there had been Russian involvement in the election process, and it risked de-legitimizing the elected presidential incumbent to the seat of government. However, in 2019, the outcome of an investigation into suspected Russian meddling in the U.S. democratic election process culminated in the Mueller Report, which upheld the original views of the U.S. Intelligence agencies. The conclusion was that a combination of cyber-attacks and a social media-facilitated disinformation drive before and during the election were used as weapons. The intent was to divide the American electorate and undermine the 2016 election process. For the cyber-attack category, APT 28 used a phishing attack against the Democrat's campaign chairman to deploy an X Agent backdoor that enabled the attackers to hack the Democratic National Committee servers (Harding, 2016; Read, 2016). Russian Intelligence then used cyber-espionage to acquire emails in order to discredit the Democrats before releasing exfiltrated emails through WikiLeaks (Embury-Dennis, 2017). Russian hackers also exfiltrated PII on half a million voters probably from the state of Illinois (Matishak, 2018). Under the social media approach, the Russian's purchased 100,000 USD worth of advertising on Facebook alone and during the following mid-term elections infiltrated groups, such as the ones aligned with the Black Lives Matter, to generate discord.

Historically, Russian interference dates back to the 1960s and more prominently, during the Republican second term presidential campaign in 1983 (Brook & Collins, 2019). However, social media platforms presented a good opportunity to propagate rhetoric as part of a mechanism to ensure that Moscow's preferred presidential candidate won (Brook & Collins, 2019). There have also been allegations of Russian Twitterbots being used to spread fake news (Herzog, 2017). During the U.S. mid-term elections of 2018, U.S.

Cyber Command temporarily took down the most prominent Russian troll farm in a bid to reduce any disinformation operation during the voting period. Subsequently, in 2019, the director of the FBI stated that Russian meddling in the U.S. democratic process is a significant counterintelligence threat as the U.S. 2020 presidential elections loom (Barnes & Goldman, 2019). The Russian president has intimated that the United States interfered with the 2012 election in Russia and denies any direct involvement in manipulating the 2016 election, although he insinuated that Russian patriotic hackers may have had a part to play (Malinowski, 2019). This is similar to previous statements that have been used to deflect nation-state involvement in cyber operations. As a result, special council Mueller indicted 13 Russians for their role in the social media-facilitated misinformation campaigns in the U.S. (Zerofsky, 2019).

The Dutch General Intelligence and Security Service (AIVD) began monitoring APT 29 after a cyber-attack against the Dutch Safety Board in 2014. By 2016, the AIVD warned of Russia's false flag operations and the manipulation of public opinion amongst a number of subversive measures applied against the Netherlands. During the 2017 elections in Holland, leaders already employed measures to avoid infiltration into the voting process by dispensing with electronic voting mechanisms and removable media transfers. Subsequently, the AIVD stated that Russia's involvement was only limited to the spreading of false information around the public debate (Brattberg & Maurer, 2018). *Time* magazine also suspects the Russians of the attempting to undermine the German elections during 2017 by using mainstream broadcast media and social media. Russian speaking communities in the country voted for the right-wing *Alternative for Germany* party, weakening the re-elected Merkel government to some degree (Shuster, 2017). In the same year, the U.S. National Security Agency stated just before the French elections that Russia had infiltrated the computer network infrastructure of the French Government. This is supported by the antivirus company Trend Micro, who attributed APT 28 to phishing emails spoofing a Microsoft storage website used by the *En Marche* centralist and liberal party. Subsequently, the Russians leaked 9 gigabytes of emails that were associated with the campaign related to the successful presidential candidate (Greenberg, 2017).

These episodes have sparked fears that Russia might have been a proponent in influencing the outcome with the United Kingdom's Brexit referendum that occurred in June of 2016 (Taylor, 2019). In a near repetition of the U.S. scenario, representatives of the Commons Intelligence and Security Committee have issued a special parliamentary report from an investigation into potential Russian influence over the Brexit vote. This report reveals there may have been an unquantifiable influence by Russia, and the report is also thought to contain an analysis into monetary donations by Russian oligarchs to the Conservative party during the same period. These were sizeable donations made by business allies of the Russian President. Like the United States, the outcome again hypothetically challenges the validity of the Brexit vote outcome (Peat, 2019; Sengupta, 2019). Ultimately, the United Kingdom's Prime Minister withheld the report until after the United Kingdom's 2019 general election, against the wishes of the Chairman of the Commons Intelligence and Security Committee. This raised accusations about political motives and almost confirmed speculation over Russian links in the findings. When it was finally released after the general election, it apparently stated that Russian influence in the Brexit Referendum could not be ruled out (Payne, 2019; Woodcock, 2019). In addition, there is also speculation over a relationship between Russia and the Leave.EU campaign (Hines, 2018).

Ironically, it is not just the Russians who are active in this sphere. The Chinese also have a history of reaching back to at least the U.S. elections of 1996. In 1997, there was speculation over the funding donations for the Democratic National Committee via a group called Asian Americans that was linked to Beijing. Then, in 1999, the Senate Select Committee on Intelligence found a direct link through a Chinese plan to conduct covert political influence (Gertz, 2018). Analysts also suspect that hackers working for the Chinese government undermined the 2008 U.S. Republican leadership campaign. The U.S. Secret Service believed that smartphones and laptops used by campaign staff had been compromised, and insisted that they were replaced (Rogin, 2010). The Australians accused China of interfering in their politics by using donations to try to influence Australia's policy over the South China Sea (Tiezzi, 2018). Incidentally, in 2018, the Global Security Review accused the People's Liberation Army of China of using blockchain technology to obfuscate payments made to public figures in both Australia and New Zealand in order to influence debates on topics that China had an interest in (Matisek, 2018). During Taiwanese local elections of 2018, China lambasted the populace with content through Facebook, Twitter, and online chat groups opposing the ruling Democratic Progressive Party (DPP). This is a fragrant attempt to use what has been dubbed a Russian-style influence campaign (Rogin, 2018). The outcome of the election was a disaster for the DPP, which was a reversal of their categorical victory in 2014. China benefited politically by discrediting the 'cross-strait policies' of the incumbent government (Bush, 2018).

Non-State Actor Influence

Following the Brexit vote of 2016 and the Presidential Election in the United States, commentators have questioned and criticized the role of psychographics in elections. Cambridge Analytica took the brunt of the negative press associated with this technology. Cambridge Analytica came from a company called Strategic Communication Laboratories (SCL), which specialized in supporting militaries around the world to gather psychological data that could ultimately be used for Psyops. Consequently, SCL created Cambridge Analytica to fulfil a role in the political arena. For example, it honed its skills over successive information campaigns in overseas elections in the Caribbean. During the Republican primary of 2012, the company was also behind the turn-around in public perception, enabling the lowest ranking Republican candidate to win the race. The British Press pursued potential threads that tied Cambridge Analytica to the Leave.EU campaign from personal associations (Mayer, 2018; Butcher, 2019). However, the United Kingdom's Electoral Commission, which was headed by the DCMS, found that the company was not directly involved with the Brexit campaign (Kanter, 2018a), albeit they undertook some preparatory work for Leave.EU prior to the referendum (Kanter, 2018b). Nevertheless, Canadian company AggregateIQ was involved on behalf of the BeLeave campaigners. This company sent micro-targeting ads to potential U.K. voters based on demographic data and interests. It is alleged that there had been a relationship between AggregateIQ and Cambridge Analytica but not during the Referendum. By 2018, the Electoral Commission found Vote Leave guilty of breaking U.K. law with respect to campaign spending and was subsequently fined (Thompson, 2018a; Davies, 2019).

Cambridge Analytica did perform personality profiling services in support of the Republican candidates in the Midterm Elections of 2014, and it provided a significant contribution to the 2016 Presidential Election as part of Project Alamo. The company was suspected of using foreign national employees during the election, contrary to U.S. law, which states that foreign contribution is illegal. Cambridge Analytica claimed that most of the Republican candidates that they worked with won their race in 2014. Interestingly, one of states in Cambridge Analytica's sights was North Carolina, which had also been subject to a Department of Homeland Security investigation into suspected Russian hacking where computer errors that were thought to be suspicious were not proven to be a cyber-attack (O'Neill, 2018; Thompson, 2018b; Paganini, 2019c).

Cambridge Analytica boasted that their big-data analytics system could access 5,000 data points on over 220 million Americans to predict people's behavior (Doward & Gibbs, 2017). Yet in reality, during 2016, Cambridge Analytica only targeted voters – allegedly in 'swing states' – who could potentially be persuaded to change their minds with content and videos (Dreyfous & Korin, 2019). This was achieved by using private data of more than 50 million American users who had been collated by an academic third-party that developed a Facebook application called 'thisisyourdigitallife' in 2015. The academic in question was affiliated with one of the top U.K. universities and also with a university in Saint Petersburg, Russia (McNamee, 2019). This academic collected the data through a personality survey generated by the Facebook research application, which had been switched into a commercial application, and the application paid respondents for their participation. By using a 120-question OCEAN quiz format, the API captured private information about the users. Just over quarter of a million users consented to their data being harvested, but in reality, up to 50 million friends were also scrapped due to the functionality provided by the API interface to the Facebook platform. The academic then discretely supplied this data to Cambridge Analytica, which used the data to map personality traits based on peoples' responses to the quiz. This data and other information, such as residential addresses, enabled Cambridge Analytica to identify at least 30 million profiles. Thus, Cambridge Analytica used ML techniques to generate psychographic profiles of personality traits against the profile dataset in order to potentially target millions of American voters within the U.S. electorate (Hern, 2018; Shephard, 2018).

Facebook held Cambridge Analytica to account about the illicit harvesting of data from their platform. Initially, Cambridge Analytica denied having any such material in their possession, but then, they admitted to having it. Later, they certified that they had destroyed the data at Facebook's request (Geneva Internet Platform Digital Watch, n.d.; Agence France-Presse, 2018; Rosenberg, Confessore & Cadwalladr, 2018; Strong, 2018). It now appears that this was not the case (Whittaker, 2018). Subsequently, after the media furor Cambridge Analytica's Chief Executive Officer was suspended, and both Cambridge Analytica and SCL went into administration (McKee, 2018; Gray, 2019). The United Kingdom's Information Commissioner's Office investigated Cambridge Analytica and concluded that it had broken U.K. law by unfairly acquiring and processing Facebook data. They called for new laws on how personal data could be collected and processed for political purposes (Satariano & Confessore, 2018).

In the interests of impartiality, it should be noted that the Democrats also employed behavioral profiling companies during the 2012 election to target American voters. Undoubtedly, the Democrats used data from the same Facebook API to realize a more modest sample size compared to that of Cambridge Analytica – a quarter of a million to be precise. The main objection in the Cambridge Analytica case is that Facebook had not authorized the use of the platform's data in the way it had been utilized, and their terms and conditions had been broken. Therefore, even though Facebook sought to remedy the situation by demanding that the data had to be deleted by Cambridge Analytica, it is also implied that Facebook was not fully aware of how the company had developed a system to propagate political misinformation at scale in a very targeted - some say weaponized - manner (Gray, 2018).

SOLUTIONS AND RECOMMENDATIONS

Arab Spring sceptics have sowed the seeds of doubt regarding the effectiveness of social media to incite rebellion. To them, social media encourages consumers to believe their participation is meaningful, but in actuality, it has a limited impact especially when there were Internet blackouts in Egypt, Libya, and Syria (Wolfsfeld et al., 2013). Yet the tables have now been turned from the user being the initiator to external influencers being the culprits. Social media has become a trillion-dollar business centered around the mining of personal data from platform users according *The New York Times* (Confessore, 2019). For good or for ill, individuals can utilize social media platforms in unforeseen ways that are not their intended purpose. For example, groups of rioters across the United Kingdom used Facebook, Twitter, and Blackberry Messenger to coordinate looting during a summer of disturbances in 2011 (Douglas, 2011). However, at that time, academics argued that the benefits of social media outweighed the negative use-cases, and commentators accused mainstream media of being equally incisive during unrest (Morton, 2012). After the 2016 presidential election debacle, one can now make a counter argument with regards to Facebook.

Facebook has a trove of data on its users and friends, which can include each users' contacts list from their smartphone if the function is enabled through the Facebook Messenger application. Since 2014, Facebook can also serve targeted advertisements based on data harvested from web surfing via tracking technologies like cookies and invisible pixels (Simonite, 2015; Chen, 2018). There has been controversy with human rights groups over the amount of data stored in cookies and the sharing of a user's browsing history through functions like the Facebook 'Like' button. Some advocate that this infringes European data protection laws (Amirtha, 2016). For almost a decade, Facebook has also created data-sharing agreements with tech-manufacturers for the use of personal data from the friends of platform users. Partners include well known smartphone producers, some search engines, streaming services, web services companies, and key online retailers. The declared intent was to integrate popular functionality into applications and thus enhance the user's Facebook experience, expand Facebook's prominence as the leading social media platform, and increase Facebook's capital from advertising. In addition, the Press surmised that Facebook saw their partners as part of their ecosystem and not as outsiders and thus gave access to user and friend personal data. This enabled Facebook to target ads, which explains why Facebook users receive ads for products that have been searched for on other online shopping platforms (Dance, Confessore, & LaForgia, 2018a).

However, U.S. lawmakers are concerned that Facebook's approach to sharing friends' data may have dishonored Facebook's privacy protection commitment to users; that is, an implied consent to the platform's terms and conditions, may have been non-compliant with the Federal Trade Commission's consent decree of 2011. They certainly lack explicit consent under General Data Protection Regulation for European users. Since the Cambridge Analytica debacle, Facebook has reportedly started to wind down some of their partnership schemes that totaled 60 partner companies in 2018 (Confessore et al., 2018a, 2018b). In 2014, Facebook decided to shut down an API that shared friends' data, if this function was enabled by the users, due to privacy concerns. Then, around April 2015, Facebook released a new API variant that required developers to migrate to a superseding version (Constine, 2015). Therefore, in the case of Cambridge Analytica the data they had acquired must have already been harvested by this point. Reportedly, Facebook had learned about the Cambridge Analytica data harvesting episode by around late 2015, and the company subsequently banned the 'thisisyourdigitallife' application (O'Neill, 2018; McNamee, 2019; Paul, 2019). By August 2016, Facebook made their demand for Cambridge Analytica to delete the data (Meredith, 2018). In all fairness, there would undoubtedly have been controls linked to the Representational State Transfer API in the form of schemas and related permissions, API authentication mechanisms controlled by Facebook, use of SSL for protecting data-in-transit, and associated policy and terms of use – in a similar vein to those of extant marketing and demographic APIs (ProgrammableWeb, 2019a, 2019b). However, Facebook had been over-trusting and short-sighted of threats regarding user data by being part of the partner ecosystem.

By being declared as a platform rather than a publisher, Facebook was able to 'police' itself on censoring user posts but had no policy or resources to seek out disinformation practices. Facebook staff discovered that Russian agents had set up fake accounts and had been using the platform illicitly in the months leading up to and during the 2016 election – but it was too late. The operation, including the use of 3,000 advertisements, went viral, reaching 126 million users. Facebook management initially played down the Russian interference story. Yet in hindsight, by late 2017, Facebook began undertaking internal changes in light of the political debate within which they had been the nonconsensual arbiter of fake news (Frenkel et al., 2018; Vaidhyanathan, 2019). Facebook rewrote the company's terms of service in plain English, clarifying how the company collects and utilizes user data (Constine, 2018). In the past, Facebook relied upon moderators to vet group posts and filter out extremist propaganda from the site. However, Facebook is now using ML to detect sexual abuse, racism, extremist propaganda, and hate crime. In response to their more recent predicament, Facebook is now building algorithms to fight the spread of fake news and to discover fake accounts in order to defeat scams (Dreyfeus, 2017; Kumar, 2018). Now, Facebook is scrutinizing developers by turning off APIs and by taking other provisions, such as Facebook applications having to go through a check process before they are hosted on the platform (Perez, 2017). Academics from the European University Institute have stated that fake news dissemination during election periods is much quicker than proper and accurate information distribution. Therefore, regulatory oversight should now be brought to bear upon online platforms that currently undertake self-regulation (Parcu, 2020).

Stakeholders acknowledged that Silicon Valley has not been as heavily regulated as other industries on the basis that the technology is fast-moving and laws could be seen as constraining to future development (Confessore, 2018). Some argue that tech-entrepreneurs have been idolized far too long in their pursuance of profit (Levy, 2019), while other mainstream media are bound by the Equal Time Rule and Fairness Doctrine to fairly represent opposing political views (University of Minnesota Libraries, n.d.). Facebook went on the record reiterating their terms and conditions are clearly stated, but as often is the case most users have not read their terms of service (Dreyfous & Korin, 2019). One positive outcome is the Honest Ads Act that was introduced to the House of Representatives. Officials will use this piece of legislation to compel tech giants to disclose the provenance of people who have paid to distribute politically orientated advertisements and thereby seek out any future and illegal foreign interference (Warner, 2019). In response to this, Facebook has released an Ads Archive API to increase advertisement transparency on their platform, albeit Mozilla (2019) has criticized their implementation for not providing an adequate level of data. In fact, an audit of the Ads Archive during the years of 2018 to 2019 has revealed that 37 million USD worth of ads still did not accurately disclose the advertisers and were likely to have originated from inauthentic communities (Lyons, 2020). However, the Capitol Hill full house hearing of 2018 exposed the magnitude of Facebook's data collection from its users and their apparent disregard for personal privacy (McNamee, 2019). Facebook reaffirmed their moral responsibility. Additionally, having been shamed by the public outcry, Facebook promised to put privacy at the top of their agenda and acknowledged the need for government regulation in the social media space. This is a complete turnaround because previously, the company had an agenda to lobby against regulation in case it conflicted with their business model (Frenkel et al., 2018; Newton, 2019).

At the RSA Conference of 2019, Schlein intimated that technology companies have a duty of care to democracy due to the apparent weaponization of social media and the Internet. Sir Tim Berners-Lee publicly declared his disappointment of how the World Wide Web (WWW) has turned out. His response to the whole debacle is his reimaging of the WWW, taking a different path from his original conception of the web in order to stop it from being used as a tool to surveil civilization as a whole (Adarsh, 2016). To this end, he has taken radical action by setting up a startup so that individuals can take control of user data away from the high-tech companies. The proposed alternative is an open source platform called SOLID, which separates user data from the applications. The data is intended to be stored in secured 'personal online data stores.' In effect, the aim is for users to decide how their data is stored and who can access their data. This, he hopes, will turn the tide, return the Internet to its original purpose, break the dominance and prominence of the tech companies, and cease division and inequality (Solid, 2019; Enquirer, 2019).

FUTURE RESEARCH DIRECTION

The next evolving threat is potentially the use of AI to misrepresent data as fake information. This is called 'deepfake technology,' and it could be a social weapon of choice for state-actors. There is potential for deepfake videos and images to be disseminated during misinformation campaigns via social media, effectively making 'deepfake technology' another method for mass manipulation. The cyber security community anticipates that the U.S. 2020 presidential elections could see the advent of deepfakes to distort people's sense of reality, causing confusion and discord. The Defense Advanced Research Projects Agency has recognized this issue, and the organization has taken a decisive step by commissioning a semantic forensics program to enhance existing statistical techniques to try to counter this problem (Conwell, 2020). Further academic research is required on the impact of 'deepfake technology' on human perception and its effect on personal bias. The author further explores human psychological vulnerabilities in Chapter 7.

CONCLUSION

Although social media was not directly to blame for the Arab Spring, it was arguably the spark that fueled public discord transcending multiple countries. Furthermore, it was enough to encourage people to continue their uprisings by other means, such as physical protests or relaying their message verbally through cellular communications (O'Donnell, 2011; Blakemore, 2019) in the knowledge that the Press could be censored. In fact, it appears that affected regimes either did not bother to block Facebook and Twitter before the dissent occurred or thought it would incite a backlash by doing so (Beaumont, 2011). In this event, a select few tech-savvy activists created and drove dissident pages on social media and the amassed readership either naïvely or radically responded to their call for reform (Hempel, 2016). Consequently, there was a fall of authoritarian regimes, such as former Egyptian president Mubarak's regime. The populace revolted in Libya, causing Colonel al-Qaddafi to respond with an iron fist. NATO was compelled to conduct airstrikes in Libya as part of a humanitarian mission, which ultimately weakened al-Qaddafi's forces, and by late 2011, Qaddafi was overthrown by Libyan rebels. Syria has been embroiled in internal conflict ever since, further exasperated by the rise of the Islamic State and resulting in President al-Assad's forces receiving and hosting support of Russian forces in the country (Editors, n.d.; Editors, 2018). Saudi Arabia has been embroiled in a military intervention against Houthi forces in Yemen since the start of their rebellion (Amnesty International, n.d.), which was initiated by the Arab Spring. The risks of social media propaganda were all too apparent to the Iranian regime, which had learned from the so called 'Twitter Revolution' of 2009. The government quelled a rebellion by leveraging an Internet blackout across the entire country (Wolfsfeld et al., 2013). Iran weathered the storm and secured its position and power in the region, which has now arguably been strengthened by the upheaval caused by the Arab Spring (British Broadcasting Corporation, 2013).

Meanwhile, with all the convenience that social media provides and profits that can be gained, the West has unwittingly been sleep walking into a situation in which the integrity of democratic process could be influenced and harmed in unintended ways (Eveleth, 2019). Critics have lambasted Facebook's leadership about the fact that the company was aware of Russian-linked infestation into Facebook, and they were powerless to stop it once the Russian operation had started discrediting the Presidential Election of 2016. Observers also accused Facebook of sacrificing its moral obligations to its users over its idyll of rapid expansionism (McNamee, 2019). Facebook has also been plagued with other annoying *faux pas,* such as the bug in the Apple iOS Facebook application that turned on the camera without an owner's permission (Binder, 2019). Another situation occurred in which two third-party developers had distributed their own SDK, which was supposed to be used for advertising purposes but was actually harvesting personal data from the Android smartphone Facebook user base. As a result, the two actors paid other developers to integrate covert functionality into Facebook and Twitter applications used on both platforms. Facebook has already removed the offending applications from its platform due to policy violations, and the two firms both received communications to desist from this type of activity (Binder, 2019; Khandelwal, 2019). Yet again, it is telling that Facebook API's that are developed for one purpose, which is to enhance the platform, could be misused by a select few in a harmful way against the wider user base.

Another potential privacy problem also looming relates to anonymized data. Based on research findings, academics from Imperial College London in the United Kingdom have stated that de-anonymization is possible in ML using 15 demographic attributes with 99.8% accuracy. Of course, demographic attributes can be a key feature of social media. Additionally, in light of recent PII legislation, anonymization methods used by companies like Facebook for their own data mining and that conducted by partners may no longer be enough (Hern, 2019). This leads directly into the realm of data protection in AI to safeguard users' privacy and errs on to the side of ethically using synthetic data for simulation rather indiscriminately using human data as part of training deep learning capabilities (Jamilly, 2018).

However, it is not only Facebook that had been conducting the practice of targeted advertising. For instance, since 2014, Google copied the Facebook approach and had been trawling through user emails hosted on their Gmail servers, not only to search for spam and malware, but also to target people with advertisements (Gibbs, 2014; Peterson, 2015). Unsurprisingly, since the uproar over targeted advertising arising out of the 2016 U.S. election, Google reversed this practice (Roettgers, 2017). Google has benefited from user trust in the past (Vise, 2005), but the company is similarly facing a bout of user mistrust over their data privacy practices (Elias, 2018). Based on the recent events, a prize-winning journalist for the U.K. *Observer* has been highlighting the issues around the unintended use of tech-platforms and the perceived spread of authoritarianism in the West. Portrayed by some as an activist, she has argued the main issue is around the amount of data held by these companies. Therefore, the issue is no longer about privacy but rather about the enormous power that the large companies wield with impunity centered around the possession of information about all users (Cadwalladr, 2019; Greene, 2019; Judah, 2019).

In a drive for growth, including expansion into augmented reality, observers have been critical of Facebook for abdicating security and policy decisions to subordinates. This outcome has seen serious reputational damage (Frenkel et al., 2018). The resultant outcome of this tech-scandal was Facebook being fined five billion USD, which caused a slowdown in new user growth on the platform (Kumar, 2019). Drawing upon the 2018 election experience, the U.S. government has stepped in. U.S. Cyber Command has already waged a Psyops campaign against Islamic State to disrupt, degrade, and frustrate the terrorist network (Lin, 2020). Now, U.S. Cyber Command has developed a cyber operations approach that includes the use of warning emails, pop-ups, and text messages to target active Russian Internet trolls before taking the source servers offline. These operations occur with a further *modus operandi* to potentially publicly publish details of offending Russian intelligence agents who are participating in such activities. In 2018, such a rouse was conducted against the now indicted Russian company Internet Research Agency, which was conducting disinformation activities and owned by a Russian businessman with close a relationship to the Russian President. In the months leading to the U.S. 2020 presidential election, there have been rumors of Russian interference in the Democratic Primaries in favor of Bernie Sanders even after 13 Russian officials were indicted for their part in a troll factory during the U.S. 2016 election campaign (Barnes & Ember, 2020).

If there is any sign of Russian cyber operations sowing discord, then U.S. Cyber Command has new authorizations to conduct 'gray zone warfare.' Yet to do so requires permission and endorsement from the Secretary of Defense because this type of operation falls short of the use of lethal force (Ted, 2019). This will act as a deterrent to foreign states that dislike Western democracies and wish to use subversion to try to change election outcomes in their favor and in line with their own national objectives (Nakashima, 2019). Since 2016, Facebook has banned foreigners from buying political advertisements in the United States. However, APT 28 operatives have shifted their activities to within the continental United States in a bid to avoid detection by elements like U.S. Cyber Command and seditiously APT 29, has been dormant since the summer of 2019. As discussed in Chapter 5, Russian APTs have been using Iranian APT infrastructure in the past, and Russia could use this type of cyber operation to obfuscate political disinformation campaigns (Rosenberg, Perlroth, & Sanger, 2020). However, for reasons other than politics, Microsoft has usefully launched an unprecedented move to take out legal proceedings in order to take control of domains linked to 70 APT 28 C2 servers and 99 domains used by the Iranian APT 35 Charming Kitten, which maliciously spoofs websites (Lyngass, 2019).

Table 1. Proposed mitigations for Facebook based on lessons learned

Mitigation	Description
Revising governance processes and practices	The process for levying advertisements on the platform needs to be more tightly controlled, and platforms need to vet advertisers in some way.
Strengthening security biased monitoring	The company is already trawling through user data for the purposes of targeted advertising, so Facebook should take the threat of platform abuse seriously and hone their data-mining practices further to potentially detect subversive anomalies during high-profile global events.
Not substituting technical controls with weaker procedural ones	Facebook must not be overly dependent on their terms and conditions in their policies with regards to partners and developers and should not trust that their terms will not be abused without proper legal recourse.
Performing code reviews prior to making applications publicly available	Platforms should not only scrutinize applications for illicit functionality but also assess third-party SDKs for maliciousness or ban their use in preference to Facebook SDKs.
Testing applications and approve them for consumption on the platform	Facebook needs to review and modify the functionality provided by APIs to combat opportunities for misuse by both partners and developers.
Increasing user awareness so user ignominy is a thing of the past	Key areas of the Facebook Terms of Service must be distilled and clearly understood by the user base for the ease of users rather than enabling users to blindly agree to a long list of terms. Perhaps an animated video explaining how Facebook collects and uses data will help to avoid any misunderstandings about data use and data privacy.

From independent research, the University College London concluded that social media and digital technologies as a whole are not liberating in their own right, but they provide additional transformative opportunities compared to offline capabilities (Miller et al. 2016). The global reach of social media enables it to be an ideal medium for misuse and the abuse of legitimate platform functionality in order to influence others. By applying a cyber security lens, a paradigm shift is required by both tech-companies and platform developers or partners as well as the users themselves. The main key to the whole Facebook scenario is six-fold, as shown in Table 1.

REFERENCES

Adarsh, V. (2016). *World wide web creator Tim Berners-Lee wants to reinvent the web.* Retrieved from https://fossbytes.com/web-inventor-tim-berners-lee-reinvent-the-web/

Agence France-Presse. (2018). *Cambridge Analytica: Firm at the heart of Facebook scandal.* Retrieved from https://www.securityweek.com/cambridge-analytica-firm-heart-facebook-scandal

Al-Abdin, A., & Costello, R. (2015). The impact of social media technologies on the revolutions. *Journal of the Humanities and Social Sciences*, *3*(3), 116–124. doi:10.11648/j.hss.20150303.13

Amirtha, T. (2016). *Facebook cookie case: Why even the 'Like' button infringes EU 'informed consent' privacy law.* Retrieved from https://www.zdnet.com/article/facebook-cookie-case-why-even-the-like-button-infringes-eu-informed-consent-privacy-law/

Amnesty International. (n.d.). *The 'Arab Spring': Five years on.* Retrieved from https://www.amnesty.org/en/latest/campaigns/2016/01/arab-spring-five-years-on/

Barnes, J., & Ember, S. (2020). *Russia is said to be interfering to aid Sanders in Democratic primaries.* Retrieved from https://www.nytimes.com/2020/02/21/us/politics/bernie-sanders-russia.html

Barnes, J., & Goldman, A. (2019). *F.B.I. warns of Russian interference in 2020 race and boosts counterintelligence operations.* Retrieved from https://www.nytimes.com/2019/04/26/us/politics/fbi-russian-election-interference.html

Beaumont, P. (2011). *The truth about Twitter, Facebook and the uprisings in the Arab world.* Retrieved from https://www.theguardian.com/world/2011/feb/25/twitter-facebook-uprisings-arab-libya

Binder, M. (2019). *Facebook bug secretly turns on iPhone camera.* Retrieved from https://mashable.com/article/facebook-camera-iphone-bug/

Bird, D. (2017). The collaborative effects of cyberspace. In S. Crabbe (Ed.), Current practices and trends in technical and professional communications (pp. 251-274). Institute of Scientific and Technical Communicators Books.

Blakemore, E. (2019). *What was the Arab Spring and how did it spread?* Retrieved from https://www.nationalgeographic.com/culture/topics/reference/arab-spring-cause/

Brattberg, E., & Maurer, T. (2018). *Russian election interference: Europe's counter to fake news and cyber attacks* [PDF document]. Retrieved from https://carnegieendowment.org/2018/05/23/russian-election-interference-europe-s-counter-to-fake-news-and-cyber-attacks-pub-76435

British Broadcasting Corporation. (2013). *Arab Spring: 10 unpredicted outcomes.* Retrieved from https://www.bbc.co.uk/news/world-middle-east-25212247

Brook, T., & Collins, M. (2019). *Mueller report: 5 things to know about Russian interference in U.S. elections.* Retrieved from https://eu.usatoday.com/story/news/politics/2019/04/22/mueller-report-what-know-russian-election-interference/3538877002/

Bush, R. (2018). *Taiwan's local elections, explained.* Retrieved from https://www.brookings.edu/blog/order-from-chaos/2018/12/05/taiwans-local-elections-explained/

Butcher, M. (2019). *'The Great Hack': Netflix doc unpacks Cambridge Analytics, Trump, Brexit and democracy's death.* Retrieved from https://techcrunch.com/2019/07/23/the-great-hack-netflix-doc-unpacks-cambridge-analytica-trump-brexit-and-democracys-death/

Cadwalladr, C. (2019). *Facebook's role in Brexit – And the threat to democracy.* Retrieved from https://www.ted.com/talks/carole_cadwalladr_facebook_s_role_in_brexit_and_the_threat_to_democracy/transcript

Chen, B. (2018). *I downloaded the information that Facebook has on me. Yikes.* Retrieved from https://www.nytimes.com/2018/04/11/technology/personaltech/i-downloaded-the-information-that-facebook-has-on-me-yikes.html

Confessor, N. (2018). *The unlikely activists who took on Silicon Valley — And won.* Retrieved from https://www.nytimes.com/2018/08/14/magazine/facebook-google-privacy-data.html

Confessore, N. (2019). *The unlikely activists who took on Silicon Valley — And won.* Retrieved from https://www.nytimes.com/2018/08/14/magazine/facebook-google-privacy-data.html

Constine, A. (2018). *Facebook rewrites Terms of Service, clarifying device data collection.* Retrieved from https://techcrunch.com/2018/04/04/facebook-terms-of-service/

Constine, J. (2015). *Facebook is shutting down its API for giving your friends' data to apps.* Retrieved from https://techcrunch.com/2015/04/28/facebook-api-shut-down/

Conwell, J. (2020). *2020: A year of deepfakes and deep deception.* Retrieved from https://www.helpnetsecurity.com/2020/01/29/deepfake-technology/

Coretti, L., & Maha, T. (2013). The role of social media in the Arab uprisings – past and present. *Westminster Papers in Communication and Culture, 9*(2), 1–22.

Dance, G., Confessore, N., & LaForgia, M. (2018a). *Facebook gave device makers deep access to data on users and friends.* Retrieved from https://www.nytimes.com/interactive/2018/06/03/technology/facebook-device-partners-users-friends-data.html

Dance, G., LaForgia, M., & Confessore, N. (2018b). *As Facebook raised a privacy wall, it carved an opening for tech giants.* Retrieved from https://www.nytimes.com/2018/12/18/technology/facebook-privacy.html

Davies, G. (2019). *Amid Brexit uncertainty and allegations, UK lawmakers consider Mueller-like inquiry.* Retrieved from https://abcnews.go.com/International/amid-brexit-uncertainty-allegations-uk-lawmakers-mueller-inquiry/story?id=62507402

Douglas, T. (2011). *Social media's role in the riots.* Retrieved from https://www.bbc.co.uk/news/entertainment-arts-14457809

Doward, J., & Gibbs, A. (2017). *Did Cambridge Analytica influence the Brexit vote and the US election?* Retrieved from https://www.theguardian.com/politics/2017/mar/04/nigel-oakes-cambridge-analytica-what-role-brexit-trump

Dreyfeus, E. (2017). *Facebook's counterterrorism playbook comes into focus.* Retrieved from https://www.wired.com/story/facebook-counterterrorism

Dreyfous, G., & Korin, J. (Producers) (2019). The Great Hack [Television broadcast]. Los Gatos, CA: Netflix.

(Ed.). (2018). *Arab Spring.* Retrieved from https://www.history.com/topics/middle-east/arab-spring

(Ed.). (n.d.). In *Encyclopedia Britannica* online. Retrieved from https://www.britannica.com/event/Arab-Spring

Elias, J. (2018). *Google will keep reading your emails, just not for ads.* Retrieved from https://www.cnbc.com/2019/11/17/people-getting-rid-of-fitbits-after-google.html

Embury-Dennis, T. (2017). *Trump-Russia probe: Mueller 'requests emails' from Cambridge Analytica firm linked to 2016 campaign and Brexit.* Retrieved from https://www.independent.co.uk/news/world/americas/donald-trump-mueller-cambridge-analytica-firm-brexit-president-election-campaign-russia-probe-latest-a8112136.html

Enquirer. (2019). *Sir Tim Berners-Lee's Inrupt startup receives £5m investment.* Retrieved from https://www.theinquirer.net/inquirer/news/3083354/tim-berners-lee-inrupt-gdp5m-investment

Eveleth, R. (2019). *The Architects of our digital hellscape are very sorry.* Retrieved from https://www.wired.com/story/the-architects-of-our-digital-hellscape-are-very-sorry/amp

Frenkel, S., Confessore, N., Kang, C., Rosenberg, M., & Nicas, J. (2018). *Delay, deny and deflect: How Facebook's leaders fought through crisis.* Retrieved from https://www.nytimes.com/2018/11/14/technology/facebook-data-russia-election-racism.html

Geneva Internet Platform Digital Watch. (n.d.). *Cambridge Analytica.* Retrieved from https://dig.watch/trends/cambridge-analytica

Gertz, B. (2018). *China vs. Russia election interference.* Retrieved from https://www.washingtontimes.com/news/2018/feb/28/inside-the-ring-china-vs-russia-election-interfere/

Gibbs, S. (2014). *Gmail does scan all emails, new Google terms clarify.* Retrieved from https://www.theguardian.com/technology/2014/apr/15/gmail-scans-all-emails-new-google-terms-clarify

Gire, S. (n.d.). The role of social media in the Arab Spring. *Pangaea Journal,* 1-10. Retrieved from https://sites.stedwards.edu/pangaea/the-role-of-social-media-in-the-arab-spring/

Gray, F. (2018). *Cambridge Analytica's use of Facebook is straight from Obama's playbook* [Weblog comment]. Retrieved from https://blogs.spectator. co.uk/2018/03/cambridge-analyticas-use-of-facebook-is-straight-from-obamas-playbook/

Gray, F. (2019). *What's the truth about Cambridge Analytica?* Retrieved from https://spectator.us/alexander-nix-cambridge-analytica/

Greenberg, A. (2017). *The NSA confirms it: Russia hacked French election 'infrastructure'.* Retrieved from https://www.wired.com/2017/05/nsa-director-confirms-russia-hacked-french-election-infrastructure/

Greenberg, A. (2019). *Here's the evidence that links Russia's most brazen cyberattacks.* Retrieved from https://www.wired.com/story/sandworm-russia-cyberattack-links/

Greene, B. (2019). *It's not about privacy — it's about power: Carole Cadwalladr speaks at TEDSummit 2019.* Retrieved from https://blog.ted. com/its-not-about-privacy-its-about-power-carole-cadwalladr-speaks-at-tedsummit-2019/

Harding, L. (2016). *What we know about Russia's interference in the US election.* Retrieved from https://www.theguardian.com/us-news/2016/dec/16/qa-russian-hackers-vladimir-putin-donald-trump-us-presidential-election

Hempel, J. (2016). *Social media made the Arab Spring, but couldn't save it.* Retrieved from https://www.wired.com/2016/01/social-media-made-the-arab-spring-but-couldnt-save-it/

Hern, A. (2018). *Cambridge Analytica: How did it turn clicks into votes?* Retrieved from https://www.theguardian.com/news/2018/may/06/cambridge-analytica-how-turn-clicks-into-votes-christopher-wylie

Hern, A. (2019). *'Anonymised' data can never be totally anonymous, says study*. Retrieved from https://www.theguardian.com/technology/2019/jul/23/anonymised-data-never-be-anonymous-enough-study-finds

Herzog, S. (2017). Ten years after the Estonian cyberattacks: Defense and adaptation in the age of digital insecurity. *Georgetown Journal of International Affairs, 18*(3), 67–78. doi:10.1353/gia.2017.0038

Hines, N. (2018). *How a journalist kept Russia's secret links to Brexit under wraps*. Retrieved from https://www.thedailybeast.com/how-a-journalist-kept-russias-secret-links-to-brexit-under-wraps

Howard, P. N., Duffy, A., Freelon, D., Hussain, M. M., Mari, W., & Maziad, M. (2011). Opening closed regimes: What was the role of social media during the Arab Spring? *Project on Information Technology and Political Islam*, 1-30.

Huang, C. (2011). Facebook and Twitter key to Arab Spring uprisings: Report. *The National, 6*, 2–3. doi:10.1038/nature09955

Jamilly, M. (2018). *Limitations of AI*. Retrieved from https://www.bcs.org/content-hub/limitations-of-ai/

Judah, B. (2019). *Britain's most polarizing journalist*. Retrieved from https://www.theatlantic.com/international/archive/2019/09/carole-cadwalladr-guardian-facebook-cambridge-analytica/597664/

Kanter, J. (2018a). *We finally have an answer about Cambridge Analytica's murky work on Brexit -- But mystery still lingers*. Retrieved from https://www.businessinsider.com.au/cambridge-analytica-did-not-work-with-leave-eu-on-brexit-2018-5

Kanter, J. (2018b). *All the times Cambridge Analytica gave brazenly contradictory accounts of its murky work on Brexit*. Retrieved from https://www.businessinsider.com/cambridge-analytica-has-contradicted-itself-on-its-work-for-leaveeu-2018-3?r=US&IR=T

Kenigsberg, B. (2019). *'The great hack' review: How your data became a commodity*. Retrieved from https://www.nytimes.com/2019/07/23/movies/the-great-hack-review.html

Khandelwal, S. (2019). *Malicious Android SDKs caught accessing Facebook and Twitter users data*. Retrieved from https://thehackernews.com/2019/11/sdk-twitter-facebook-android.html

Kumar, M. (2019). *Facebook agrees to pay $5 billion fine and setup new privacy program for 20 years*. Retrieved from https://thehackernews.com/2019/07/ftc-facebook-privacy-program.html?m=1

Levy, S. (2019). *The 2010s killed the cult of the tech founder. Great!* Retrieved from https://www.wired.com/story/the-2010s-killed-the-cult-of-the-tech-founder/

Lin, H. (2020). *On the integration of psychological operations with cyber operations*. Retrieved from https://www.lawfareblog.com/integration-psychological-operations-cyber-operations

Lyngass, S. (2019). *Microsoft uses court order to shut down APT35 websites*. Retrieved from https://www.cyberscoop.com/microsoft-uses-court-order-shut-apt-linked-websites/

Lyons, K. (2020). *NYU researchers say Facebook advertisers lied about their identity*. Retrieved from www.theverge.com/platform/amp/2020/3/6/21167714/facebook-ads-nyu-identify-lies-political-disclosure-pages

Malinowski, T. (2019). *Did the United States interfere in Russian elections?* Retrieved from https://www.washingtonpost.com/news/democracy-post/wp/2017/07/21/did-the-united-states-interfere-in-russian-elections/

Markham, T. (2014). Social media, protest cultures and political subjectivities of the Arab spring. *Media Culture & Society, 36*(1), 89–104. doi:10.1177/0163443713511893

Mathieson, S. (2017). *Trump, Brexit, and Cambridge Analytica – not quite the dystopia you're looking for*. Retrieved from https://www.theregister.co.uk/2017/03/07/cambridge_analytica_dystopianism/

Matisek, J. (2018). *Is China weaponizing blockchain technology for gray zone warfare?* Retrieved from https://globalsecurityreview.com/china-weaponizing-blockchain-technology-gray-zone-warfare/

Matishak, M. (2018). *What we know about Russia's election hacking*. Retrieved from https://www.politico.com/story/2018/07/18/russia-election-hacking-trump-putin-698087

Mayer, J. (2018). *New evidence emerges of Steve Bannon and Cambridge Analytica's role in Brexit*. Retrieved from https://www.newyorker.com/news/news-desk/new-evidence-emerges-of-steve-bannon-and-cambridge-analyticas-role-in-brexit

McKee, R. (2018). *Alexander Nix, Cambridge Analytica CEO, suspended after data scandal.* Retrieved from https://www.theguardian.com/uk-news/2018/mar/20/cambridge-analytica-suspends-ceo-alexander-nix

McKeran, L. (Producer). (2019). *Christmas sales: Super shoppers special* [Television broadcast]. London: Channel 4.

McNamee, R. (2019). *Zucked: Waking up to the Facebook catastrophe.* Harper Collins.

Meredith, S. (2018). *Here's everything you need to know about the Cambridge Analytica scandal.* Retrieved from https://www.cnbc.com/2018/03/21/facebook-cambridge-analytica-scandal-everything-you-need-to-know.html

Miller, D., Costa, E., Sinanan, J., Haynes, N., Nicolescu, R., ... McDonald, T. (2016). *Why we post: The anthropology of social media.* Training course retrieved from https://www.futurelearn.com/courses/anthropology-social-media

Morton, J. (2012). *The role of social media in the 2011 London riots: A critical analysis Article* [PDF document]. Retrieved from https://www.researchgate.net/publication/283641849_The_role_of_social_media_in_the_2011_London_riots_A_critical_analysis

Mozilla. (2019). *Facebook's ad archive API is inadequate* [Weblog comment]. Retrieved from https://blog.mozilla.org/blog/2019/04/29/facebooks-ad-archive-api-is-inadequate/

Nakashima, E. (2019). *U.S. Cybercom contemplates information warfare to counter Russian interference in the 2020 election.* Retrieved from https://www-washingtonpost-com.cdn.ampproject.org/c/s/www.washingtonpost.com/national-security/us-cybercom-contemplates-information-warfare-to-counter-russian-interference-in-the-2020-election/2019/12/25/21bb246e-20e8-11ea-bed5-880264cc91a9_story.html?outputType=amp

Newton, J. (Producer). (2019). Insider the social network: Facebook's difficult year [Television broadcast]. London: British Broadcasting Corporation.

O'Donnell, C. (2011). *New study quantifies use of social media in Arab Spring.* Retrieved from https://www.washington.edu/news/2011/09/12/new-study-quantifies-use-of-social-media-in-arab-spring/

O'Neill, B. (2018). *The great Cambridge Analytica conspiracy theory* [Weblog comment]. Retrieved from https://blogs.spectator.co.uk/2018/03/the-great-cambridge-analytica-conspiracy-theory/

Paganini, P. (2019a). *Russian APT groups are targeting European governments for cyber-espionage purposes ahead of the upcoming European elections.* Retrieved from https://securityaffairs.co/wordpress/82772/apt/russian-apt-groups-may-elections.html

Paganini, P. (2019b). *The evolutions of APT28 attacks.* Retrieved from https://securityaffairs.co/wordpress/94747/apt/evolutions-apt28-attacks.html

Paganini, P. (2019c). *DHS report – Voting systems in North Carolina county in 2016 were not hacked.* Retrieved from https://securityaffairs.co/wordpress/95805/hacking/north-carolina-voting-systems-investigation.html

Parcu, P. (2020). *Culture in the Digital Age.* Training course retrieved from https://www.futurelearn.com/courses/culture-in-digital-age/2/todo/60314

Paul, K. (2019). *Ocasio-Cortez stumps Zuckerberg with questions on far right and Cambridge Analytica.* Retrieved from https://www.theguardian.com/technology/2019/oct/23/mark-zuckerberg-alexandria-ocasio-cortez-facebook-cambridge-analytica

Payne, A. (2019). *The report that Boris Johnson is refusing to publish says it cannot rule out Russian interference in the Brexit referendum.* Retrieved from https://www.businessinsider.com/report-russia-report-cannot-rule-out-interference-in-brexit-referendum-2019-11?r=US&IR=T

Peat, J. (2019). *Russia report suppressed because Downing Street is concerned it raises questions over validity of referendum result.* Retrieved from https://www.thelondoneconomic.com/politics/russia-report-suppressed-because-downing-street-is-concerned-it-raises-questions-over-validity-of-referendum-result/18/11/

Perez, S. (2018). *Facebook rolls out more API restrictions and shutdowns.* Retrieved from https://techcrunch.com/2018/07/02/facebook-rolls-out-more-api-restrictions-and-shutdowns/

Peterson, T. (2015). *Google to use email addresses for ad targeting, like Facebook and Twitter do.* Retrieved from https://adage.com/article/digital/google-people-s-email-addresses-ad-targeting/300533

ProgrammableWeb. (2019a). *Facebook marketing REST API v5.0.* Retrieved from https://www.programmableweb.com/api/facebook-marketing-rest-api-v50

ProgrammableWeb. (2019b). *Facebook graph REST API v5.0.* Retrieved from https://www.programmableweb.com/api/facebook-graph-rest-api-v50

Read, R. (2016). *Meet the Russian hacking groups that fooled Clinton and the Democrats.* Retrieved from https://dailycaller.com/2016/10/30/meet-the-russian-hacking-groups-that-fooled-clinton-and-the-democrats/

Roettgers, J. (2017). *Google will keep reading your emails, just not for ads.* Retrieved from https://variety.com/2017/digital/news/google-gmail-ads-emails-1202477321/

Rogin, J. (2010). *The top 10 Chinese cyber attacks (that we know of).* Retrieved from https://foreignpolicy.com/2010/01/22/the-top-10-chinese-cyber-attacks-that-we-know-of/

Rogin, J. (2018). *China's interference in the 2018 elections succeeded — In Taiwan.* Retrieved from https://www.washingtonpost.com/opinions/2018/12/18/chinas-interference-elections-succeeded-taiwan/

Rosenberg, M., Confessore, N., & Cadwalladr, C. (2018). *How Trump consultants exploited the Facebook data of millions.* Retrieved from https://www.nytimes.com/2018/03/17/us/politics/cambridge-analytica-trump-campaign.html

Rosenberg, M., Perlroth, N., & Sanger, D. (2020). *'Chaos is the point': Russian hackers and trolls grow stealthier in 2020.* Retrieved from https://www.nytimes.com/2020/01/10/us/politics/russia-hacking-disinformation-election.html?smid=nytcore-ios-share

Satariano, A., & Confessore, N. (2018). *Cambridge Analytica's use of Facebook data broke British law, watchdog finds.* Retrieved from https://www.nytimes.com/2018/11/06/technology/cambridge-analytica-arron-banks.html

Schlein, T. (2019). *Weaponization of the Internet.* Retrieved from https://www.youtube.com/watch?v=wVbteTdrnQY

Sengupta, K. (2019). *We have no objections': Security officials say secret Russia report being blocked by Boris Johnson government can be published immediately.* Retrieved from https://www.independent.co.uk/news/uk/politics/russia-conservative-party-brexit-intelligence-uk-report-national-security-money-a9185116.html

Shephard, A. (2018). *Cambridge Analytica is shady. But Facebook is shadier.* Retrieved from https://newrepublic.com/article/147559/cambridge-analytica-shady-facebook-shadier

Shuster, S. (2017). *How Russian voters fueled the rise of Germany's far-right.* Retrieved from https://time.com/4955503/germany-elections-2017-far-right-russia-angela-merkel/

Simonite, T. (2015). *Facebook's like buttons will soon track your web browsing to target ads.* Retrieved from https://www.technologyreview.com/s/541351/facebooks-like-buttons-will-soon-track-your-web-browsing-to-target-ads/

Solid. (2019). *Welcome to solid.* Retrieved from https://solid.inrupt.com

Sputnik News. (2019). *Next gen warfare: Cyber conflict between US & Russia 'can skirt the edges of the unknown' – Author.* Retrieved from https://sputniknews-com.cdn.ampproject.org/c/s/sputniknews.com/amp/analysis/201912271077883053-next-gen-warfare-cyber-conflict-between-us--russia-can-skirt-the-edges-of-the-unknown--author/

Strong, A. (2018). *How Cambridge Analytica used machine learning to mine Facebook data.* Retrieved from https://news.codecademy.com/cambridge-analytica-machine-learning-facebook-data/

Taylor, A. (2019). *Did Russia interfere in Brexit?: An unpublished report roils U.K. politics before election.* Retrieved from https://www.washingtonpost.com/world/2019/11/05/did-russia-interfere-brexit-an-unpublished-report-roils-uk-politics-before-election/

Ted. (2019). *Laura Galante: Cyberspace analyst.* Retrieved from https://www.ted.com/speakers/laura_galante

Thompson, I. (2018a). *Could the Cambridge Analytica scandal save Britain from itself?* Retrieved from https://www.vanityfair.com/news/2018/03/could-the-cambridge-analytica-scandal-save-britain-from-itself

Thompson, I. (2018b). *The Cambridge Analytica scandal is going global.* Retrieved from https://www.vanityfair.com/news/2018/03/cambridge-analytica-scandal-is-going-global

Tiezzi, S. (2018). *Is China Really Interfering in the US Elections?* Retrieved from https://thediplomat.com/2018/09/is-china-really-interfering-in-the-us-elections/

University of Minnesota Libraries. (n.d.). *15.3 The law and mass media messages.* Retrieved December 27, 2019, from https://open.lib.umn.edu/mediaandculture/chapter/15-3-the-law-and-mass-media-messages/

Vaidhyanathan, S. (2019). *Mark Zuckerberg needs to shut up.* Retrieved from https://www-wired-com.cdn.ampproject.org/c/s/www.wired.com/story/mark-zuckerberg-needs-to-shut-up/amp

Vise, D. (2005). *The Google story: Inside the hottest business, media and technology success of our time.* Macmillan.

Wang, Y., Lakkaraju, H., Kosinski, M., & Leskove, J. (n.d.). *Psycho-demographic analysis of the Facebook rainbow campaign* [PDF document]. Retrieved from https://arxiv.org/pdf/1610.05358.pdf

Warner, M. (2019). *The honest ads act.* Retrieved from https://www.warner.senate.gov/public/index.cfm/the-honest-ads-act

Whittaker, Z. (2018). *Trump-linked data firm Cambridge Analytica harvested data on 50 million Facebook profiles to help target voters.* Retrieved from https://www.zdnet.com/article/facebook-suspends-analytics-firm-that-helped-trump-campaign/

Wolfsfeld, G., Segev, E., & Sheafer, T. (2013). Social media and the Arab Spring: Politics comes first. *The International Journal of Press/Politics,* *18*(2), 115–137. doi:10.1177/1940161212471716

Woodcock, A. (2019). *Boris Johnson approves release of Russian interference report following election win.* Retrieved from https://www.independent.co.uk/news/uk/politics/boris-johnson-russia-report-brexit-interference-general-election-release-a9248446.html

Zerofsky, N. (2019). *The investigator.* Retrieved from https://www.cjr.org/special_report/guardian-carole-cadwalladr.php

ADDITIONAL READING

Arthur, C. (2012). *Digital wars: Apple, Google Microsoft & the battle for the Internet*. Kogan Page Limited.

Hobsbawm, J. (2017). *Fully connected: Surviving and thriving in an age of overload*. Bloomsberry Publishing PLC.

Keen, A. (2012). #digital vertigo: How today's online social revolution is dividing, diminishing, and disorientating us. London: Constable.

MacKinnon, R. (2012). *Consent of the Networked: Worldwide struggle for Internet freedom*. Basic Books.

Ryan, J. (2010). *A history of the Internet and digital future*. Reaktion Books.

KEY TERMS AND DEFINITIONS

Brexit: A synonym used during the EU Referendum in the United Kingdom to mean Britain's exit from the EU. Ironically, the vote and the impact of the result effects the whole of the United Kingdom: England, Scotland, Wales, and Northern Ireland.

Glavnoye ypravleniye General'nogo shtaba Vooruzhonnykh Sil Rossiyskoy Federatsii: The main directorate of General Staff for the Russian Federation is the Russian Military Intelligence arm also known by its previous Soviet acronym GRU.

OCEAN: A method to categorize and score key personal attributes for research purposes based on the following categories: openness, conscientiousness, extraversion, agreeableness, and neuroticism.

Psyops: The art of persuading and in some cases educating a non-combative populace with suspected allegiances with the enemy in a warzone to not to take up arms and fight. This approach avoids bolstering the numbers of fighters in the fray.

Troll: A means to disseminate falsehoods about someone or something. Normally associated with attacks against individuals on social media that is hurtful and categorized as cyber-bullying by some nations but has now transitioned into a coordinated means of conducting political misinformation campaigns.

Chapter 7
A Socio–Technical Perspective

ABSTRACT

Chapter 7 uses a philosophical approach to discuss the frailty of the human psyche with regards to the implementation and use of systems through our engagement with cyberspace. Our constant exposure to newsworthy cyber security events can desensitize people to the warnings that are either apparent or subliminal. A number of key topical subject areas are discussed exploring human psychology: why people are susceptible to psychological vulnerabilities, characteristics of the human psyche that facilitate errors, how these traits can be exhibited through flawed actions causing mistakes and preventative measures to stop deliberate and accidental actions. This analysis is of vital importance and relevance in order to combat the risks, which to the computer end-user may appear distant and intangible.

INTRODUCTION

This chapter uses a sociological analysis in a technological context to discern the common differentiator in many security breaches – the human. From research conducted between 2009 and 2017 in the U.S. Healthcare Industry, Doctors of Philosophy from Michigan State University and Johns Hopkins Carey Business School concluded that the majority of security breaches are caused unintentionally and through carelessness. A small minority of breaches were classed as intentional acts extrapolating information for unauthorized use, such as fraud (Worth, 2018). However, a study conducted by Verizon using 2015 and 2016 statistical data surmised that 95% of breaches can be

DOI: 10.4018/978-1-7998-3979-8.ch007

categorized by nine patterns – two thirds of which are technology enabled attacks and one third being human facilitated. Strikingly, the patterns with the highest percentile scores were human behaviors, comprising: miscellaneous errors, insider and privilege misuse, and physical theft and loss (Verizon, 2016). While organizations are keen to adopt technology, the human appears to be trailing behind because of misunderstandings in the challenges of implementing technology and the consequences of getting it wrong (Editor, 2016). This has led the U.K. NCSC to call for business boards to take more responsibility and recognize that cyber risk is one of the business risks that can affect enterprises (Ashford, 2019). However, in order to understand this problem more thoroughly, researchers must explore the psychology of the human mind. Hence, the rest of this chapter establishes the reasons behind some user failings and ways of remedying them.

BACKGROUND

In recent years, the Press has reported on users being the major contributory factor in organizational data breaches. The contagion of phishing and spear phishing campaigns from outsiders have fueled this. Insider password re-use that are both exploitable by hackers and state actors alike have also caused data breaches. Users and executives are arguably targets as they are the most exposed within organizations who have access to the Internet on a daily basis and potentially the most naïve or ignorant. Thus, they are targeted like low hanging fruit by the attackers. The employee does not need to be using a higher privilege level for an attack to be a success. Instead, all it needs is an exploitable weakness in unpatched software for an attacker to escalate privileges in a compromised user account (Winkler, 2015). When it comes to taking shortcuts, employees may circumvent technical controls because they are just trying to be more efficient and harbor no malicious intent (Wyatt, 2017).

Passwords are one contributing factor to security breaches. RSA Security's second survey - conducted by the company set named after co-founders Rivest Shamir and Adleman, reported that password overload was a significant cause of security breaches in 2006; thereby indirectly encouraging password re-use to make things simpler for the users (Savvas, 2006). By 2016, advice on password constitution changed from the traditional 'upper, lower case, number and special character passwords' to random three-letter words in order to make them more memorable (Ian M., 2016). In the same year, the Mirai botnet, as discussed in Chapter 1, was able to infiltrate default IoT devices by scanning for open telnet ports and trying to login using 61 pre-established username and password combinations based on default passwords (Fruhlinger, 2018). In 2018, security researchers identified that hackers had acquired details of the U.S. MQ-9 Reaper UAVs because the default passwords associated with file transfer protocol on Netgear routers had not been changed at some military installations (Cimpanu, 2018). Then, there is the more recent password spraying method of cycling through a list of compromised passwords to try and then brute force credentials for the anticipated wider user account base of a target organization. In 2019, Iran proved this technique to be successful, as shown in Chapter 4. Yet in 2019, 64% of people using the Internet still use and re-use the same password for some or all of their online accounts (Helpnet Security, 2019a). Academics in China concluded Chinese passwords are more vulnerable to online trawling attacks (Wang et al., 2016) due to the cultural use of birthdays or mobile phone numbers as passwords of choice – and sometimes alternatively default passwords (Feng, 2011; Wang et al., 2015).

Other reports, like the one from Risk Based Analysis, highlight that hacking is the most common attack type. However, shrouded underneath this is the human element that facilitates a cyber-attack; so, in reality misconfigured services or data handling mistakes can expose more data than external attackers are able to exfiltrate (Constantin, 2019). In 2019, the insider threat was deemed the biggest risk to businesses because of mistakes and/or poor cyber security hygiene (Helpnet Security, 2019b). The Facebook example in Chapter 6 identified that lapses in data protection can enable bad actors to transgress policy and use unexpected behaviors to misuse data (Kang, 2019). This has resulted in more discussion and public dissemination about how advertisements can be managed responsibly (Animalz, 2020). Key mitigations for people tend to be employee security education, the strengthening of technical controls as well as reinforcement procedures. However, the overall situation is more complicated than that; it amounts to the employee's sense of responsibility and organizational security focused culture (Schweber, 2016).

ANALYSIS OF HUMAN PSYCHOLOGY

A key area is sensory perception. This is the act in which people process information gleaned from their environment through their senses, then interpret the input from sensory stimulus and decide necessary responses based on interpretation and conclusions. This is very similar to a technological ICS context in which sensors distribute data for backend processing and resultant physical outcomes performed from the computation. There are two important aspects of perception: top-down and bottom-up. The former is reactive, based upon a person's prior experience of encountering such a stimulus and how they deal with the input data. On the other hand, the latter is deductive, based on an understanding of the stimuli that is formulated through past knowledge (Doring & Hua, 2019a). These facets enable humans to develop over their lifetime and simultaneously influence human behavior.

Emotional development is a strong influencer on human behavior that is drawn from the experience of other people, professional and personal relationships, and cultural influences. Cognition is another relevant aspect that allows individuals to assimilate categorize and reason and learn how to deal with situations when they encounter them. Non-associative learning can occur. This form of learning desensitizes humans due to their constant exposure to stimuli and how they respond to that input. That is when humans can become less responsive through repeated exposure or stimulation; this is called habituation. Another state is dishabituation, which is the state in which humans can become more reactive to a stimulus due to their assimilation of whether it is related to a perceived threat. Spontaneous recovery is a state in which desensitization from habituation is adjusted due to a change in circumstances or an external influence (Doring & Hua, 2019b).

Underlying Human Psyche

Psychologists and academics have formulated a number of theories regarding human development over the years. Pertinent aspects include the following:

- Piaget believed that information and skills can be learned by experiencing successive development stages: (a) sensorimotor stage; (b) preoperational stage; (c) concrete operational stage; and (d) formal operational stage. Conversely, Lev Vygotsky expressed his view that fundamentally, skills need to be acquired before one can develop (Doring & Hua, 2019c).

- Edward Thorndike proposed that consequences can condition people's behavior. For example, a satisfying stimulus through reflex or verbal encouragement strengthens the human response; but an unpleasant stimulus, such as pain or verbal abuse, causes dissatisfaction so that they do not intentionally seek to repeat it. A reward is a reinforcer that can drive humans' desire for something they like, and punishment can disincentivize them from repeating something deemed unsatisfactory; both can encourage their behavior to change (Doring & Hua, 2019c).

- Albert Bandura developed social theory regarding self-efficacy of what humans have learned from situations and their expectancies from these experiences. Julian Rotter built upon this to devise a theory of their belief system and what they believe is inside and outside the control of their abilities – called the locus of control. Through his research, Walter Mischel found that a person's behavior would be more consistent in situations that were similar but inconsistent across situations that are unfamiliar. Sigmund Freud determined that the human brain has a defense mechanism that subconsciously transitions states of mind. As a means of stress reduction, it operates on a range of unconscious thoughts of self-interest or self-preservation versus egotistical perception of morality regarding what is right and wrong (Doring & Hua, 2019d).

In the 19th century, Auguste Kerckhoffs formulated a series of principles pertaining to a cryptosystem and the pertinent aspects for people comprised: (a) ease of use; (b), should not be too hard to think about; and (c) not be bound by a list of complicated rules. In 1975, Jerome Saltzer and Michael Schroeder stated that there are various aspects that need to be considered from a user perspective: (a) humans need to be able to apply specific procedures and policy; (b) security mechanisms involving people should be as few as possible; and (c) the rigor of security measures should exhaust the resources or rewards reaped by an attacker. Therefore, by implication, if users are overly dependent upon applying security through the use of procedural controls, such as a voluminous set of security operating procedures, then humans could make mistakes when they are overwhelmed (Rashid, Chivers, Danezis, Lupu, & Martin, 2019).

Another connotation, provided by Daniel Kahneman and Amos Tversky in the 1970s, is that people have cognitive biases and unconsciously apply short-cut thinking to different situations as a way of slicing through irrelevance in order to focus on what is important (Hallas, 2018). This can also be termed desire lines – the path of least resistance (National Cyber Security Centre, 2019). This is the scenario in which people may not conform to set paths like pathway designs in public parks. Instead, they unconsciously take unsanctioned shortcuts where they deem it necessary in their own mind – thereby circumventing the established norm (Kohlstedt, 2016).

In the 1980s, Curt and Anne Bartol (Source: Rao, 2007) performed an analysis of human nature and devised the following from a criminological context that is still useful for cyber security:

- **Conformity:** Humans are fundamentally good, are influenced by societal values, and will naturally 'do the right thing'.
- **Non-Conformist:** Assumes people are undisciplined and, if given the chance, will abandon society's norms and commit acts of criminality.
- **Neutral:** People are neutral at birth and learn their behaviors, beliefs, and tendencies from their environment in society.

Under a 'conformist' perspective, criminologists expect people to follow security and organizational policies because the natural state of mind would be to remain compliant; therefore, any subsequent non-confirmative actions are the result of human error. Under the 'non-conformist' viewpoint, if individuals are given an opportunity, they would circumvent rules or flaunt the norms of society in order to achieve an aim, whether it be to complete their work on time or hack a system for illicit gain. From the 'neutral' perspective, a person's outlook regarding their ways of working or outlook on life generally depends on a person's upbringing and their mentors. Thus, by using the psychology from all three, an attacker would seek to exploit human weakness by altering their perception of the right course of action and persuade or pressurize them to disregard what they know, forcing errors to occur. The time to achieve such manipulation may depend on the target's experience in their environment or their perspective from life. Hackers apply examples of these techniques during social engineering or through phishing campaigns.

Then there is the problem of 'stupidity,' in which both intellectually gifted people and the average person can make significant errors of judgement due to personal biases. This occurs by the way phrasing is used to explain a dilemma, which may cause some people to be more gullible than others; rationalizing rather than using a deliberate thought process. Keith Stanovich called this problem dysrationalia. There is also the phenomenon of 'motivated reasoning,' in which people can build arguments that justify their own views, and knowledgeable people can generate convincing arguments. Dogmatism is also a problem in which egotistical people can over-estimate their own self-worth and dismiss the views of others based on personal biases. This has the effect of deflating others or defeating collective intelligence in groups, and it can then be the catalyst for underperformance (Robson, 2019). Yet historically, homosapiens have been successful over other humanoid species because of the complete opposite trait – their ability to communicate and cooperate in groups (Schneier, 2012).

Attacker Motivations

One must also consider the psyche of the attackers and what motivates them (Parenty & Domet, 2019). In the case of hackers, Parker (2000) believed that for some, the incentive is the emotional thrill of exploiting a weakness, whereas for others, it could be criminal intent, their personal belief system, or political or quasi-political influences (Shinder, 2010). According to Hodson (2019), the motivations for cyber-crime are no different from that of physical criminality, apart from a greater feeling of impunity by using computer hacking techniques. He also holds a similar view to Parker in that motivations can comprise: (a) financial gain; (b) espionage or sabotage; (c) political advantage; (d) ideological cause; (e) revenge; or (f) kudos.

Maslow's hierarchy of needs provides a means of contextualizing human nature. The hierarchy is in the form of a pyramid. Working from bottom to top: (a) psychological needs are fundamentally paramount; (b) followed by safety needs; (c) then by belonginess and love; (d) esteem and accomplishment; and (e) the pinnacle is self-actualization. It is stipulated that the aforementioned needs at the bottom-end of the scale must be met so the latterly needs can be attained towards the top (McLeod, 2018). But Maslow's motivational theory also provides good insight to understand opportunistic endeavors by cyber-crime; that is, how targeting the higher levels of personal needs, criminals by alluding to a promise or desire, or through coercion are able to persuade people into making mistakes or doing something out of character. Nurse (2018) provided a perspective that cyber-criminals play upon a combination of criminal motivations and manipulatable needs on the part of the victim:

- Humans' trusting nature enables criminals to defraud via phishing campaigns;
- Humans' need for attention or affection through romance scams;

- Humans' biases that can insight poor decisions such as giving criminals remote access to their computers, or,
- Humans' sentimentality or attachment to their data assets that are susceptible to blackmail through the use of ransomware.

The Royal United Services Institute also added to this list from an analysis that Russian state-actors are emulating the *modus operandi* of cybercriminals to obfuscate their own activities in order to make them less attributable (Sullivan, 2018). In this regard, the fundamentals of espionage today still rely on the human psychology and concerted state-level determination that it did in the pre-Internet age, albeit modern technology and techniques have espoused a shift in methods to arguably a more efficient tradecraft (Gray, 2015). The infamous Google incident of 2009 features prominently under this category. In this incident, the company's China office was attacked. The attackers were able to move laterally through Google's infrastructure and continue their cyber-attack against Google's headquarters in the United States (Buchanan, 2010). This cyber-attack is known as Operation Aurora, and the company blamed Chinese government actors. Their intent was not only to acquire intellectual property but also to access the Gmail accounts of dissidents and human rights activists (ARN Staff, n.d.). The source of the attack was originally geo-located to Taiwan, but Google actually thought it to have originated in Beijing (Buchanan, 2010). Subsequently, experts attributed Chinese APT 1 and APT 17 to this attack (Zetter, 2010; Price Waterhouse Coopers, 2017).

ANALYSIS OF HUMAN NATURE WITH THE BENEFIT OF HINDSIGHT

In 2019, nearly half of cyber security leaders in the three largest European economies opined that their cyber security professionals were losing the skills race to cyber-criminality (Helpnet Security, 2019c). Separate evidence from the financial sector from 2018 indicates that there is some credence to such a view in which human errors occurred, spanning procedural, policy, process, and technical contexts (British Broadcasting Corporation, 2019). There is nothing that cyber security leaders can do to affect the psychology of scheming threat actors. However, humans can learn from past security breaches to avoid repeating their mistakes. This section looks into two crucial attacks: the first is cryptanalytic in nature, performed by the British during the 1940s; the other is the first known case of ICS being targeted to deliberately sabotage safety mechanisms with intent to cause significant physical damage.

Learning from LORENZ

An incident during the operation of LORENZ cryptography is a perfect scenario that contextualizes human psychological traits. During the early stages of World War II, the National Socialist German Workers' Party (Nazi) High Command used the SZ40 cipher machine, codenamed LORENZ, to encode plaintext and decode ciphertext messages. The famous Enigma machine averaged three to four wheels depending on the use-case and was orientated around the 26 letters of the alphabet, whereas the LORENZ cipher was fundamentally different because it operated using the 32-symbol Baudot code. Enigma converted encrypted messages electromechanically from plaintext to ciphertext, character-by-character. Operators wrote down the messages, then transmitted them by hand over radio using Morse code. SZ40 was a cipher enhancement to the teleprinter in which the operators set up a cipher key using wheel settings including specific pin selections - 501 pins in total - that formed an electrical circuit. The operator then inputted plaintext input to a keystream of obscured letters to symmetrically encrypt or decrypt messages.

The LORENZ machine was based on the Vernam Scheme cipher, which was constructed from 12 wheels that were arranged as five *psi*-wheels, five *chi*-wheels, and two motor-wheels. in 1941 the arrangement of the *chi*-wheels were changed monthly, the *psi*-wheels quarterly and the motor-wheels daily. The transmitting operator used 12-character word indicators at the start of the message to denote the wheel settings to the receiving operator. The receiving operator determined the settings, otherwise known as the cipher key, by using an out-of-band device called a grille. The transmitter then encrypted messages by typing in the plaintext using the teleprinter keyboard and encipherment. This would occur automatically, advancing the wheels on each key stroke producing cipher text in Baudot code. This either occurred as a live transmission or as an offline perforated tape for later transmission over telegraphic cable or by radio signal. Part of the encipherment procedures were never to send the same message twice using the same settings. This configuration method provided 1.6 quadrillion cryptographic variations compared with the 3-wheel Enigma that produced 150 million million cryptographic variations (Cryptographic

Museum, 2019). The Nazis thought the SZ40 to be uncrackable, and the British codenamed this form of encryption Tunny (Sale, n.d.a; Copeland, 2010; Roberts, 2017; Science Museum, 2019).

British codebreaker Brigadier John Tiltman (later awarded Commander of the Order of the British Empire) specialized in teleprinter encryption and knew of the Vernam Scheme. He speculated that if a mistake was made and the same start positions were used for two messages, which was called a depth, then it might be possible to use modulo-2 addition of both ciphertexts character by character to discern the obscured characters. In 1941, a German radio operator thought to be in Athens sent an almost identical teleprinter message over the radio twice because the recipient in Vienna was unable to decrypt the message properly. However, for both messages, the German operator used the same preceding 12-character indicator, and therefore, the wheels were in the same start position for the second message as they were for the first. The act of not changing to a new wheel arrangement for the cipher key was forbidden and contrary to defined telegraphy practice. The first message was 4,000 characters, but the second was only 3,500 because the sender took shortcuts in abbreviating certain words for expediency when typing the message. This was particularly relevant because the obscured letters were not executed in exactly the same way, providing a depth. The British intercepted the two resultant teleprinter transmissions, initially on undulator tapes, and they subsequently provided them to John Tiltman likely as 5-bit Baudot-Murray code paper tapes (Wikpedia, 2019). Tiltman began comparing them, and as a consequence, he was able to identify the obscured characters.

In 1942, Alan Turing started to formulate a method of obtaining the start settings based on the length of key. He did so by using an iterative process based on depths and differencing when there were no depths. This approach enabled Turing to achieve some manual decryption. Advancing this initial analysis, Bill Tutte (later awarded Fellow of the Royal Society (FRS)) formulated the patterns from the repetition periods of the obscured characters. In reality, they represented the number of pins on the wheels. From this analysis, he produced a manual double-delta method to cross-correlate the originally obscured but now-recovered characters and also the ciphertext. This allowed him to crack the system and provide plaintext. The mathematician Max Newman FRS then became involved, building a prototype mechanical system to prove whether the double-delta method could be automated. Newman used this to measure the cross correlation by processing two teleprinter tapes and trying to find the start positions in order to decrypt messages. This proved successful, but it was a slow way of performing this function. Any message decipherment would be of no tactical importance by the time it had been cracked. In 1943, Bletchley Park brought in Tommy Flowers (later awarded Medal of the British Empire) to build what amounted to a 1,500 thermionic valve computer codenamed Colossus that would completely automate the process. By January 1944, ten Colossi were located in Bletchley Park. These Colossi were employing cryptanalysis by utilizing the double-delta algorithm and by breaking intercepted Nazi High Command teleprinter messages in a timelier fashion than before. This gave the Allies the advantage for the remainder of the war even when the Nazis changed their procedures and introduced the modified SZ42A and SZ42B later on (Sale, n.d.a, n.d.b; Copeland, 2010; Carey, 2018).

Rotter's, Mischel's and Freud's findings apply to this scenario. The sending operator had control over the re-use of the 12-character indicator within his sphere of influence. He also looked towards the impact upon himself with regard to re-sending of the entire 4,000-character message again to the recipient. The situation he was confronted by might well have been out of the norm too. Consequently, it influenced a poor decision not to change the SZ40 wheel settings. Even though it was wrong according to the procedures, it was assuredly a nuisance to change the settings, and it is asserted this encouraged operator carelessness (Heath, 2017). A major failing from the operator's perspective was the tinge of arrogance from the Nazi's belief of the system's infallibility, which heightened the operator's ignorance towards the intangible nature of radio intercept. This then provided him with the confidence to abbreviate some of the message contents for efficiency when sending the same message, the second time. This echoes what other signalers had had from the start of the war generating bad habits and probably influenced his actions, such as not changing the settings when they were supposed to displaying non-conformism. The mistake of taking shortcuts and disregarding procedural controls – only once – compromised the entire LORENZ cipher system. The initial cracking of the cipher was the beginning that allowed continued decrypts, providing insight into Hitler's thought process and Nazi High Command strategy. Ultimately, this proved to be invaluable at the tail-end and most critical period of World War II.

Lessons from TRITON

Another example of multiple human failures is the TRITON cyber-attack on the SIS of the Saudi Arabian petrochemical plant, which the author discussed in Chapters 4 and 5. The TRITON malware framework, which comprised of a number of components, including a remote access trojan (Higgins, 2018). FireEye identified that threat actor had been using this framework in an effort to subvert part of the modular Schneider Triconex safety controller system. The intent appears to have been wanton destruction of parts of the plant. However, in the event, the attacker's actions inadvertently triggered the SIS to instigate a safety feature that shut down the plant's actuators (Lough & Caban, 2019). Luckily, this was an unintended consequence of the attacker's actions that left residual traces of the malware framework on the SIS workstation. A year later, FireEye based attribution traced the malware to the IP address of the Russian Central Scientific Research Institute of Chemistry and Mechanics in Moscow (FireEye Intelligence, 2018; Khandelwal, 2018). Dragos (2020) also identified the attackers as the group Xenotime, who in 2018, had been actively targeting oil and gas companies beyond the Middle East.

Fundamentally, the plant operators made errors that enabled the attack to occur in the first place. One of the first errors of judgement was the 'dual homing' of the workstation to the DCS when it had actually been designed to operate on the separate SIS network. Simply put, the function of the DCS is to control sensors and actuators in the plant, and the role of the SIS is to independently shutdown actuators if a hazard condition is detected. As it happened, the DCS had already been subverted by the attackers, and it would have been used to pivot across to other network segments. Computers generally advertise their services across the network when they are interrogated. In this case, attackers can distinguish open and even closed ports when probed, using scanning tools. In the Triconex scenario, it would have been apparent to the attackers, who had already subverted the DCS, that the workstation was operating software client(s) for a SIS. It could not have been hardened with additional lockdown measures because by being dual homed, it was in effect acting as an uncontrolled bridge between the two networks. Therefore, the identification of these services would have sparked the interest of the attackers as they enumerated the DCS. This can be characterized by the analogy of someone visibly leaving valuables on view in a car. Even though they are protected by the locked car doors, they could be seen through the glass windows, thereby enticing an opportunist or professional thief to smash the window and steal the valuable item. 'Dual homing' has a similar connotation in the computing world.

A combination of psychology, sociology and anthropology drives organizational behavior. The first two are based on human traits associated with individual membership of groups, followed by the relationships within the social order of groups. The latter is based on the culture of organizations within which groups belong (Mullins, 1996). If less stagnating attitudes are prominent within groups, then attitudes for 'thinking out of the box' may not be as apparent in people. This can then drive a biased organizational outlook towards established engineering practices, and at the same time, it can stifle related aspects, such as security awareness culture. In this case, poor decisions were made or approved by committees, such as connecting up networks that had been implemented as separate architectures for specific reasons. Engineers can be so process-driven that they may not see the wood for the trees in a complex inter-disciplined domain. This can potentially blind people to the obvious that could just be reasoned with some common sense. According to Benson et al. (2018), human behavior and decision-making processes are multifaceted and unpredictable. This supposition is supported by Trist and Bamforth, who in 1951, proposed that changes to a technological system must also be complemented by changes in social systems.

The working environment of the ICS world operates in a 'safety first' regime, which trumps cyber security for various reasons to ensure continued safe operation of the system. For example, ICS implementations can default to 'fail open' to avoid an inadvertent pressure that might cause an explosion at the plant. Typically, components of traditional IT network systems 'fail closed' in order to reduce the attack surface (ThreatPress, 2018). Thus, the workforce could have become indoctrinated into a single-dimensional way of thinking around the function of the plant rather than the wider threat environment. In the 1950s, Leon Festinger stated that people filter information to formulate a more comforting cogitative consonance of opinion that influenced their perceived reality. However, this could also be a catalyst of ignorance towards the intangible and asymmetric cyber threats in which a user does not consider the wider perspective. For example, Robert Winston (2003) pointed out our brains make decisions on what to concentrate on and what to disregard; misperceptions can misguide people into underestimating what they do not truly know and typically unconsciously gravitating to things they do (Duffy, 2019). This might well have been behind the second erroneous decision by one of the end-users to leave the manual key-enabled failsafe switch in the program state rather than Run mode. This provided the attackers an opportunity to try to reprogram the SIS, allowing them to cause an unsafe condition. On the other hand, a user potentially left the switch in Run because there may not have been any apparent outright safety issue beyond bad practice for doing so. Either way, in actuality such a bad decision had obvious cyber security implications. This could be attributed to some misplaced perception that ICS is first and foremost safety critical systems, and therefore, it is innocuous to cyber threats, when in fact, the opposite is true. On the other hand, cyber security practitioners could relate it to the combining of the two different worlds of ICS and ICT. In this scenario, complexity and skills gaps in the ICT domain can cause fissures in cyber hygiene and security posture (Goldfarb, 2019).

Inherently, some engineers are suspicious of the intentions of the cyber security discipline, fearing that it makes their job harder and can over-complicate things. Yet the reality is that the role of a cyber security practitioner is to protect the organization from cyber threats as a supporting function of the business (Goldman, 2019). Individuals might be influenced by the perception of other people, situations, and issues. Hence, misinterpretations and negative bias can actually generate counterintuitive ways of working (Bignell & Fortune, 1984) in which people display poor attitudes, like paying 'lip-service' to cyber risks. The author has encountered this issue many times – too many for it to be dismissed as personal views. Rather, it appears to be an emotional or irrational impulse that is more aligned with a perception problem across the industry. In this example, Curt and Anne Bartol may classify human nature associated with this incident as neutral: engineers are influenced by the culture of the work environment, where a committee like a change control board would have undoubtedly agreed 'dual homing.' Perhaps it was for practicality and the ease of updating software on the SIS via the workstation instead of performing air-gap installations using removable media. By ignoring the moral reasons and focusing on the practicalities, any recognition that SIS network was designed to be isolated from the main DCS for specific reasons was lost. This is a perfect example of an established adage that human factors clearly influence failure not only in human activity systems, consisting of people and group work activities, but also in socio-technical systems in which people design, implement, interact, and update technological sub-systems (Bignell & Fortune, 1984).

SOLUTIONS AND RECOMMENDATIONS

The Information Security Forum (ISF) produced a paper focusing on human-centered security to counter the flaws exhibited from the human factor. Its main purpose is to draw together pertinent psychological aspects in order to defeat counterproductive human weaknesses. The thrust of their approach is to focus on the following:

- **Mental Shortcuts:** People inherently use subconscious mental processes, or heuristics, to process information and make decisions. This can involve ignoring some information to decomplexify a situation, especially if individuals are under pressure to solve another problem.
- **Cognitive Bias:** Errors in reasoning can incite poor decision making or poor judgments that, depending on the context, could be gravely impactful upon an organization. Cognitive bias enables the most prominent facts to be recognized, causing other, more relevant facts to be discarded. Other examples are bounded rationality based on time, decision fatigue from repetitive decision making, optimism bias (i.e., 'it will never happen to me'), polarization whilst making decisions that are not necessarily clear cut; and missing that there could be a grey area.

There is a relationship between mental shortcuts and cognitive bias, so when a situation applies external pressure or stress, threat actors can fix or force errors by using 'social power.' An example of the former is the use of repetitive attacks, such as lambasting a target with phishing emails, so that the subconscious starts to ignore an inkling of any suspicious activity. Cognitive bias could be triggered by using social engineering techniques to incite stress and then coerce a target into performing actions they would normally not consider doing. Such methods are similar to those discussed in Chapter 6, in which Facebook ads were used to prey upon people's fears in an attempt to influence a target audience's voting habits.

The ISF recommends that organizations implement a change to their culture, erring towards a human-centered approach for information security. Organizations should initiate this through the board to embrace education and awareness; this should be coupled with buy-in from support functions to help change people's perspective of cyber risk (Information Security Forum, 2019). Already, the Human Resource (HR) profession is voicing viewpoints about how HR can be supportive in reinforcing the cyber security message (Abbott, 2019). There should also be an understanding that millennials and centennials have a different outlook on technology. Older generations may be less knowledgeable than younger generations and oblivious in certain areas of understanding, but they do have the benefit of experience. On the other hand, the younger generation may be blinded to the risks, having grown up with the technology from an early age. Hallas reinforces the argument that organizations need to change their awareness and training programs to cater to the human factor (Haren, 2018). Bird and Curry (2018) have portrayed the need for a wider ecosystem of education and blended training delivery for technology industry practitioners that, when applied in the workplace, should enable competencies to be built up. When ably assisted by professional institutions, it should allow broader cyber orientated intelligence to percolate more widely. This would enable better cyber immersion in the national curriculum, facilitate knowledge growth as part of people's careers paths, enhance experience, and increase skills across the technology community. The author therefore expects investment in education and training to increase cyber security focused skills, which may well reverse the skills shortage that individuals are currently experiencing (Zorz, 2018). Figure 1 shows the interrelationship between all the facets that form the human factor discussed

Figure 1. Contributing elements to the human factor

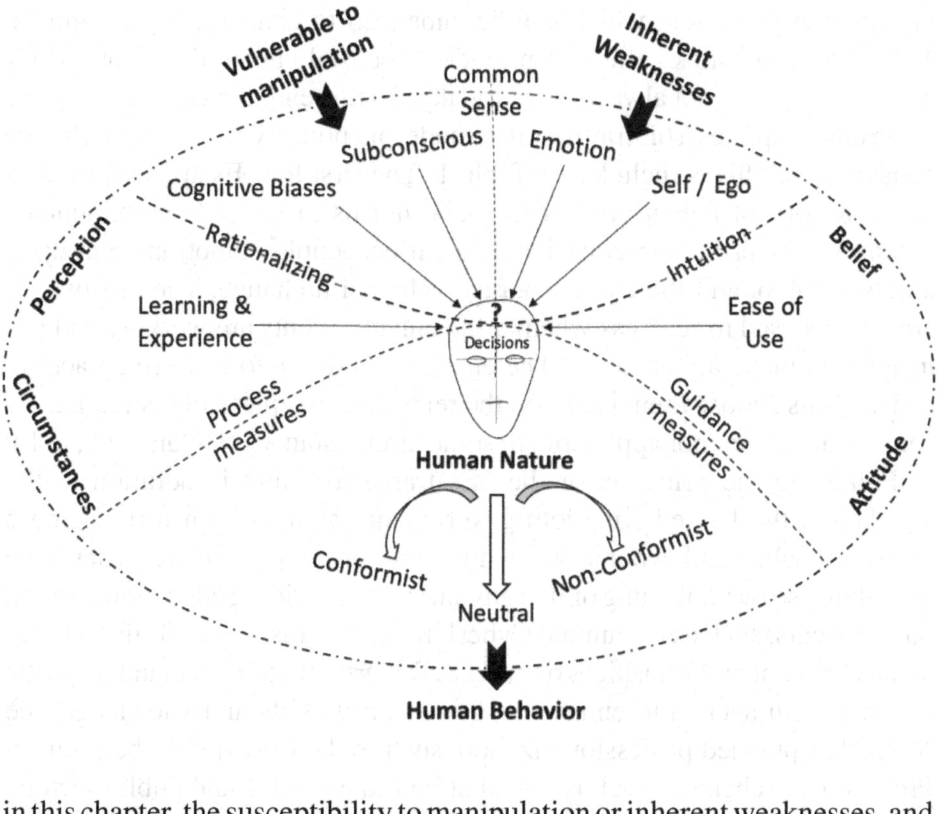

in this chapter, the susceptibility to manipulation or inherent weaknesses, and their influence on behavioral outcomes.

As already inferred in Chapter 6, advertisers are manipulating consumers online when they make choices to purchase or choose content. This is called digital nudging and is based on the principles of playing on people's sub-conscious, cognitive biases or rationalizing to influence their heuristics and decision-making. Advertisers can perform this through rewards and decoys to swing or re-affirm item selection, thereby encouraging purchases. Other techniques, such as subliminal advertising, 'hard selling,' or emphasizing the scarcity effect used offline, are still relevant online. Academics are analyzing the art of nudging, and researchers have found that users are more willing to disclose information but contrastingly, are more reticent to accept default options (Schneider, Weinmann, & Vom Brocke, 2018). There is not a 'one-size-fits-all' option for digital nudging, which is why Cambridge Analytica unethically targeted groups of persuadable voters based on a number of different criteria, including bias (Osbourne, 2018; Remnick, 2018)

Governments also use influencing behavior, in which nudging citizens is purportedly used as a technique. Examples of this are incentivization and information provision, which can be enhanced to change peoples' minds. The 'carrot and stick' effect to provide a focused choice does not always work as people do not always act rationally. To this end, the United Kingdom government applies a 6E framework to underpin policy with an aim to change behavior, and this is included in Table 1. The first four Es are actions used as an armory of enhancements to social norms in order to communicate commitments, prime sub-conscious cues, affect peoples' emotions, play upon a person's ego, and thereby encourage behavioral change. The last two Es are actions used to reassess whether the enhancements are working and use insights to make adjustments. The enablers are tools to achieve an action, and analysts choose them based on the relevance of a particular situation, so some enablers are not applicable in some circumstances (Dolan et al., n.d.).

Following the principle of the 6Es framework and in addition to the legislation, the United Kingdom government has also been influencing a change of habits and cyber security direction through the NCSC. They have been doing so by publishing online guidance and providing education through public events, such as the annual CyberUK event. This is in a similar fashion to the CISA under the auspices of the U.S. Department of Homeland Security. As part of an agenda to enhance cyber security skills and knowledge, the NCSC has pursued professionalization, such as the Certified Cybersecurity Professional scheme, which is aimed at both the private and public sectors. More recently, the NCSC collaborated with academia to provide a foundational Cybersecurity Body of Knowledge. In addition, following a similar approach to the United States the NCSC has been evaluating and certifying university degrees, creating academic centers of excellence (Bird & Curry, 2018; National

Table 1. 6E framework

Actions	Enablers
Enable	· Infrastructure · Facilities · Design · Resources
Encourage	· Legislation · Regulation · Incentives · Information
Engage	· Deliberation · Permission · Co-production
Exemplify	· Leading by example · Policy consistency · Organizational learning
Evaluate	· Evidence-based innovation
Explore	· Insights

Source: Dolan et al., n.d.

Security Agency, 2019; DHS, 2020). The U.S. Federal Information Systems Security Educators' Association (2017) identified culture and training aspects as being crucial influencers. These factors are among the top nine important considerations for reducing the insider threat (Widdowson, 2019). Another U.K. strategy has been to release a formalized government security profession framework for civil servants working in the public sector including the cyber security domain (Cabinet Office, 2020). These considerations are important because the Verizon Data Breach investigations report highlighted that 25% of breaches in 2016 were attributed to the human factor, and by 2018, this had increased to 34% (EKRAN, 2019). The Fortinet Insider Threat Report (2019) reinforced the fact 68% of organizations were more concerned about the internal threat.

FUTURE RESEARCH DIRECTION

AI-based technology is a pervasive and disruptive force that is being billed as a solution to many problems that are experienced in the world. Yet one must be careful. The advent of AI and human desire to achieve AGI may be problematic, especially when humans are finding it difficult to understand their own psychology. More importantly, humans are still involved in developing algorithms as well as collecting, enriching, cleaning, and preparing data for AI systems to process (CloudFactory, n.d.). As such, some organizations are implementing ML-facilitated monitoring of their staff as their answer to the cyber security problem – a technology-centered approach rather than a human-centered one (Booth, 2019). China, for example, has been using AI to measure people's behavior, thereby further imposing Orwellian ideals onto their society. U.S. law enforcement has already encountered ethnicity bias within face recognition systems due to the apparent prejudice of its creators (Coldicutt & Harding, 2018; Best, 2019). There is also a drive to emulate the human brain using AI through the implementation of spiking neural network system-on-a-chip technology, whereby the neural network spikes in a similar fashion to real neurons. This process thereby mimics this function of the human brain and the Spiking Neural Network Architecture, which transmits data in a comparable way to the brain. Thus, this enables researchers to simulate a network of tens of thousands of spiking neurons that can process sensory input and generate motor output in real time (Best, 2019). This is the first stage of learning, according to Piaget. Researchers have recognized the firing of neurons in the brain as the basis for human intelligence.

Alarmists will be particularly concerned with visions of marrying the human brain with machines in order to control machines through human thoughts. For instance, Silicon Valley has ambitions of using Brain Computer Interfaces (BCI) to enable humans to type words into Facebook using just their thoughts. Sceptics think this use-case is slightly fanciful, and questions are already arising about how these sorts of developments would need to be regulated. Society should treat the resultant BCIs in a similar way to invasive medical devices (The Economist, 2018a; Perez, 2019). Where would that leave humans? As discussed in Chapter 6, high-tech companies have already been harvesting our personal data. So what are the consequences of being directly plugged into one's thoughts (The Economist, 2018b)? There have already been calls for people to have more control of their own information based on the way technology companies have been appropriating and using their data. Humanity should also take stock of previous research based on AI-based human-machine interaction and the differences in human perception and the lack of perception by machines. One case in particular was Microsoft's experiment using an AI powered chatbot called Tay. Tay gained knowledge by using Twitter conversations with 18- to 24-year old young adults. However, the AI system started to mimic its followers and converse using strong right-wing bias that had been learned from the attitudes of the human subjects (Hunt,

2016; Reese, 2016). It raised the issue that a sense of empathy was missing, and the inability to perceive right from wrong was obvious (West, 2016).

Therefore, governance and safeguarding controls need to be applied to the AI sphere, not just for the AI technology itself but because of the amassed datasets that are required (Bird, 2018). Ethics also need to be tuned within the field of AI to define what is and what is not acceptable (Shanahan & Singler, 2017). Society should do so whilst being cognizant that ethics is not a level playing field around the world. Without these safeguards, low public trust in technology may be engendered, causing societal discrimination towards machines rather than the people behind them. Such concerns will only be exasperated by predictions that over the next two decades, 47% of jobs will become automated (McNeal, 2018), and of course, AI will be controlling them. On the assumption that BCI is a long way away, more research is required on how society can preserve data quality and algorithmic integrity to avoid an AI electronic arms race. Chapter 8 attempts to answer this very question, among other important deliberations regarding authenticity and integrity.

CONCLUSION

Academic and psychologist Bruce Hood (2012) from the University of Bristol in the United Kingdom believes that people are a collection of conflicting messages, signals, and thought processes that holistically form 'our unified self.' This means that humans have the ability to either operate as individuals or engage in a group where one might also decide to disengage. Professor of psychology Martin Conway of City University of London believes that humans have a distorted self-image that might over-inflate their capabilities and self-perpetuate an illusion about themselves (Lange, 2019). Schneier (2004) stated that people do not understand subtle threats, and academics identified a weaker cyber security mindset of employees as a general catalyst for cyber security breaches (Benson et al., 2018). While defensive cyber security professionals may put controls in place, a human lack of perception of the threats, oblivious human subconscious actions, or lackadaisical attitudes play into the hands of attackers (Snook, 2020). Any mischievousness used to bypass policy and procedures in order to get the job done may weaken the security regime. Reliance on procedural controls without due consideration of technical options facilitates circumvention. Some would say this is just human nature, but conditioning like this is counter-intuitive and it is a fallacy of human nature. One must remember that the human factor in some way has been the common denominator in untold system failures and cyber security breaches. This is why companies like AWS are trying to automate processes as much as possible and thereby remove the human to avoid any mistakes (Worrell, Tomic, & Case, 2019). This approach defeats a security delusion from the intangibility factor of cyber and the risks that lie therein.

Misapprehension towards the cyber security discipline and a lack of understanding of fundamental security precepts can be detrimental to an organization. Typically, when users engage with the Internet, their outlook might be mostly positive regarding the experience it can provide us. Their perception might be more of comfort rather than distrust, and therefore, they lose their awareness to the intangible dangers that lurk within cyberspace. Internet consumers seem to have been quite trusting with regard to their interaction online (Bird, 2013). People can tune out and, through a lack of concentration, accept what appears to be more annoying prompts that may in fact be the start of a cyber-attack. Perhaps only when something bad happens to each individual personally – such as an online account being hacked – does the fog of obliviousness lift enabling, users to be more responsive because of the distress that was caused. Another risk that remains aloof is that Internet addiction and compulsion can psychologically affect the younger generation (Vitelli, 2016), and this trend forced the United States to introduce new measures to counter social media addiction (Burton, 2019).

To reduce the risks, organizations should implement systems using secure-by-design principles, such as: (a) minimizing the attack surface area; (b) implementing security-by-default; (c) applying principles of least privilege avoiding the use of default or weak passwords; (d) using of defense-in-depth concepts but not over complicating security measures; (e) not inherently trusting services and validating ingested data; (f) employing separation of duties regimes; (g) avoiding security by obscurity; and (h) correctly fixing security issues (Duffy, 2019). From a user's perspective, simple measures can make all the difference in making it more difficult for remote attackers or rogue insiders. These measures include:

- Avoiding screen-locking computers overnight – if subverted, they could be used as a 'staging server for data exfiltration';
- Remaining wary of phishing emails and stay vigilant;
- Being on guard against redirection attacks;
- Maintaining focused when responding to computer-based prompts;
- Not taking shortcuts and bypassing procedural controls and processes. They are there for a reason even if one may think differently.

Civilization as a whole must take heed of why experts have considered cyber warfare to be a threat multiplier and why this has been a factor for advancing the Doomsday Clock closer to midnight than was the case during the Cold War (Ranger, 2020). The image of people being the 'weakest link' needs to change to a more positive one akin to a 'human firewall,' and thus, a cultural shift is required. Organizations need to move away from a dependence on tomes of policies that many do not read and instead communicate inciteful cyber security messages more than once so that the average person not only hears them but truly absorbs the information (May, 2017). Reliance on myths about the risks, ignorance of the threats, inadequate cyber behaviors, and uninformed views only perpetuate a counter-intuitive delusion of what is relevant in the threat landscape and what is not. This makes an organization's information assets ripe for abuse, misuse and flagrant exploitation. This means education and training is a necessity to bridge the perception gap because at the end of the day, cyber security is not only a technical issue but also a people problem.

REFERENCES

Abbott, J. (2019). *Five ways HR can improve cyber security.* Retrieved from https://www.personneltoday.com/hr/hr-role-in-cyber-security/

Animalz. (2020). *Facebook ad placements: 4 ways to control it (and why you should!) + a guide.* Retrieved from https://adespresso.com/blog/facebook-ad-placements/

ARN Staff. (n.d.). *Top 10 most notorious cyber attacks in history.* Retrieved from https://www.arnnet.com.au/slideshow/341113/top-10-most-notorious-cyber-attacks-history/

Ashford, W. (2019). *Weak cyber security top challenge, says NCSC chief Ciaran Martin.* Retrieved from https://www.computerweekly.com/news/252464679/Weak-cyber-security-top-challenge-says-NCSC-chief-Ciaran-Martin

Benson, V., McAlaney, J., & Baranowski, L. (2018). *Emerging threats for the human element and countermeasures in current cyber security landscape* [PDF document]. Retrieved from https://repository.uwl.ac.uk/id/eprint/4448/1/Human%20element%20Editorial%20Chapter_v3.pdf

Best, J. (2019). *This million-core supercomputer inspired by the human brain breaks all the rules*. Retrieved from https://www.zdnet.com/article/this-million-core-supercomputer-inspired-by-the-human-brain-breaks-all-the-rules/

Bignell, V., & Fortune, J. (1984). *Understanding systems failures*. Open University.

Bird, D. (2013). Open or closed? *ITNOW*, *55*(2), 32–33. doi:10.1093/itnow/bwt014

Bird, D. (2018). AI in the cloud. *ITNOW*, *60*(2), 38–39. doi:10.1093/itnow/bwy048

Bird, D., & Curry, J. (2018). A case for using blended learning and development techniques to aid the delivery of a UK cybersecurity core body of knowledge. *International Journal of Systems and Software Security and Protection*, *9*(2), 28–45. doi:10.4018/IJSSSP.2018040103

Booth, R. (2019). *UK businesses using artificial intelligence to monitor staff activity*. Retrieved from https://amp.theguardian.com/technology/2019/apr/07/uk-businesses-using-artifical-intelligence-to-monitor-staff-activity

British Broadcasting Corporation. (2019). *Cyber-incident reports from UK finance sector spiked by 1,000% in 2018*. Retrieved from https://www-bbc-co-uk.cdn.ampproject.org/c/s/www.bbc.co.uk/news/amp/technology-48841809

Buchanan, K. (2010). *Google hacked the Chinese hackers right back*. Retrieved from https://gizmodo.com/google-hacked-the-chinese-hackers-right-back-5449037

Burton, G. (2019). *US Bill introduced to ban 'addictive' social media features*. Retrieved from https://www.computing.co.uk/news/3079817/social-media-addiction-law

Cabinet Office. (2020). *Career framework: For security professionals in government* [PDF document]. Retrieved from https://assets.publishing.service.gov.uk/government/uploads/system/uploads/attachment_data/file/864752/Government_Security_Profession_career_framework.pdf

Carey, J. (Producer). (2019). Code-breakers: Bletchley Park's lost heroes preview [Television broadcast]. London: British Broadcasting Corporation.

Cimpau, C. (2018). *Hacker steals military docs because someone didn't change a default FTP password.* Retrieved from https://www.bleepingcomputer.com/news/security/hacker-steals-military-docs-because-someone-didn-t-change-a-default-ftp-password/

CloudFactory. (n.d.). *Humans in the AI tech stack.* Durham, NC. *CloudFactory Limited.*

Coldicutt, R., & Harding, V. (2018). *The ethics of artificial intelligence.* Paper presented at The Times Science Festival, Cheltenham, UK.

Constantin, L. (2019). *Data breaches exposed 5 billion records in 2018.* Retrieved from https://www.csoonline.com/article/3341317/data-breaches-exposed-5-billion-records-in-2018.html

Copeland, J. (Ed.). (2010). *Colossus: The secrets of Bletchley Park's codebreaking computers.* Oxford University Press.

Crypto Museum. (2019). *Working principle of the Enigma.* Retrieved from https://cryptomuseum.com/crypto/enigma/working.htm

Department of Homeland Security. (2020). *Cybersecurity.* Retrieved from https://www.dhs.gov/topic/cybersecurity

Dolan, P., Hallsworth, M., Halpern, D., King, D., & Vlaev, I. (n.d.). *Mindspace: Influencing behavior through public policy* [PDF document]. Retrieved from https://www.instituteforgovernment.org.uk/publications/mindspace

Doring, N., & Hua, P. (2019a). *Introduction to psychology: Sensation and perception.* Training course retrieved from https://www.futurelearn.com/courses/sensation-perception/6/steps/615466

Doring, N., & Hua, P. (2019b). *Introduction to psychology: Developmental psychology.* Training course retrieved from https://www.futurelearn.com/courses/developmental-psychology/6/steps/601640

Doring, N., & Hua, P. (2019c). *Introduction to psychology: The psychology of learning.* Training course retrieved from https://www.futurelearn.com/courses/psychology-of-learning/6/steps/601615

Doring, N., & Hua, P. (2019d). *Introduction to psychology: The psychology of personality.* Training course retrieved from https://www.futurelearn.com/courses/psychology-personality/6/steps/615432

Duffy, B. (2019). *The perils of perception.* Atlantic Books.

(Ed.). (2016). *Insider threats: A persistent and widespread problem.* Retrieved from https://www.welivesecurity.com/2016/04/26/insider-threats-persistent-widespread-problem/

Ekran. (2019). *Insider threat statistics for 2020: Facts and figures.* Retrieved from https://www.ekransystem.com/en/blog/insider-threat-statistics-facts-and-figures

Federal Information Security Educators Association. (2017). *Cybersecurity – The human factor prioritizing people solutions to improve the cyber resiliency of the federal workforce* [PDF document]. Retrieved from https://csrc.nist.gov/CSRC/media/Events/FISSEA-30th-Annual-Conference/documents/FISSEA2017_Witkowski_Benczik_Jarrin_Walker_Materials_Final.pdf

Feng, D. (2011). *Bad passwords with Chinese characteristics.* Retrieved from https://www.techinasia.com/bad-passwords-china

FireEye Intelligence. (2018). *TRITON attribution: Russian government-owned lab most likely built custom intrusion tools for TRITON attackers.* Retrieved from https://www.fireeye.com/blog/threat-research/2018/10/triton-attribution-russian-government-owned-lab-most-likely-built-tools.html

Fortinent. (2019). *Insider threat report* [PDF document]. Retrieved from https://www.fortinet.com/content/dam/maindam/PUBLIC/02_MARKETING/08_Report/2019_Insider%20Threat%20Report_Fortinet_1.8.pdf

Fruhlinger, J. (2018). *The Mirai botnet explained: How teen scammers and CCTV cameras almost brought down the Internet.* Retrieved from https://www.csoonline.com/article/3258748/the-mirai-botnet-explained-how-teen-scammers-and-cctv-cameras-almost-brought-down-the-internet.html

Goldfarb, J. (2019). *Technology is not our problem.* Retrieved from https://www.securityweek.com/technology-not-our-problem

Goldman, E. (2019). *Developers need to stop fearing the InfoSec Mafia.* Retrieved from https://medium.com/jettech/developers-need-to-stop-fearing-the-infosec-mafia-f61f4b8b8ba5

Grey, S. (2015). *The new spymasters: Inside espionage from the Cold War to global terror.* Penguin Books.

Hallas, B. (2018). *Re-thinking the human factor: A philosophical approach to information security awareness behaviour and culture. The Hallas Institute.* Hallas.

Haren, J. (2018). *A review of 're-thinking the human factor: A philosophical approach to information security awareness behaviour and culture by Bruce Hallas*. Retrieved from https://www.linkedin.com/pulse/re-thinking-human-factor-philosophical-approach-security-john-haren?article Id=6475702980351004672

Heath, N. (2017). *Cracking Hitler's unbreakable code: How the Colossus computer helped beat the Nazis*. Retrieved from https://www.techrepublic.com/article/cracking-hitlers-impossible-code-how-the-colossus-computer-helped-allies-beat-the-nazis/

Helpnet Security. (2019a). *Despite warnings, most people still don't change their passwords*. Retrieved from https://www.helpnetsecurity.com/2019/05/13/people-password-habits/

Helpnet Security. (2019b). *Internal user mistakes create large percentage of cybersecurity incidents*. Retrieved from https://www.helpnetsecurity.com/2019/10/08/internal-user-mistakes/

Helpnet Security. (2019c). *Cybersecurity professionals are outgunned and burned out. Retrieved* from https://www.helpnetsecurity.com/2019/06/28/cybersecurity-burnout/

Higgins, K. (2018). *Schneider Electric: TRITON/TRISIS attack used 0-day flaw in its safety controller system, and a RAT*. Retrieved from https://www.darkreading.com/vulnerabilities---threats/schneider-electric-triton-trisis-attack-used-0-day-flaw-in-its-safety-controller-system-and-a-rat/d/d-id/1330845

Hodson, C. (2019). *Cyber risk management: Prioritize threats, identify vulnerabilities and apply controls*. Kogan Page Ltd.

Hood, B. (2012). *What is the self illusion?* Retrieved from https://www.psychologytoday.com/us/blog/the-self-illusion/201205/what-is-the-self-illusion

Hunt, E. (2016). *Tay, Microsoft's AI chatbot, gets a crash course in racism from Twitter*. Retrieved from https://www.theguardian.com/technology/2016/mar/24/tay-microsofts-ai-chatbot-gets-a-crash-course-in-racism-from-twitter

Ian, M. (2016). *Three random words or #thinkrandom*. Retrieved from https://www.ncsc.gov.uk/blog-post/three-random-words-or-thinkrandom-0

Information Security Forum. (2019). *Human-centred security: Addressing psychological vulnerabilities.* Retrieved from https://www.securityforum.org/research/human-centred-security/

Kang, C. (2019). *F.T.C. approves Facebook fine of about $5 Billion.* Retrieved from https://www.nytimes.com/2019/07/12/technology/facebook-ftc-fine.html?smid=nytcore-ios-share

Khandelwal, S. (2018). *FireEye: Russian research lab aided the development of TRITON industrial malware.* Retrieved from https://thehackernews.com/2018/10/russia-triton-ics-malware.html?m=1

Kohlstedt, K. (2016). *Least resistance: How desire paths can lead to better design.* Retrieved from https://99percentinvisible.org/article/least-resistance-desire-paths-can-lead-better-design/

Lange, C. (2019). The Self. *New Scientist, 244*(3260), 38. PMID:31618788

Lough, V., & Caban, D. (2019). *Triton malware case-study: FireEye, Schneider Electric.* Paper presented at CyberUK Conference, Glasgow, UK.

May, R. (2017). Y*our human firewall – The answer to the cyber security problem.* Paper presented at TEDxWorking, Surrey, UK.

McLeod, S. (2018). *Maslow's hierarchy of needs.* Retrieved from https://www.simplypsychology.org/simplypsychology.org-Maslows-Hierarchy-of-Needs.pdf

McNeal, M. (2018). *Rise of the machines: The future has lots of robots, few jobs for humans.* Retrieved from https://www.wired.com/brandlab/2015/04/rise-machines-future-lots-robots-jobs-humans/

Mullins, L. (1996). *Management and organisational behaviour* (4th ed.). Pitman Publishing.

National Cyber Security Centre. (2019). Cloud: The latest thinking from the NCSC on Cloud. Paper presented at CyberUK Conference, Glasgow, UK.

National Security Agency. (2019). *NSA congratulates Centers of Academic Excellence.* Retrieved from https://www.nsa.gov/resources/students-educators/#cae

Nurse, J. (2018). *Cybercrime and you: How criminals attack and the human factors that they seek to exploit* [PDF document]. Retrieved from https://arxiv.org/pdf/1811.06624.pdf

Osbourne, H. (2018). *What is Cambridge Analytica? The firm at the centre of Facebook's data breach.* Retrieved from https://www.theguardian.com/news/2018/mar/18/what-is-cambridge-analytica-firm-at-centre-of-facebook-data-breach

Parenty, T., & Domet, J. (2019). *Sizing up your cyberrisks.* Retrieved from https://hbr.org/2019/11/sizing-up-your-cyberrisks

Parker, J. (2000). *Total surveillance: Investigating the big brother world of E-spies, eavesdroppers and CCTV.* Piatkus Publishers Ltd.

Perez, C. (2019). *Elon Musk's 'Neuralink' could merge human brains with computers by 2020.* Retrieved from https://nypost.com/2019/07/17/elon-musks-neuralink-could-merge-human-brains-with-computers-by-2020/?utm_medium=SocialFlow&sr_share=facebook&utm_campaign=SocialFlow&utm_source=NYPFacebook

Price Waterhouse Coopers. (2017). *Operation cloud hopper* [PDF document]. Retrieved from https://www.pwc.co.uk/cyber-security/pdf/cloud-hopper-report-final-v4.pdf

Ranger, S. (2020). *The Doomsday Clock just moved closer to midnight again. Tech is getting some of the blame.* Retrieved from https://www.zdnet.com/article/the-doomsday-clock-just-moved-closer-to-midnight-again-tech-is-getting-some-of-the-blame/

Rao, S. (2007). Psychiatrist and the science of criminology: Sociological, psychological and psychiatric analysis of the dark side. *Indian Journal of Psychiatry, 49*(1), 3–5. doi:10.4103/0019-5545.58886 PMID:20640058

Rashid, A., Chivers, H., Danezis, G., Lupu, E., & Martin, A. (Eds.). (2019). *The cyber security body of knowledge version 1.0* [PDF document]. Retrieved from https://www.cybok.org/media/downloads/CyBOK-version_1.0.pdf

Reese, H. (2016). *Why Microsoft's 'Tay' AI bot went wrong.* Retrieved from https://www.techrepublic.com/article/why-microsofts-tay-ai-bot-went-wrong/

Remnick, D. (2018). *Cambridge Analytica and a moral reckoning in Silicon Valley.* Retrieved from https://www.newyorker.com/magazine/2018/04/02/cambridge-analytica-and-a-moral-reckoning-in-silicon-valley

Roberts, J. (2017). *Lorenz: Breaking Hitler's top secret code at Bletchley Park.* The History Press.

Robson, D. (2019, February 23). How to upgrade your thinking and avoid traps that make you look stupid (Electronic ed.). New Scientist.

Sale, T. (n.d.a). *The Lorenz Cipher and how Bletchley Park broke it*. Retrieved from https://www.codesandciphers.org.uk/lorenz/fish.htm

Sale, T. (n.d.b). *The Colossus its purpose and operation*. Retrieved from https://www.codesandciphers.org.uk/lorenz/colossus.htm

Savvas, T. (2006). *Password overload causes security breaches and non-compliance*. Retrieved from https://www.computerweekly.com/news/2240078379/Password-overload-causes-security-breaches-and-non-compliance

Schneider, C., Weinmann, M., & Vom Brocke, J. (2018). Digital nudging: Guiding online user choices through interface design. *Communications of the ACM, 61*(7), 67–73. doi:10.1145/3213765

Schneier, B. (2004). Secrets & lies (Paperback ed.). Hoboken, NJ: Wiley Publishing.

Schneier, B. (2012). *Liars & outliers: Enabling the trust that society needs to thrive*. Wiley Publishing.

Schweber, A. (2016). *The root cause of most data breaches* [Weblog comment]. Retrieved from https://blogs.absolute.com/human-error-still-root-cause-of-data-breaches/

Science Museum. (2019). *Top secret: From ciphers to cyber security* [Exhibition]. British Science Museum.

Shanahan, M., & Singler, B. (2017). *The machine mind*. Paper presented at The Times Science Festival, Cheltenham, UK.

Shinder, D. (2010). *Profiling and categorizing cybercriminals*. Retrieved from https://www.techrepublic.com/blog/it-security/profiling-and-categorizing-cybercriminals/

Sullivan, J. (2018). *Russian cyber operations: State-led organised Crime* [Weblog comment]. Retrieved from https://rusi.org/commentary/russian-cyber-operations-state-led-organised-crime

The Economist. (2018a). Thought experiments. *The Economist, 426*(9073), 1-12.

The Economist. (2018b). Taming the titans. *The Economist, 426*(9075), 11-12.

ThreatPress. (2018). *Security by design principles according to OWASP*. Retrieved from https://blog.threatpress.com/security-design-principles-owasp/

Verizon. (2016). *2016 data breach investigations report* [PDF document]. Retrieved from https://enterprise.verizon.com/resources/reports/2016/DBIR_2016_Report.pdf

Vitteli, R. (2016). *Can compulsive Internet use affect adolescent mental health?* Retrieved from https://www.psychologytoday.com/us/blog/media-spotlight/201601/can-compulsive-internet-use-affect-adolescent-mental-health

Wang, D., Cheng, H., Gu, Q., & Wang, P. (2015). *Understanding passwords of Chinese users: Characteristics, security and implications* [PDF document]. Retrieved from http://wangdingg.weebly.com/uploads/2/0/3/6/20366987/chinesepassfull15.pdf

Wang, D., Zhang, Z., Wang, P., Yan, J., & Huang, X. (2016). Targeted online password guessing: An underestimated threat. In *Proceedings of the 23rd CM Conference on Computer and Communications Security*. Vienna, Austria: Association of Computing Machinery. 10.1145/2976749.2978339

West, J. (2016). *Microsoft's disastrous Tay experiment shows the hidden dangers of AI*. Retrieved from https://qz.com/653084/microsofts-disastrous-tay-experiment-shows-the-hidden-dangers-of-ai/

Widdowson, A. (2019). *How people affect cyber security*. The Ergonomist. The Chartered Institute of Ergonomics and Human Factors.

Winkler, I. (2015). *Awareness lessons from the Sony hack*. Retrieved from https://www.csoonline.com/article/2919050/awareness-lessons-from-the-sony-hack.html

Winston, R. (2003). *The human mind and how to make the most of it*. Bantam Books.

Worrell, C., Tomic, A., & Case, N. (2019). *How to get started with security response automation on AWS*. Retrieved from https://aws.amazon.com/blogs/security/how-get-started-security-response-automation-aws/

Worth, T. (2018). *The threat from within: Most breaches due to employee errors* [Weblog comment]. Retrieved from https://blog.hipaavideo.net/2019/04/1564/

Wyatt, C. (2017). *Security breaches are inevitable...Or are they?* Retrieved from https://www.infosecurity-magazine.com/opinions/security-breaches-inevitable/

Zetter, K. (2010). *Google hack attack was ultra sophisticated, new details show*. Retrieved from https://www.wired.com/2010/01/operation-aurora/

Zorz, Z. (2018). *What can we do to reverse the cybersecurity skills shortage?* Retrieved from https://www.helpnetsecurity.com/2018/09/10/reverse-cybersecurity-skills-shortage/

ADDITIONAL READING

Harper, R. (2010). *Texture: Human expression in the age of communications overload*. Massachusetts Institute of Technology Press. doi:10.7551/mitpress/7856.001.0001

Hodges, A. (2012). *The enigma*. Vintage.

Lewin, R. (2008). *Ultra goes to war*. Pen & Sword Military.

Schneier, B. (2008). *Schneier on security*. Wiley Publishing.

Sebag-Montefiore, H. (2000). *The battle for the code*. Weidenfeld & Nicholson.

Snook, A. (2020). *11 cybersecurity threats for 2020 (Plus 5 solutions)*. Retrieved from https://i-sight.com/resources/11-cybersecurity-threats-for-2020-plus-5-solutions/

KEY TERMS AND DEFINITIONS

Defense-in-Depth: The process of architecting computer systems by laying various different types of controls from the outer-boundary to the core.

Desire Lines: A scenario in which people deviate from the established path to take a shortcut that is more desirable and potentially expedient.

Secure-by-Design: A concept in which information and cyber security principles are considered from the outset of system design and feature through system implementation into operations.

Security by Obscurity: A term synonymous to when mechanism(s) like an obscure proprietary protocol is used in place of a cyber security control, such as end-to-end encryption.

Senses: Sight, touch, hearing, smell, and taste are all facets that enable people to process, assess and perform actions from interpretation.

Vernam Scheme: Developed for teleprinters used Modulo-2 addition to add together obscured characters with the associated plaintext character, which then generated the ciphertext character-by-character in an automated manner.

Chapter 8

Blockchain as an Enabler for Zero–Trust Architectures

ABSTRACT

From the lessons that can be learned so far in this book, the author justifies why a new strategy is required to refocus our perception and utilization of computerized capabilities in the future. Chapter 8 focuses on the advancement of the cyber security discipline by determining trust-less control-sets – a fourth dimension if you will, comprising blockchain technology. Blockchain has been implemented in fungible forms, such as public bitcoin and Ethereum, and in a non-fungible manner like private keyless signature infrastructure. It is the latter that is of particular interest, where proven implementations have the potential to demonstrably act as a verifiable trust anchor, embellishing cyber security controls in a number of critical areas to ensure (1) preservation of data integrity, (2) digital finger printing of IoT assets to prove the source of data is trustworthy, (3) validation of identity and access management mechanisms, and (4) software provenance in the supply chain for not only traditional code-bases but also AI algorithms.

INTRODUCTION

A trust-less technology like blockchain could be an answer to a considerable number of technical challenges already highlighted over successive chapters in this book. This is because historically systems must apply levels of access control based on trust which is at the center of many security incidents –

DOI: 10.4018/978-1-7998-3979-8.ch008

whether it be human or automated machine processes. Examples already covered include: (a) data losses through insider misuse; (b) abusing or exposing data; and (c) outsiders gaining traction through cyber-attacks against computer systems using privilege elevation to cause nefarious damage or conduct data exfiltration. According to John Kindervag (Greengard, 2018), relying on outdated or improperly thought through trust models has been the main catalyst for most data breaches. He advocates a 'zero-trust' approach that can enable organizations to focus on determining which assets are important and need protecting, such as properly applying a need-to-know and least-privilege model supported by monitoring and log inspection (Greengard, 2018). AWS already advocates an approach in which one set of credentials and privileges do not enable users full trusted access; rather, there is a granular approach for human access control by: (a) roles and groups; (b) MFA; (c) least privilege allocation coupled with permissions; (d) supported by network access control; and (e) auditable logs (Columbus, 2019; Gerritz, 2020).

Gault (2019) justified how a mechanism like PKI requires an additional measure to assure data integrity based on a verifiable state of truth (Gault, 2019a). Integrity is a particularly important control that is generally shrouded by the need for confidentiality, in which the use of cryptography generally covers both aspects. However, this can create a « *double entendre problème* » because encryption can affect performance. Gault makes a compelling case, quoting Schneier (2016) to say that since the 90s, there has been a fixation on the protection of data-in-transit, but there has been less focus on protecting data-at-rest. Consequently, there have been many security breaches or events discussed in the first six chapters of this book, in which attackers or abusers have exfiltrated data. When data-in-transit is protected with mutual authentication and encryption through PKI, for example, there can be a performance hit. This fact is especially true for ICS systems. In some way, this explains some of the weaknesses found in CNI systems, notwithstanding some oversights in secure-by-design architectural deployments that may have also occurred. The TRITON case in Chapter 4 is a perfect example of this.

This chapter focuses on a fourth dimension: the advent of blockchain technology that could become a game changer for cyber security. By focusing on the integrity aspect of the CIA triad, blockchain technology changes the stereotypical confidentiality heavy view of cyber security. The technology also provides a trail of immutable transactions, coupled with transparency in a trust-less manner.

BACKGROUND

There are examples where blockchain technology has been implemented in fungible forms, like Bitcoin and Ethereum, and in a non-fungible format, such as Keyless Signature Infrastructure (KSI). First, to understand the fundamental concepts of this technology, one needs to explore public blockchains first. This will be followed by delving into private blockchain approaches and gaining an understanding of the differences between them. It is the latter that forms the main crux of the argument toward the adoption of blockchain for cyber security. A salient private blockchain model with the correct non-fungible attributes can have a number of advantages, such as: (a) providing an alternative form of trust and authenticity verification; (b) facilitating transactional privacy through a permissioned approach; and (c) providing an irrefutable and auditable record of transactions (Datta, 2019). The use-cases for a KSI type blockchain are diverse, can be advantageous, and provide demonstrable security and privacy-focused properties. Therefore, organizations could also use it to: (a) provide proof of peoples' identities online; (b) ensure data or object trustworthiness; (c) provide a record of any data alterations; and (d) operate in a zero-trust manner.

PUBLIC BLOCKCHAINS

The disruptive blockchain technology paradigm has been synonymous with the Bitcoin cryptocurrency that was introduced in 2009. Bitcoin is an example of a public permissionless blockchain implementation that, at its core, relies on a series of decentralized databases, called ledgers, residing in nodes on the network. The main elements of each block comprise: (a) user credentials based on asymmetric elliptic curve digital signature algorithm (ECDSA) cryptography; (b) digital digest or hash to verify the transaction state; (c), digital signatures to validate the transaction; and (d) inclusion of the hash of the previous block in the chain (Bitcoin.it, 2018). The mechanisms involved in these transactions provide pseudo-anonymity, instead of revealing the users' full identity. Before a block is added to the chain, a consensus mechanism operated by other nodes on the network ratifies it and then an entity that first achieves consensus signs it before systematically updating a series of distributed ledgers with a record of the validated transaction (Pujoldevall, 2019).

The Bitcoin example employs a Proof of Work (PoW), in which the blockchain uses nodal algorithms to form the consensus mechanism, and miners operate as nodes on the network. The miners have to complete a mathematical puzzle as part of the validation process before blocks can be added to the chain. Therefore, PoW is hugely computationally intensive and time consuming, and it underpins the worth of the entire process. Once the consensus mechanism deems the associated transaction and proof of authenticity to be valid, the successful node can create a new block. When the block is created, a hash of the transaction record is included as well as the preceding block's hash that forms the chain. Yet this action is only performed after a predefined time hiatus to avoid double-spending, which is a weakness associated with cryptocurrencies. This generation of blockchain always utilizes the longest chain as it has the longest path of integrity compared to more recent forked chains. The blockchain community apportions remuneration to participating owners who ratified the block via PoW in the form of a block reward. The robustness of the Bitcoin framework and model encourages participants not to cheat the system. The blockchain system will detect any tampering within blocks on the chain, which will result in entities being financially penalized (Lipovyanov, 2019).

An enhancement to the Bitcoin approach is known as the second generation blockchain. Ethereum is an example of this type of decentralized platform that utilizes tokenization. This approach enables participating entities to produce Decentralized Applications (DApps) in Turing-Complete Virtual Machines and establish smart contracts for automated self-enacting transactions between entities. The tokens used by Ethereum is called Ether and is a form of cryptocurrency (Jha, 2019). A Proof of Stake (PoS) consensus model is used instead of PoW. Ethereum still uses miners and decentralized ledgers for consensus purposes, but computer processing for each transaction is substantially less demanding. Therefore, the interoperable period to achieve consensus is substantially quicker that PoW (Lipovyanov, 2019). Ethereum is an open source platform that enables application development, while Bitcoin has an established codebase that has to comply with stringent rules. Both Bitcoin and Ethereum use software-based wallets to hold their respective crypto-assets and PKI private keys. Ethereum provides a capability for decentralized autonomous organizations to raise funds from investors or entities by implementing Initial Coin Offerings for a new deregulated cryptocurrency. The owners of the nodes who undertake PoS are rewarded by taking a percentage of the transaction fees. Bitcoin and Ethereum have also set up their own respective test networks that allow developers to test their code rather than validate it centrally. These test harnesses help preserve the resilience of the main systems and also help the developers evade financial penalties by introducing coding errors on the live systems. Both Bitcoin and Ethereum are known as public blockchains.

Alternative Blockchains

Waltonchain blockchain provides an approach to apply valuation to IoT assets through a PoS and Trust consensus mechanism. This model follows a fungible value-based approach related to the Radio Frequency Identifiers (RFID) of assets in the supply chain so that consumers can purchase them (Maio, 2018). Alibaba Cloud provides a Blockchain-as-a-Service (BaaS) for customers who rely on a supply chain for their business, such as individuals working in finance, logistics, distribution, and consumption services. Alibaba's offering promises integration with IoT and anti-counterfeiting technologies with traceable visibility to multiple distributors. The transactions are transparent as well as being tamper-resistant (Alibaba, n.d.). The Chinese company Baidu launched their BaaS called 'Baidu Trust'. Like another Chinese company, Tencent, both use a TrustSQL platform, which consists of a core chain, product service, and applications to beat fraud in value exchanges and transfers. This enables customers to perform and trace transactions associated with the following list (Suberg, 2017; Sundararajan, 2018; Chi et al., 2019a):

- Digital currency
- Digital billing
- Bank credit management
- Insurance management financial auditing
- Identity systems
- Digital rights management
- Supply chain provenance

Microsoft established an Azure Blockchain that utilizes the Confidential Consortium Framework, which interoperates with their Trusted Execution Environments in their Azure cloud platform (Microsoft, n.d.). AWS is also offering a BaaS model, which is based on two components: (a) Quantum Ledger Database, which allows customer to use a ledger service whilst acting as a central trusted authority; or (b) Managed Blockchain that enables customers to implement a blockchain network from a choice of the public Ethereum framework for building DApps or a private and permissioned variant through

Hyperledger Fabric in order to build blockchain applications in Docker containers. Ethereum provides transaction standards for using the fungible Ether cryptocurrency or Non-Fungible Tokens (NFT) (Crypto Influence, 2018). Hyperledger blockchain is based on Practical Byzantine Fault Tolerance, uses transactional smart contracts between enrolled participants and enables users to create separate ledgers for privacy (Bryson, Penny, Goldenburg, & Serrao, 2018). AWS lists examples of blockchain implementations as trading and asset transfer, retail, and supply chain (Amazon Web Services, 2019). IBM also provides a platform to track assets using RFIDs as a non-fungible asset in order to monitor car sales (Hamilton, 2018a).

Some Issues With Public Blockchains

Of course, poor implementations or flaws within dependent components could put blockchain technologies at risk. For example, one-way hashes are supposed to be a function in which the output is unique; this makes them a deterministic discriminator in digital signatures on X.509 certificates for instance. However, over time digital digests can be found to be vulnerable, like the first generation of SHA, in which more than one identical hash can be generated through what is known as a collision; generally, this can be instigated on legacy hashes where special conditions can be met using GPU acceleration. Experts also found MD5 to be susceptible in 2009, and Iran already used it in Flame malware to spoof digital signatures in certificates as if they were from Microsoft; and thereby fool computers into accepting fake certificates as legitimate ones (Eddy, 2017). Fake hashes or duplicates would be extremely catastrophic to blockchain technologies that rely on these digital digests, and this is why blockchain systems use more robust variations like SHA-256 so that hackers cannot undermine their integrity – but this may not remain so forever.

Supporters of the technology consider blockchain to be the panacea for IoT security, in which smart contracts can be used for driving sensor condition-based processing, potentially leading users down the road of autonomous decision-making based on the resultant data analysis collected from such actions (Groopman & Owang, n.d.). Notwithstanding the security of the IoT devices themselves and the data-in-transit aspects, at its source, blockchains carry out smart contracts when a specific condition has been met but is not validated by the Ethereum virtual machine. If there is an issue like a bug in the DApp or some malicious alteration, then the smart contract will still be executed. Yet users must take heed of the warnings from hacks against traders in the cryptocurrency world. In this case, virtual tokens - such as 'bitcoins' or in the case of Ethereum, ethers - are stored in their respective software-based wallets. Of course, electronic wallet type technology uses asymmetric private key that is attributable to the owner and a public key that allows owners to trade in virtual assets. These wallets are not cold wallets and are thereby accessible online, so they can be prone to software vulnerabilities.

In 2017, hackers exploited a weakness in an Ethereum wallet and performed a 'recursive call' attack that enabled them to drain at least 30 million USD worth of Ether before the bug was fixed (Castillo, 2016; Wong, 2017). This was a form of de-anonymization, and the vulnerability enabled the hackers to avoid stealing the credentials and still gain access to the assets in the wallet (Clarke et al., 2019). In the same year, a bug in another wallet type caused 70 multi-signature wallets to be frozen, resulting in many owners being denied access to their cryptocurrency (Thompson, 2017). Some have speculated that this might have been fraud by the developer rather than a mistake. There are also indirect risks if keys are stored offline inappropriately. For instance, the legitimate owner of numerous Bitcoin private keys contracted a cyber security researcher to break the Infozip encryption used to protect them. He had forgotten his password, and the bitcoins protected by the zip file were worth 300,000 USD. Reportedly, the researcher cracked the password due to insufficient rigor in password entropy, and it took only a few months using the compute power of a medium sized graphic processing unit farm (Smith, 2020).

By 2018, cyber-criminals attacked a number of DNS servers, which redirected users from myetherwallet.com to a phishing website. The attackers then used credentials harvested from this malicious website to steal Ether from the users' wallets (Johnson, 2018). Then, in early 2019, nefarious actors conducted a 51% attack against a spin-off Ethereum currency that forced a double-spend situation. The attackers were able to rewrite transactions in the decentralized ledgers that should not have been possible. It transpires that where the blockchain is reasonably short, a number of miners could conspire together to beat the system and conduct fraudulent transactions (Brandom, 2019). Another apparent attack is known as an eclipse attack, in which an actor could monopolize the connections used by a legitimate node and abuse the behavior of the network, thereby having an impact on the crucial consensus mining mechanism. DDOS is another potential weakness, in which nodes in a Bitcoin economy could be attacked. In this case a number of distributed nodes could be starved of resources, and this could affect consensus functions.

In 2017, researchers revealed that at least seven percent of Bitcoin operators had experienced such attacks (Martinovic, Kello, & Sluganovic, 2018).

Furthermore, there was the saga related to the Cyptoqueen in which a Bulgarian businesswoman Dr Ruja Ignatova started a supposed cryptocurrency called OneCoin. Based out of Sofia, she toured the world in 2016, publicizing her cryptocurrency, which was promoted as being capable of surpassing Bitcoin. Her sales pitch was to be part of a community that had the power to change the world. Many people from around the globe invested in OneCoin. Investors ranged from low- to high-earners, and this enabled the value of this alleged deregulated currency to reach 4 billion USD at its height. However, after Igantova disappeared in 2017, OneCoin was revealed to be more like a multi-level marketing scheme and no more than a pyramid-selling scam to peddle fake coin. There was no blockchain behind OneCoin just a traditional database. The scam worked by playing on people's desire to be a part of 'the next big thing' in the cryptocurrency market or to quickly earn a large amount of money. Some did in fact achieve the latter at its height. Soon, OneCoin came under the microscope of the United Kingdom's Financial Conduct Authority (FCA), and they issued warnings about the risks that OneCoin posed to consumers. Subsequently, City of London Police collaborated with foreign law enforcement organizations and issued statements for victims of the scam to contact Action Fraud online. In 2019, the Federal Bureau of Investigation arrested Ignatova's brother, Konstantin, for fraud when he was visiting the United States. Ruja Ignatova was also charged in absentia for wire fraud and money laundering. The Press surmised that the scam grew far larger than was expected and that Ignatova decided to jump ship before the fraud was discovered. Reporters also speculated that perhaps organized crime groups from Eastern Europe were involved (British Broadcasting Corporation, 2019).

The wider financial institutions have been particularly slow to accept cryptocurrencies. Cryptocurrency analysts say this is due to the decentralized nature of blockchain-based currencies that pose a threat to existing financial models. This has led to rumors of a ban of cryptocurrencies in the United Kingdom. For instance, the FCA previously stated that cryptocurrencies have no intrinsic value, they are extremely volatile, and investors could suffer harm from unexpected losses. Therefore, cryptocurrencies are not covered by the Financial Services Compensation Scheme. The U.S. standpoint from the White House appears to be general reticence towards cryptocurrencies (Davies, 2019; Bambrough, 2019). The United Kingdom is a leader in the financial markets but has languished behind Asia and other European counterparts on regulating cryptocurrency. However, a U.K. cryptocurrency firm could be on the verge of receiving FCA approval as the first large-scale crypto asset manager (Chowdhury, 2019). Furthermore, the U.K. Jurisdiction Taskforce, consisting of Her Majesty's Treasury, the Bank of England, and the FCA, published a statement calling for some consideration towards developing legislation relating to cryptocurrencies, blockchain, and smart contracts under English and Welsh common law (Cryptomoney News, 2019). Certainly, regulation would be required especially in relation to the inter-market purchases of energy, as well as the monitoring and controlling of CNI utilities. It appears that the challenge will be jurisprudence around smart contracts that would enable multi-party transactions to be fulfilled without any arbitration through a single coordinating organization (Marvin, 2016; Lielacher, 2019). This is only likely to be amplified by the threats from cyber-criminality and quantum computers that may be able to crack ECDSA in the not-so-distant future. Fungible blockchain implementors use ECDSA to create the asymmetric public key for investors to trade in cryptocurrencies. Perhaps this is why the number of ICOs have depleted by 72% between 2018 and 2019 (Leonard, 2019).

NON-FUNGIBLE PERMISSIONED BLOCKCHAIN

Setting fungible cryptocurrencies and the value-chain aside, private blockchain technologies are also available, but they do not attract the limelight. They can be implemented for closed communities to safeguard their transactional data in which public scrutiny is not needed. Private blockchains are permission-orientated, so entities must be invited into membership of the community, which places trust in peers to control access to the blockchain. This type of approach sets the scene for the concept of NFT, in which non-cryptocurrency assets are able to be transacted (Garner, 2018; Vision Times, 2018). Permissioned blockchains generally exist in two forms: consortium-based and fully private. The former relies on trusted owners, such as financial institutions or government departments, to manage transaction readability using public/private permissions controlled through layers of abstraction. A fully private blockchain is centralized and managed by a single organization, which only issues permissions to read publicly. Private blockchains are more efficient, use trusted peers and networks, and can provide a greater level of privacy than public blockchains (Martinovic, Kello, & Sluganovic, 2017).

An example of a fully private NFT blockchain is the KSI-based blockchain that was created in 2008. KSI employs Hash and Publish operations and a proof of participation consensus model to provide an irrefutable chain of trust. Guardtime from Estonia invented and developed KSI in response to a government initiative after their country had suffered from significant cyber-attacks in 2007. As an online-reliant society, the Estonian government was keen to adopt private blockchain technology to protect information systems underlying their important national services. Additionally, the Estonian government sought to validate the integrity of data stored by government systems as a protective measure against external attackers and insider threats (e-estonia, n.d.a; Herzog, 2017). From the outset, the KSI model is based on the Merkle Hash Tree, in which non-leaf nodes are a recursive concatenation of hashes from child nodes that starts from an originating node. The Merkle Hash Tree approach can use a one-time signature scheme and/or a few times signature scheme. In the former, the KSI creates one signature from an instance's signing function. The latter remains secure because not too many signatures are generated. Merkle Hash Trees can be stateful or stateless. This binary tree approach uses an ordered hierarchy of sibling nodes to compute the leaf-to-root path, where the system can verify the leaf signature by calculating the path to the root node (Accredited Standards Committee X9, 2019).

The core functionality of KSI is keyless because it does not rely on the secrecy of keys within the blockchain itself. Rather, the system gleans trust through the secure architecture, starting with the gateways going up the network hierarchy to the core. A crucial feature of KSI is that customer data is not stored on the blockchain. Instead, it stores hashed representations of that data. The hierarchical structure of the KSI system from the bottom up comprises the following:

- **Application:** Unique hashes that represent the record of the original source data are produced and stored on the blockchain. The blockchain only stores hashes of that data and not the source data. The application then raises a signing and time stamp request. In the end-to-end system context, the application is the originating node and hash onboarding component at the start of the KSI onward hashing process. The application is treated as an untrusted element in the system;
- **KSI Gateways:** These are trusted nodes that interact with the application layer in OpenKSI format. The gateways accept requests for the records to be aggregated onto the KSI global hash tree based on originator identity and permissions. The gateways also contain an extender service, the author describes its role next;

- **Aggregation and Delivery Network:** Child-servers publish the requests and progress the requests up the binary tree of the distributed and scalable aggregator network. The requests received for each aggregation round are aggregated onto the same hash tree and root hashes passed to upstream servers in the calendar hash chain. Each hash has the identity of each downstream server appended until consensus of the top root hash from each aggregation period is calculated by the next tier. The resultant time stamped KSI Signature (KSig) is generated in the core cluster and then cascaded back down the Delivery Network to the Extender Service for verification. The minimum amount of data necessary to recompute the top root hash of the global hash tree is contained in each KSig token provided with the child-server's identity. Each KSig acts as 'proof of existence,' linked to the original hashed record on the permissioned hash chain in accordance with its publishing time. The application can store the verified token and use it to recreate the hash chain by creating an 'extended token'. This token is the leaf and provides a verifiable cryptographic link to the original data record;
- **Core Parent-Server Cluster:** The top of the aggregator hierarchy is called the calendar hash chain, which is also responsible for the time synchronization of the system. This is a distributed state machine that is responsible for reaching consensus of the top root hashes. The top root hash is then promoted to the calendar hash chain within a consistent and measurable time period and forms part of the KSig token that is returned to the aggregation network. The core cluster operates in a stateful manner and effectively acts as the calendar database, or ledger system, across redundant nodes that provides the append-only blockchain of cryptographically linked events. The resultant top root value is signed per round by parent-servers of the top root hashes. The top root value is corroborated into a publication code that is then advertised in a widely witnessed manner and is therefore extremely hard to modify (Buldas, Kroonmaa, & Laanoja, n.d.; Martinovic, Kello, & Sluganovic, 2017).

KSI Blockchain to Enhance Cyber Security

The KSig token derivation is based on peer reviewed mathematical proofs and keyless cryptographic functions approved by the EU. In reality, KSI operates in a multi-signatory fashion. For example, a single signature endorses many records during each round. The underlying functionality of the KSI itself relies on online-only signing, the accurate time stamping function of the federated hashes on the calendar hash chain, and the time interval between signatures to denote the integrity of the system. KSI overcomes two major weaknesses of other blockchain technologies: it is highly scalable and grows linearly over time; and it is extremely quick at reaching consensus within one second by limiting the number of trusted participants (Guardtime Federal, n.d.).

Therefore, KSI depends on the collision-freeness of the hash functions, and that is why this blockchain uses second and third generation SHA digital digests. KSI publishes all transactions on the blockchain and removes none. Therefore, the system will detect any tampering or meddling with the blockchain to remove entries, making this technology secure against back-dating attacks. Ultimately, in this zero-trust environment, any forgery attempts against the blockchain will be revealed even when event clocks are tampered with or rounds skipped. In 2016, the U.S. Defense Advanced Research Projects Agency (DARPA) contracted Galois to undertake a mathematical proof verification (similar to an audit) of the Guardtime's KSI trust model, and then very shortly afterwards, it announced its adoption of KSI as part of its strategy to monitor and protect DoD data from APTs (Ogundeji, 2016; Wong, 2016).

Quantum Immunization

Asymmetric approaches use what is called trapdoor functions, which are used to easily compute a number in one direction, but a threat actor will find it difficult to compute it in the other direction with traditional computation. With the advent of the quantum computing era, asymmetric cryptography is prone to being cracked due to proponents like Shor's algorithm. This technique can factor large numbers exponentially faster than traditional machines, so it can break down and work out the prime factors of numbers much quicker than traditional computers. For example, Google's 56 quantum bit Sycamore computer used random sampling to calculate a number in just over three minutes, and yet, this task would take the world's most powerful classical computer 10,000 years to achieve (Cossins & Crane, 2019). Academics have predicted that in 25 years, it may be possible to build a 20 million qubit computer that can break 2048-bit Rivest-Shamir-Adleman-based cryptographic asymmetry in 8 hours (Jurvetson, 2019). In response, the world is quickly seeking quantum proof encryption techniques using new cryptographic approaches, like one developed by IBM called Cryptographic Suite for Algebraic Lattices (Bushwick, 2019).

In contrast, hashes are one-way functions that do not use trapdoor functions. That is, the cryptographic function should not calculate the hash by inverting a hash function through a flaw, for example. Bernstein (2009) stated that the speed differential between quantum computers and traditional computers used to calculate hash collisions is approximately the same. Therefore, in his judgement, irreversible one-way hash functions appeared to be resistant to quantum cracking, unlike PKI algorithms, which current academic knowledge has deemed not to be quantum immune. In his paper, Buldas justified that the Merkle-based signature schemes, as well as other hash-based signature schemes, showed existential non-forgeable post-quantum resistance under reasonable attack approaches and assumptions (Buldas, Kroonmaa, & Laanoja, n.d.; e-estonia, n.d.b; Buldas, 2017; Gault, 2019b).

SOLUTIONS AND RECOMMENDATIONS

As a comparison, the ledgers for both KSI and Bitcoin grow at an approximately similar rate of 2Gbytes per year. Yet in the case of KSI, this is based on the significantly larger amount of consecutive transactions compared to Bitcoin. The KSI blockchain can undertake billions of transactions per second due to its hierarchical hash chain model; and still, it provides the ability to verify hash representations of the original data input to detect whether any alterations or deletions have been made to the original dataset(s). As a result, governments and corporations are adopting the proprietary KSI model for a variety of uses, such as:

- **Data Security:** Guardtime's flagship product is its Blockchain-as-a-Service. On behalf of the Information System Authority, Gateways are located at multiple customer sites, while the KSI Aggregation and Core server levels underpin the Estonian X-Road technology that act as the interoperability backbone for the Estonian government. X-Road integrates various interfaces and security services, and it operates within a regulatory framework to provide a secured transport for authenticated and logged access. This system facilitates citizens' and government servants' abilities to search official databases (depending on the level of access) and enables civil authorities to transmit large datasets over an encrypted data-in-transit system. Beyond the confidentiality protection mechanism, the benefits of KSI are authenticity, integrity, and non-repudiation of exchanged data, in which KSI digitally signs hashes of data, files, access and transaction logs. Therefore, KSI provides Estonian health records, document registries, and legal databases with a tamperproof auditable trail of hashed logs that can be used to detect any changes to the original data sets (Lõhmus, 2017);

- **PII:** Guardtime implemented a VOLTA gateway for the singular purpose of taking snapshots of PII related transaction histories using process policy maps, comma-separated values or REST API rules. Associated workflows comprise schemas, classification mechanism, and pseudonymization rules. The system tracks transactions in accordance with state, source, destination, and context that are recorded on the KSI blockchain. Where VOLTA is installed on customers' site and pseudonymization is not required, then a 'mirrored' signed copy of PII data is retained for audit purposes. When VOLTA is hosted remotely, the node uses restricted identity information to pseudonymize the identities of people, and KSI publishes signed copies of vital transactions. In effect, the VOLTA database keeps a record of PII-related data events that are registered onto the onward KSI blockchain, which, when using KSI verification, enables tampering to be detected and notified in near real-time.

This approach provides an auditable, immutable history of signed and time-stamped transactions associated with each workflow rather than the original PII data itself. The system allows the initiation of EU General Data Protection Regulation (GDPR) compliant reporting based on role and is in line with data handling requirements. This includes the capability to conduct consent tracking and policy violation analytics that is verifiable against their associated hashes and signatures on the KSI blockchain (Shorthouse, 2017). Subsequently, the companies Instant Access Medical and Ethical GmbH are using KSI to provide not only immutability of each patient record but also auditable traceability for compliance with GDPR (AIT News Desk, 2018; Sturman, 2018).

- **Access Management:** Organizations use PKI hierarchies to establish a form of trust, but unlike KSI, PKI depends on the secrecy of the private key. PKI is based on the assumption that both parties implicitly trust each other's computing equipment that holds the private key. However, the private key could be compromised by the users or by hackers who can acquire them during a cyber-attack. This is especially problematic in a root of trust where the private key is used to sign an asymmetric exchange (Lacerda, n.d.). Customers can use the Guardtime Black Lantern authentication and security appliance as a gateway to augment a PKI system in an access management use-case. It comprises application-specific integrated circuits and high integrity Green Hills real-time operating system combined with anti-tamper protection features, which are effectively protected against physical and remote attacks. Common Criteria has independently validated the product, and it is installed within the customer perimeter. Exchanges are implemented against Federal Information Processing Standards using robust cryptographic algorithm suites to provide encrypted TLS connections (Guardtime, 2017).

In an access management use-case, organizations historically can use PKI for two-way authentication, relaying on a Certificate Authority (CA) as a signatory of the certificates that are used. In support of this, KSI offers an accurate time-stamping service at its core. This system can be used to monitor the client's key validity against revocation information aligned by time. KSI can also underwrite the integrity of PKI CA configuration files, providing evidence of authenticity and integrity. One feature of a Man-in-the-Middle (MITM) attack is that the time stamp is adjusted, enabling a compromised and potentially revoked private key to authenticate the exchange. However, KSI protects against such back-dating attacks, even when PKI certificates have been revoked. Therefore, time difference between exchanges can be discerned, and reveal any discrepancies that are indicative of MITM attacks (Buldas, 2017; Johnson & Treccani, 2019). In a related context, Guardtime announced its implementation of a chain-of-custody solution for DoD Identity and Access Management functions in 2018 (Bishop, n.d.). Furthermore, telecommunications company Verizon implemented KSI as part of a system to authenticate identities on their network through self-enacting code that will either grant or deny read access to their network system (Crypto Influence, 2018).

In addition, it is also possible to integrate KSI with other systems to provide an integrity validation mechanism. Examples consist of the following:

- **Supply Chain:** KSI blockchain can underpin a collaborative group of organizations that have a need for multi-organizational interoperability through a common association, like a software supply chain. A community can use a system of 'dockets' for software assurance purposes to track and trace the order placement authenticity, software verification, and testing all the way through to order fulfillment. The 'dockets' house data related to transactional data and context, parameters, and KSigs. In effect, the 'dockets' act as self-contained micro-ledgers that are irrefutably verifiable by the community of stakeholder organizations, who are a party to the permissioned KSI blockchain (Zawicki, 2018). In 2018, Guardtime declared it was using its KSI technology to protect the integrity of the Joint Strike Fighter F-35 supply chain (Hamilton, 2018b);

- **Asset Validation:** In collaboration with Guardtime's partner, Intrinsic-ID, KSI can be used to store verifiable hashes that represent the fingerprints of IoT asset physical attributes. The integrated system achieves this by using Static Random Access Memory Physical Unclonable Function (SRAM PUF) to create IoT asset identities from meta-data authenticated using a PKI signing mechanism. This identity is in the form of a device-unique cryptographic key, which is then hashed and signed using KSig before the record is published on a ledger system (Guardtime, n.d.). SRAM PUF is a scalable technology that does not rely on non-volatile memory. It can uniquely authenticate a device, and when the registered ownership is published on a ledger, the provenance of that asset is cryptographically linked to the device at the chip level (Intrinsic-ID, 2016). General Electric (GE) and Ericsson collaborated to create a micro-service in GE's Predix cloud platform. At its heart, the platform is designed to verify the integrity of ICS hardware states using SRAM PUF. Customers can use this approach to ensure that the software state has not been altered or modified. In addition, the provenance of software and firmware is traceable from build, compilation, and development of updates (Ruubel, 2019). Additionally, it is an answer to IoT sensor trustworthiness discussed earlier in the book;

- **Assured AI:** Whilst KSI blockchain cannot influence the cleanliness of AI algorithmic training and the input data itself, the system can be used to provide evidence of the fingerprinted state of data quality used by AI platforms. Hashes of AI rules or algorithms of known provenance could also be registered on the blockchain to show any transgressions, such as unauthorized modifications and the times at which any alterations took place. The state of AI-based logs can be registered on the blockchain to prove that they are genuine and have not been tampered with. Blockchain ledgers can be implemented as a shared trust anchor of hash values for the original data sets, training schemes, software libraries, and pretrained models. The KSI blockchain can be used to provide an immutable, and distributed data-synchronization trust fabric between test-simulation systems containing the final code baseline and a real-world system upon which it will be run. This protects the integrity of the database, logs, and data that are shared between the two systems (Guardtime Research, 2019).

FUTURE RESEARCH DIRECTION

Today, the adoption of AI algorithms is popular from open source projects; however, at present, the context in which they were trained and tested is not necessarily available. Rather, only the code commits themselves. Therein lies a problem for the integrity of AI algorithms in the future, and as the complexity grows, then do-it-yourself approaches with open source may become a false economy. Gartner believes that in 2020 customers will seek Industry 4.0 algorithms from algorithmic marketplaces (Gartner, 2017) This implies that customers may purchase AI algorithms from third-party software houses. KSI blockchain can resolve the problem of assurance in the AI sphere, and it has applications in IoT, as discussed in Chapter 1. This would allow customers to track AI code against a blockchain ledger system that proves code traceability and authenticity, and it provides a verifiable level of trust. Blockchain technologies also brings about a multi-chain opportunity that is already being explored by Ethereum. In a software supply chain context (Vollumer, n.d.), multi-chaining could take private KSI blockchain to the next level in the AI sphere.

A private blockchain could provide an assurance of the following: the state of an algorithm's integrity and source data provenance through non-fungible tokenization. A public blockchain could be used to pay for the algorithms using cryptocurrency, which acts as a notary function (Williams, 2019). For this to work, an off-chain processing node would be required in between the two chains to translate the fungible transaction on one side and correlate to NFT on the other side as proof of the integrity pertaining to the AI assets. There could be a risk of code translation errors between the two chains via the broker entity, so consistency in the message transmission method would be critical. The advantage of this approach is that it would provide global transparency and traceability of purchases on the public blockchain, whilst ensuring trust in the global AI supply chain via the private blockchain. If this is achievable, it would provide confidence in the quality and reliability of the algorithm source data, code provenance, integrity of the test results, and training history. Customers can use this to prove the quality and thereby provide more confidence in the resultant AI decision-based outcomes when used in the real-world. This concept would also limit access to unregulated open source AI technology by illicit and malevolent actors, thus reducing the risk of this capability being misused in an adversarial manner (Vision Times, 2018; Bryk, 2017; Crypto Influence, 2018; Jakobson, 2019) for nefarious purposes. Fungible to non-fungible off-chain processing in this context is worthy of future research.

CONCLUSION

Imperial College London has articulated that the public and private blockchain paradigms have a number of applications, such as: (a) crypto currency; (b) financial and logistical assets; (c) legal, insurance and supply chain contracts; (d) data integrity and auditability; (e) point-to-point transactions (Mulligan, n.d.). Certainly, with calls for a decentralized Internet, including decentralized messaging and decentralized data-storage (Simonite, 2018), blockchains will prove most useful. For example, public blockchains can be used to execute smart contracts in a fungible manner to lease aircraft, purchase autonomous deliveries, and lease autonomous carriers in a trust-less transparent and irrefutable manner (Kehoe & Hallahan, 2017, DAV, 2019). In fact, it might have wider connotations, contributing toward a more efficient drone tracking capability as part of efforts to combat illegal drone activity and help with regulating them (Civil Aviation Authority, 2015; Wyman, 2018). Blockchain is being heralded as a game changer in the aircraft engineering industry, where an immutable record of aircraft maintenance history would benefit air industry stakeholders and customers who lease the airframes. However, there are concerns over governance of the blockchain platform at scale and legal implications pertaining to safety of aircraft leasing in this manner (Kehoe & Hallahan, 2017).

From a security perspective, the cyber security profession may well prefer private and permission-orientated blockchain technologies. According to O'Reilly and the NCSC, the following factors shown in Table 1 are deemed to be true for fully fledged zero-trust environments. Gartner stated that Chief Information Officers are expecting blockchain technology to gain more traction by 2023 (Panetta, 2019). Blockchain is being expressed as transformative yet at the same time, disruptive. Certainly, Ethereum developers are researching the concept of off-chain processing, which might enable a number of transactions between two parties to be undertaken before writing it onto the chain at the end of business. This approach is centered around Cryplet Fabric processing on a confidential computing framework that uses different programming constructs to the blockchain itself (Beiler & Bennet, 2016). For this to be achieved a trust relationship between the blockchain and the transacting entities would be required; perhaps gauged from each trader's reliability gleaned from a history of previous transactions (The Doppler, 2018).

KSI as a private and industry-scale permissioned blockchain goes a long way toward fulfilling the specifications needed to prove authenticity and integrity in a non-fungible way. Yet it is a proprietary technology, and therefore, any organization wishing to buy its services should assess lock-in. However, KSI does meet the functional and non-functional specifications for zero-trust domains shown in Table 1. The cyber security community can learn from Estonia's leading global digital economy (Heller, 2017) that is underwritten by KSI. Unlike asymmetric PKI technologies, academia has asserted that KSI's hash-based cryptography is quantum immune. It does not rely on traditional asymmetric keys or revocations as part of the blockchain itself or elliptic curve cryptography like blockchain currencies do, and therefore, it has quantum immutability. KSI hashes can provide a level of transparency and permanence (Mire, 2018), which this system can be used to detect any unauthorized changes to original data and associated logs in which representative hashes have been registered and signed on the blockchain. This is particularly useful for compliance audits and real-time verification of state recorded by the blockchain (Shorthouse, n.d.). The founding nations of the Digital 5 (the United Kingdom, South Korea, Israel, New Zealand, Estonia, and the United States as an observer) have studied KSI (Lacerda, n.d.). The adoption of KSI by DARPA and U.S. space and defense companies (Lõhmus, 2017) is vilification that the company presents a credible and worthwhile capability that is adept at enhancing cyber security controls. Guardtime is also working in partnership with the U.K. Future Cities Catapult to develop prototype applications to enhance resiliency, security, and reliability of CNI through blockchain-based services (Emlin Media, 2016).

Recently the Press has been consistently reporting on cyber security failings that could give the impression that the profession is failing society. Before cyber security becomes an antonym, zero-trust networks can provide a solution that is not a cure-all solution to fix all cyber security woes, but the

Table 1. Categories and key elements of zero-trust networks

Categories for Zero-Trust Networks	Key Elements
The network is always assumed to be hostile with external and internal threat actors being ever present.	• One should build in trust to devices and services. • One should build in support for zero-trust network architectures. • One should monitor health of devices and services. • One should monitor to ensure devices are in the most secure state.
The network functions are insufficient in determining trust of a network.	• All data sources and computing services are considered resources. • Communication is secured regardless of location. • One should control access to one's services and data. • One should undertake threat protection of devices and services.
Every device, user, and dataflow must not be inherently trusted and must be authenticated and authorized.	• One should implement accounts linked to individuals in a user directory. • Not all resources are part of enterprise-owned architecture. • One should ensure all devices are identifiable against a device directory. • One should map transaction flows. • One should trust in the requestor is evaluated before being granted access. • One should authenticate all connections.
Policies must be dynamic and derived from as many sources as possible.	• One can use policy agents to coordinate connections to gateways and onward data resources that may reside in enclaves. • One can use portal gateways supported by policies to facilitate access to data sources individually or within an enclave. • The data plane and management plane in the zero-trust domain are logically separate. • One should adequately define policies in relation to the value of services or data. • Policies should authorize access against assigned privileges in a scalable manner.

Source: Barth & Gilman, 2017; National Cyber Security Centre, 2019; Gerritz, 2020; Rose et al., 2020.

architectural concepts are a considerable step in the right direction. However, organizations need to carefully think through and integrate implementations into compatible architectures that are not constrained by legacy designs. So, zero-trust architectures are not a bolt-on but rather an investment (Haber, 2019). A private blockchain technology like KSI provides another dimension that can enhance existing technologies and goes some way to resolve some of the technological weaknesses discussed in this book at the enterprise level. The use of such a non-fungible blockchain arguably provides benefit as a contributing factor to zero-trust networks through its adoption of zero-trust principles, as outlined in Table 1. Together with its management structures, governments and industry can integrate KSI blockchain in various ways to meet disparate technology implementation use-cases. As technology has developed, Guardtime has proven the advantages of KSI through its scalability to assist in the protection of data sources and services from a variety of threats, which is a significant step in the right direction for cyber defense.

REFERENCES

Accredited Standards Committee X9. (2019). *ASC X9 TR 50–2019 Quantum techniques in cryptographic message syntax* [PDF document]. Retrieved from https://x9.org/wp-content/uploads/2019/03/ASC-X9-TR-50-2019-Quantum-Techniques-in-Cryptographic-Message-Syntax-1.pdf

AIT News Desk. (2018). *Ethical eAdjudication integrates with Guardtime KSI-blockchain.* Retrieved from https://www.aithority.com/technology/blockchain/ethical-eadjudication-integrates-with-guardtime-ksi-blockchain/

Alibaba. (n.d.). *Blockchain as a service.* Retrieved from https://www.alibabacloud.com/products/baas

Amazon Web Services. (2019). *Amazon managed blockchain.* Retrieved from https://aws.amazon.com/managed-blockchain/

Bambrough, B. (2019). *Bitcoin has 'no intrinsic value,' as U.K. 'moves towards' crypto ban.* Retrieved from https://www.forbes.com/sites/billybambrough/2019/08/01/bitcoin-has-no-intrinsic-value-as-uk-moves-towards-crypto-ban/

Barth, D., & Gilman, E. (2017). *Zero trust networks.* O'Reilly Inc.

Beiler, D., & Bennett, M. (2016). *Blockchain and the Internet of Things: The IoT blockchain opportunity and challenge.* Retrieved from https://www.i-scoop.eu/blockchain-distributed-ledger-technology/blockchain-iot/

Bishop, R. (n.d.). *Introduction to Guardtime and KSI Blockchain* [PDF document]. Retrieved from Lecture Notes Online Web site https://cred-c.org/sites/default/files/slides/PNW-IW17_7.2_Bishop_Panel2_Emerging-Tech_Keyless-Signature.pdf

Bitcoin.it. (2018). *How bitcoin works.* Retrieved from https://en.bitcoin.it/wiki/How_bitcoin_works

Brandom, R. (2019). *Why the Ethereum Classic hack is a bad omen for the blockchain.* Retrieved from https://www.theverge.com/2019/1/9/18174407/ethereum-classic-hack-51-percent-attack-double-spend-crypto

British Broadcasting Corporation. (2019). *Cryptoqueen: How this woman scammed the world, then vanished.* Retrieved from https://www-bbc-co-uk.cdn.ampproject.org/c/s/www.bbc.co.uk/news/amp/stories-50435014

Bryk, A. (2017). *Blockchain: Cyber security pros and cons*. Retrieved from https://www.apriorit.com/dev-blog/462-blockchain-cybersecurity-pros-cons

Bryson, D., Penny, D., Goldenburg, D., & Serrao, G. (2018). *Blockchain technology for government* [PDF document]. Retrieved from https://www.mitre.org/publications/technical-papers/blockchain-technology-for-government

Buldas, A., Kroonmaa, A., & Laanoja, R. (n.d.). *Keyless signatures' infrastructure: How to build global distributed hash-trees* [PDF document]. Retrieved from https://guardtime.com/files/BuKL13.pdf

Buldas, A., Laanoja, R., & Truu, A. (2017). Keyless Signature Infrastructure and PKI: Hash-tree signatures in pre- and post-quantum world. *International Journal of Services Technology and Management, 23*(1/2), 117. doi:10.1504/IJSTM.2017.081881

Bushwick, S. (2019). *New encryption system protects data from quantum computers*. Retrieved from https://www.scientificamerican.com/article/new-encryption-system-protects-data-from-quantum-computers/

Castillo, M. (2016). *The DAO attacked: Code issue leads to $60 million ether theft*. Retrieved from https://www.coindesk.com/dao-attacked-code-issue-leads-60-million-ether-theft

Chi, C., Yu, G., Yeh, J., Li, X., Pen, J., … Kai-Fu, L. (2019a). *China Internet report 2019*. Hong Kong, China: South China Morning Post.

Chowdhury, H. (2019). *UK crypto scene set for boost as London firm poised for FCA approval*. Retrieved from https://www.telegraph.co.uk/technology/2019/06/30/uk-crypto-scene-set-boost-london-firm-poised-fca-approval/

Civil Aviation Authority. (2015). *Recreational drone flights*. Retrieved from https://www.caa.co.uk/Consumers/Unmanned-aircraft/Recreational-drones/Recreational-drone-flights/

Clarke, D., Emms, M., Morisset, C., Shahandashti, S., & Coopamootoo, K. … Mehrnezhad, M. (2019). *Bitcoin: a cryptocurrency*. Training course retrieved from https://www.futurelearn.com/courses/cyber-security/1/steps/97943

Columbus, L. (2019). *6 Best practices for increasing security in AWS in a zero trust world*. Retrieved from https://www.forbes.com/sites/louiscolumbus/2019/01/04/6-best-practices-for-increasing-security-in-aws-in-a-zero-trust-world/#17ece2d07439

Cossins, D., & Crane, L. (2019). Google reigns supreme. Special report quantum supremacy. *New Scientist*, *244*(3254), 6–9. doi:10.1016/S0262-4079(19)32037-8

Crypto Influence. (2018). *4 powerful non-cryptocurrency uses for blockchain technology*. Retrieved from https://medium.com/boosto/4-powerful-non-cryptocurrency-uses-for-blockchain-technology-bb190106d785

Cryptomoney News. (2019). *New report on crypto's legal status in UK lays out regulation options*. Retrieved from https://www.cryptomoneynew.com/2019/11/22/new-report-on-cryptos-legal-status-in-uk-lays-out-regulation-options/

Datta, A. (2019). *Blockchain in the government technology fabric*. Retrieved from https://arxiv.org/abs/1905.08517

DAV. (2019). *Blockchain-based transportation protocol*. Retrieved from https://dav.network

Davies, R. (2019). *FCA proposes ban on cryptocurrency products*. Retrieved from https://www.theguardian.com/technology/2019/jul/03/fca-proposes-ban-on-cryptocurrency-products

e-estonia (n.d.a.). *Security and safety*. Retrieved from https://e-estonia.com/solutions/security-and-safety/

e-estonia. (n.d.b.). *Healthcare*. Retrieved from https://e-estonia.com/solutions/healthcare/e-health-record/

Eddy, M. (2017). *Researchers reveal secrets of SHA-1 hash collision*. Retrieved from https://uk.pcmag.com/news-analysis/90490/researchers-reveal-secrets-of-sha-1-hash-collision

Emlin Media. (2016). *Guardtime, future cities catapult join forces to develop blockchain-based cybersecurity*. Retrieved from https://www.econotimes.com/Guardtime-Future-Cities-Catapult-Join-Forces-to-Develop-Blockchain-Based-Cybersecurity-140819

Garner, B. (2018). *What are NFTs? Non-fungible tokens, explained.* Retrieved from https://coincentral.com/nfts-non-fungible-tokens/

Gartner. (2017). *Gartner says by 2020, at least 30 percent of Industrie 4.0 projects will source their algorithms from leading algorithm marketplaces.* Retrieved from https://www.gartner.com/en/newsroom/press-releases/2017-03-21-gartner-says-by-2020-at-least-30-percent-of-industrie-4-projects-will-source-their-algorithms-from-leading-algorithm-marketplaces

Gault, M. (2019). *Six reasons security will fail on the industrial Internet* [Weblog comment]. Retrieved from https://guardtime.com/blog/6-reasons-security-will-fail-on-the-industrial-internet

Gault, M. (2019). *Quantum computing, KSI and flat-earthers* [Weblog comment]. Retrieved from https://guardtime.com/blog/quantum-computing-ksi-and-flat-earthers

Gerritz, C. (2020). *5 considerations for building a zero trust IT environment.* Retrieved from https://www.helpnetsecurity.com/2020/03/02/building-zero-trust/

Greengard, S. (2018). *SRT interview: John Kindervag says 'put your trust in zero trust'.* Retrieved from https://www.securityroundtable.org/john-kindervag-put-trust-zero-trust/

Groopman. J. & Owang, J. (n.d.). *Blockchain use cases where IoT and distributed ledger technology meet.* Retrieved from https://www.i-scoop.eu/blockchain-distributed-ledger-technology/blockchain-iot-distributed-ledger-technology/

Guardtime. (2017). *Black lantern security target version 1.2* [PDF document]. Retrieved from https://www.commoncriteriaportal.org/files/epfiles/st_vid10838-st.pdf

Guardtime Federal. (n.d.). *Keyless signature infrastructure.* Retrieved from https://www.guardtime-federal.com/ksi/

Guardtime. (n.d.). *Internet of Things authentication: A blockchain solution using SRAM physical unclonable functions* [PDF document]. Retrieved from https://m.guardtime.com/files/gt_KSI-PUF-web.pdf

Guardtime Research. (2019). *Convergence of blockchain and artificial intelligence* [PDF document]. Retrieved from Lecture Notes Online Web site https://m.guardtime.com/files/blockchain_and_ai.pdf

Haber, M. (2019). *Why zero trust is an unrealistic security model?* [Weblog comment]. Retrieved from https://www.beyondtrust.com/blog/entry/why-zero-trust-is-an-unrealistic-security-model?

Hamilton, D. (2018a). *The growing world of non-fungible tokens*. Retrieved from https://coincentral.com/non-fungible-tokens/

Hamilton, D. (2018b). *DARPA blockchain programs*. Retrieved from https://coincentral.com/darpa-blockchain-programs/

Heller, N. (2017). *Estonia, the digital republic*. Retrieved from https://www.newyorker.com/magazine/2017/12/18/estonia-the-digital-republic

Herzog, S. (2017). Ten years after the Estonian cyberattacks: Defense and adaptation in the age of digital insecurity. *Georgetown Journal of International Affairs*, *18*(3), 67–78. doi:10.1353/gia.2017.0038

Intrinsic-ID. (2016). *Intrinsic-ID and Guardtime announce alliance on IOT blockchain*. Retrieved from https://www.intrinsic-id.com/intrinsic-id-guardtime-announce-alliance-iot-blockchain/

Jakobson, L. (2019). *Defense Department turns to blockchain to secure communications*. Retrieved from https://modernconsensus.com/technology/defense-department-turns-to-blockchain-to-secure-communications/

Jha, P. (2019). *Is Ethereum a private or public blockchain?* Retrieved from https://www.btcwires.com/round-the-block/is-ethereum-a-private-or-public-blockchain/

Johnson, M., & Treccani, A. (2019). *Hardening PKI to address the IoT and mobile devices* [Weblog comment]. Retrieved from https://guardtime.com/blog/part-1-hardening-pki-with-ksi

Johnson, R. (2018). *$140,000 in Ethereum stolen in wallet hack*. Retrieved from https://cryptodaily.co.uk/2018/04/140000-ethereum-stolen-wallet-hack

Jurvetson, S. (2019). *How a quantum computer could break 2048-bit RSA encryption in 8 hours*. Retrieved from https://www-technologyreview-com.cdn.ampproject.org/c/s/www.technologyreview.com/s/613596/how-a-quantum-computer-could-break-2048-bit-rsa-encryption-in-8-hours/amp/

Kehoe, L., & Hallahan, J. (2017). *Blockchain – A game changer in aircraft leasing?* Retrieved from https://www2.deloitte.com/content/dam/Deloitte/ie/Documents/Tax/ie-blockchain-a-game-changer-in-aircraft-leasing.pdf

Lacerda, E. (n.d.). *The second era of the internet, digital signature infrastructures and trusted entities. KSI, PKI and Permissioned Blockchain* [PDF document]. Retrieved from http://www.iti.gov.br/images/repositorio/publicacoes_tecnicas/The_second_era_of_the_internet_digital_signature_infrastructures_and_trusted_entities_KSI_PKI_and_Permissioned_Blockchain.pdf

Leonard, J. (2019). *Blockchain latest news: A state-owned quantum computer could break blockchains in as little as three years.* Retrieved from https://www.computing.co.uk/ctg/news/3033006/state-owned-quantum-computer-break-blockchains-three-years

Lielacher, A. (2019). *Crypto assets to be classified as property in the UK.* Retrieved from https://bravenewcoin.com/insights/crypto-assets-to-be-classified-as-property-in-the-uk

Lipovyanov, P. (2019). *Blockchain for business 2020: The new industrial revolution.* Training course retrieved from https://www.udemy.com/course/blockchain-for-business-the-new-industrial-revolution/

Lõhmus, I. (2017). *Securing public services with blockchain* [PDF document]. Retrieved from Lecture Notes Online Web site https://www.maaamet.ee/pcc2017/docs/PCC_11_Lohmus_Estonia_Blockchain_Guardtime.pdf

Maio, M. (2018). *Waltonchain (WTC) – The blockchain technology for the Internet of Things.* Retrieved from https://tokeninvestoronline.com/waltonchain-wtc-blockchain-technology-for-the-internet-of-things/

Martinovic, I., Kello, L., & Sluganovic, I. (2017). Blockchains for Governmental Services: Design Principles, Applications, and Case Studies. Oxford University Centre for Technology and Global Affairs, 7, 1-16.

Marvin, R. (2016). *Blockchain in 2017: The year of smart contracts.* Retrieved from https://www.pcmag.com/article/350088/blockchain-in-2017-the-year-of-smart-contracts

Microsoft. (n.d.). *Confidential consortium framework.* Retrieved from https://www.microsoft.com/en-us/research/project/confidential-consortium-framework/

Mire, S. (2018). *Blockchain for smart cities: 12 possible use cases.* Retrieved from https://www.disruptordaily.com/blockchain-use-cases-smart-cities/

Mulligan, C. (n.d.). Blockchain – a brief overview [PDF document]. Retrieved from https://na.eventscloud.com/file_uploads/b4d722450d854c8b9fdaf14823c49a0c_MULLIGAN_Blockchain-brief-overview.pdf

Ogundeji, O. (2016). *US DARPA takes blockchain for military use*. Retrieved from https://www.ccn.com/us-darpa-takes-blockchain-for-military-use/

Panetta, K. (2019). *The CIO's guide to blockchain*. Retrieved from https://www.gartner.com/smarterwithgartner/the-cios-guide-to-blockchain/

Pujoldevall, O. (2019). *Blockchain in the energy sector*. Training course retrieved from https://www.futurelearn.com/courses/blockchain-energy-sector

Rose, S., Borchert, O., Mitchell, S., & Connelly, S. (2020). Zero trust architecture. *National Institute of Science and Technology*, Special Publication 800-207. doi: . doi:10.6028/NIST.SP.800-207-draft2

Ruubel, M. (2019). *GE and Ericsson launch KSI blockchain based cloud assurance for the industrial Internet* [Weblog comment]. Retrieved from https://guardtime.com/blog/ge-and-ericsson-launch-ksi-blockchain-based-cloud-assurance-for-the-industrial-internet

Schneier, B. (2016). *Data at rest vs. data in motion* [Weblog comment]. Retrieved from https://www.schneier.com/blog/archives/2010/06/data_at_rest_vs.html

Shorthouse, D. (2017). *GDPR compliance using KSI® blockchain* [PDF document], Lecture Notes Online Website. Retrieved from https://m.guardtime.com/files/Guardtime-whitepaper-Volta.pdf

Shorthouse, D. (n.d.). *Redefining audit and compliance with blockchain*. Retrieved from https://guardtime.com/compliance

Simonite, T. (2018). *The decentralized Internet is here, with some glitches*. Retrieved from https://www.wired.com/story/the-decentralized-internet-is-here-with-some-glitches/

Smith, T. (2020). *Bitcoins worth $300,000 recovered by 'breaking zip encryption'*. Retrieved from https://bitcoinist.com/bitcoin-worth-usd-300000-recovered/

Sturman, C. (2018). *The first comprehensive blockchain-supported personal care record platform has been launched.* Retrieved from https://www.healthcareglobal.com/public-health/first-comprehensive-blockchain-supported-personal-care-record-platform-has-been

Suberg, M. (2017). *Tencent joins China's blockchain race with new TrustSQL platform.* Retrieved from https://cointelegraph.com/news/tencent-joins-china-blockchain-race-with-new-trustsql-platform

Sundararajan, S. (2018). *Chinese web search giant Baidu has launched its own blockchain-as-a-service (BaaS) platform.* Retrieved from https://www.coindesk.com/search-giant-baidu-launches-blockchain-as-a-service-platform

The Doppler. (2018). *Enterprise smart contracts and the rise of off-chain processing.* Retrieved from https://www.cloudtp.com/doppler/enterprise-smart-contracts-and-the-rise-of-off-chain-processing/

Thompson, I. (2017). *Parity's $280m Ethereum wallet freeze was no accident: It was a hack, claims angry upstart.* Retrieved from https://www.theregister.co.uk/2017/11/10/parity_280m_ethereum_wallet_lockdown_hack

UKNCSC. (2019). *Zero trust architecture design principles.* Retrieved from https://github.com/ukncsc/zero-trust-architecture/blob/master/README.md

Vision Times. (2018). *DARPA now exploring blockchain for military applications.* Retrieved from.

http://www.visiontimes.com/2018/12/07/darpa-now-exploring-blockchain-for-military-applications.html

Vollmer, J. (n.d.). *Blockchain and SCM* [PDF document]. Retrieved from https://www.academia.edu/36159602/Blockchain_and_SCM_HOW_WILL_BLOCKCHAIN_REVOLUTIONIZE_GLOBAL_SUPPLY_CHAINS_Blockchain_and_SCM

Williams, S. (2019). *Blockchain: The next everything.* Charles Scribner's Sons.

Wong, J. (2016). *Even the US military is looking at blockchain technology—to secure nuclear weapons.* Retrieved from https://qz.com/801640/darpa-blockchain-a-blockchain-from-guardtime-is-being-verified-by-galois-under-a-government-contract/

Wong, J. (2017). *A coding error led to $30 million in Ethereum being stolen.* Retrieved from.

https://qz.com/1034321/ethereum-hack-a-coding-error-led-to-30-million-in-ethereum-being-stolen/

Wyman, O. (2018). *Why the use of drones still faces big regulatory hurdles.* Retrieved from https://www.forbes.com/sites/oliverwyman/2018/09/10/why-the-use-of-drones-still-faces-big-regulatory-hurdles/#5fd8bb921c0d

Zawicki, K. (2018). *Keyless signature infrastructure (KSI): Blockchain technology for the defense industry* [PDF document]. Retrieved from https://potomacinstitute.org/images/VITAL/2018-08-16-KSI---Blockchain-Tech-for-DoD.pdf

ADDITIONAL READING

Greenfield, A. (2017). *Radical technologies.* Verso.

Harkness, T. (2016). *Big data: Does size matter?* Bloomsberry Publishing.

Mayer-Schönberger, V., & Cukier, K. (2013). *Big data: A revolution that will transform how we live, work and think.* John Murray Publishers.

Schmidt, E., & Cohen, J. (2013). *The new digital age: Reshaing the future of people, nations and business.* John Murray Publishers.

Zuboff, S. (2019). *The age of surveillance capitalism: The fight for a human future at the new frontier of power.* Hachette Books Group.

KEY TERMS AND DEFINITIONS

Asymmetric Cryptography: Another term for public key cryptography that uses public key and private key associations through a mathematical proof to underpin PKI.

Blockchain: Fundamentally, blockchains comprise a sequence of blocks in a chain from the genesis block onwards. If a block is tampered with, it will be detected as invalid by other nodes on the network.

Chain-of-Custody: A framework to protect evidential data that could be used during an investigation and legal cases. Typically used in the digital forensics field as a method of tracking and preserving physical media and computer assets, the approach has been adopted for logically preserving auditable logs for computer network defense purposes.

Cold Wallet: A digital wallet that is isolated from the internet.

Cryptographic Suite for Algebraic Lattices: An asymmetric cryptography technique using equations to produce public and private keys called lattice problems that is deemed to be classical and quantum proof.

Docker Containers: Docker is a PaaS software platform that provides a common kernel that supports a series of containers each hosting an application, application libraries and runtime. This is in contrast to traditional IaaS method, which employs a hypervisor to manage and connect hosted operating systems and applications, libraries, and runtime. AWS uses security groups and permissions to control access to customer docker applications to alleviate weaknesses of using a common kernel potentially between multiple customers.

Drone: A remotely controlled unmanned aerial system that is significantly smaller than a UAV. UAVs are controlled using satellite uplinks and downlinks over long distances, while drones have significantly shorter range and are normally controlled using WiFi transceivers.

Practical Byzantine Fault Tolerance: Allows nodes on a decentralized network to irrefutably enable message distribution to all recipients even when the network is unreliable.

Proof of Stake: A consensus model used to prove that each entity has adequate digital capital in the form of Ether tokens as proof of value.

Proof of Work: The arbitrator of 'value' in Bitcoin digital currency demonstrated through the investment in electricity to solve an assigned mathematical problem block-by-block.

Round: The time interval of equal duration (1 second) to calculate root hashes.

SHA-256: A second-generation SHA digital digest that has been adopted because the first generation of SHA hashes and MD5s can now be prone to collisions, which enables one or more exact hashes to be created affecting their integral value as a unique one-way cryptographic function.

State: Stateful means a system tracks each transaction, whereas stateless would mean there is no record of the system's transactions.

About the Author

David Anthony Bird has worked in multiple technical disciplines within both the public and private sectors for over 33 years. Over the past 11 years, David has worked on many complex consortia-based projects and programs for a number of leading IT integration companies as an information security specialist. He also brings to bear his additional experience in business and training consultancy as well as performing cybersecurity research in his own time. He has had many articles published in several reputable magazines comprising topical, technical, and information security subject matter that includes: the British Computer Society ITNoW and Digital Leaders editions, CyberTalk and the Institute of Information Security Professionals Pulse Magazine. David has also provided a published chapter entitled "The Collaborative Effects of Cyberspace" in a book published by the Institute of Scientific and Technical Communicators. Between 2018 and 2020, he published three proceedings papers in the following: IEEE Xplore, ACM digital library, and Springer. During the same period, David also published journal articles with the *International Journal of Systems and Software Security and Protection* at IGI Global and *Current Analysis on Communication Engineering* at Mesford.

Index

Ensure Quality Research is Introduced to the Academic Community

Become an IGI Global Reviewer for Authored Book Projects

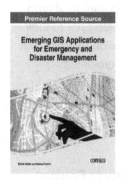
Premier Reference Source

Emerging GIS Applications for Emergency and Disaster Management

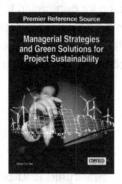
Premier Reference Source

Managerial Strategies and Green Solutions for Project Sustainability

Premier Reference Source

Comparative Approaches to Using R and Python for Statistical Data Analysis

Premier Reference Source

Solutions for High-Touch Communications in a High-Tech World

The overall success of an authored book project is dependent on quality and timely reviews.

In this competitive age of scholarly publishing, constructive and timely feedback significantly expedites the turnaround time of manuscripts from submission to acceptance, allowing the publication and discovery of forward-thinking research at a much more expeditious rate. Several IGI Global authored book projects are currently seeking highly-qualified experts in the field to fill vacancies on their respective editorial review boards:

Applications and Inquiries may be sent to:
development@igi-global.com

Applicants must have a doctorate (or an equivalent degree) as well as publishing and reviewing experience. Reviewers are asked to complete the open-ended evaluation questions with as much detail as possible in a timely, collegial, and constructive manner. All reviewers' tenures run for one-year terms on the editorial review boards and are expected to complete at least three reviews per term. Upon successful completion of this term, reviewers can be considered for an additional term.

If you have a colleague that may be interested in this opportunity, we encourage you to share this information with them.